Keto Made Easy

Fat Adapted 50-Day Guide

D1418355

MEGHA BAROT *AND* **MATT GAEDKE**

First published in 2019 by Victory Belt Publishing Inc.

ISBN-13: 978-1-628603-72-9

The author is not a licensed practitioner, physician, or medical professional and offers no medical diagnoses, treatments, suggestions, or counseling. The information presented herein has not been evaluated by the U.S. Food and Drug Administration, and it is not intended to diagnose, treat, cure, or prevent any disease. Full medical clearance from a licensed physician should be obtained before beginning or modifying any diet, exercise, or lifestyle program, and physicians should be informed of all nutritional changes.

The author claims no responsibility to any person or entity for any liability, loss, or damage caused or alleged to be caused directly or indirectly as a result of the use, application, or interpretation of the information presented herein.

Front and back cover photography by Tatiana Briceag

Cover design by Kat Lannom and Justin-Aaron Velasco

Interior design and illustrations by Yordan Terziev and Boryana Yordanova

Additional contributions provided by Lara Clevenger and Cassandra Cardy

Printed in Canada

TC 0219

To our siblings, Akash, Michelle, and Marie, who have helped shape us into who we are today.

And to our beautiful son, Theo, who will change the world for all of us!

Contents

Introduction

By now everyone is familiar with the story. Record numbers of people are struggling with obesity, type 2 diabetes, heart disease, depression, and many other problems that fall under the heading "diseases of modern civilization." The first time we heard that term, it was illuminating. *These problems are modern? We haven't always dealt with these types of issues to some degree?* We started analyzing our daily lives to see exactly how they were different from the daily lives of our ancestors. If we were to avoid these "diseases of modern civilization," it was important for us to understand all the ways that modern civilization was ingrained in our lives.

A few thousand Google searches and a handful of books later, this is still the question that interests us more than any other. It has led us to the ketogenic diet and opened our eyes to the harmful way people are living today. The "easy" fix would be to buy a cabin in the woods somewhere and live off the land, but what's more interesting—and more doable for most people—is to find a way to enjoy modern conveniences while minimizing their negative effects.

In this book, we'll be focusing on diet, but we think you'll find that once you start to take an ancestral approach to your diet, it will carry over into other aspects of life. You may find yourself asking, How much time do I spend staring at a screen each day? How much do I move my body? Do I get out in the sun enough? All of these questions are worth considering, but the questions with the most important and significant answers by far are these: What am I supposed to eat, and how do I get myself to eat it? These are the questions that we set out to answer in this book.

What am I supposed to eat? This is the sexy question. It's the question that gets most of the attention and marketing and has the most businesses built on top of it. There are hundreds of diets with flashy names and dozens of berries from exotic lands, and don't forget about the detoxes and cleanses! But the truth is pretty simple. We are supposed to eat what humans have always eaten: whole, natural foods, not processed, man-made foods. Historically, these foods came from within a few miles of home. The idea that we need foods shipped in from around the world on a daily basis to achieve a balanced diet is a very new concept. It's safe to say we will not be discovering a magical berry that changes everything we know about human nutrition anytime soon. We've already discovered coffee and chocolate, and that's about as good as it's going to get. But we'll talk more about the specifics of what to eat in part 1.

How do I get myself to eat it? This is the question we love talking about and the one that is plaguing most of us. Maybe you don't know exactly what to eat, but you probably have a general idea of what is healthy and what is bad for you. Even with this knowledge, though, we eat more of the bad stuff than ever before. Why is that? Why do we eat things that we know will make us sick and tired and will eventually lead to chronic disease? Why is it so hard to eat healthy foods? Why do we stick to a diet for a few weeks and then fall off the wagon? These are the most important questions. We'll explore the answers in the following pages, and in part 2 we'll offer a practical week-by-week guide to transitioning to a healthy diet.

FAT ADAPTATION IS KEY

Fat adaptation is the missing puzzle piece that you've been searching for all these years. Most of us rely primarily on sugar to fuel our bodies. Developing the ability to use fat for fuel instead will break your reliance on carbs and put you back in the driver's seat of your dietary choices.

Why is it so hard to eat the foods that we know are good for us? Why do we always go back to foods that provide temporary pleasure but cause long-term problems? It's because we are disconnected from the foods humans traditionally ate and rely instead on the quick fix of carbohydrates every couple of hours. We have become conditioned to eat this way, and most of us have never known anything else. At an early age most of us woke up to breakfast cereals, orange juice, whole-grain toast, and other "healthy" options. A lifetime of bad habits built on the food guidelines provided by our government is difficult to overcome. It doesn't happen overnight, but consistent progress over extended periods of time will lead to incredible results.

Simply put, being fat adapted—being efficient at using primarily fat for fuel instead of sugar—gives you consistent energy throughout the day, freedom from food cravings, and the ability to once again see food as a fuel source to power you through your life.

Up until very recently, humans had a much greater degree of metabolic flexibility. Historically, we were able to use carbs as a fuel source when fruits and grains were abundant, typically in the summer. We were also able to use fat for fuel when plant foods were not available, typically in colder climates and during the winter. In the Western world today, all we know how to use is carbohydrates. In the absence of carbs, we become tired and angry. This can happen when you skip a meal or even if it's just been a few hours since you last ate. We burn through carbs extremely quickly and need to constantly refuel. This can lead to overeating, weight gain, and a perpetual ride on the blood sugar roller coaster (it's not as fun as it sounds).

Adapting to using primarily fat as fuel takes some real effort in the modern food environment. You have to avoid the vast majority of packaged and processed foods and stick to lower-carb real, whole foods. If you do this over an extended period of time, your body begins to recognize that it will no longer be getting carbs as it used to and begins fueling with fat instead. At first it has no idea what it's doing, like a child trying to ride a bike for the first time. Over a few weeks it starts figuring things out, and by the end of the fifty days laid out in this book, it will be burning fat like a pro.

There are some people who don't think much about food; it isn't a driving factor in their lives. But for most of us, being brought up on Cinnamon Toast Crunch takes a toll. Controlling our food choices and intake can seem impossible. Becoming fat adapted is the best way to fix this issue. Four months into starting the keto diet, we didn't make it into the clean plate club for the first time in our lives, and we have never been prouder of not making a club. If you take these fifty days to lay the groundwork for the rest of your life, your control over food and, in turn, over all aspects of your life will greatly improve.

ABOUT US

We met the way most people our age meet: online dating! (Not all modern conveniences are bad after all.) We first bonded over our shared love of food and cooking. There are two types of people in the world: those who eat to live, and those who live to eat. We both fall firmly into the second group. Some of our fondest memories are walking to the Ferry Plaza farmers market in San Francisco and picking out ingredients for a homemade dinner that we would prepare later that day. We loved visiting all the different booths and coming up with ideas for dinner based on what caught our eye on that particular day.

When we first met, we were both health conscious in the sense that we watched what we ate. We tried not to eat too much, and we mostly ate foods that were considered healthy, like kale, bananas, berries, and sweet potatoes. That was as far as our interest in nutrition went. We simply accepted conventional nutritional wisdom at face value. We never asked, "What is it about a banana that makes it healthy?" *Of course a banana is healthy. Everyone says it's healthy.*

It wasn't until we watched the documentary *That Sugar Film* that something clicked. The movie shows how much sugar is found in what the typical nutritional guidelines would call a healthy diet. Say you have a breakfast of yogurt, granola, and a glass of orange juice. For lunch, you have a sandwich on whole-wheat bread and a glass of milk. For dinner, a large salad with chicken and fat-free dressing. Throw in a few snacks throughout the day, and you're looking at around 150 grams of sugar! That's more sugar than early humans would have been eating in the span of a few *months.* That documentary inspired us to dramatically reassess our eating habits.

With the new information that our current diet, healthy by modern standards, contained such an abundance of sugar, we began searching for low-sugar diets. We didn't know much about them at the time. Was this something people did? Not eat sugar? How would our bodies and minds perform if we started giving them close to 0 grams of sugar every day when they were used to getting 150 grams?

It didn't take long for us to stumble upon the keto subreddit. Reddit.com is a website that hosts thousands of different message boards for specific interest groups. Reddit.com/r/keto is one of the most popular message boards on the entire site and is the best place to go to learn about keto.

Soon after finding the keto subreddit and learning from all of the experienced keto dieters who posted there, we decided to give the keto diet a try and see how we felt. We read numerous posts about how important it was to supplement with electrolytes, but we figured that everyone was exaggerating and decided not to. Big mistake! For the first five days we had no energy at all and were only able to sit around and watch TV. We began questioning whether this diet worked, or would work for us. The thought that kept us going through the tough times was this: *It shouldn't be this hard for our bodies to go without sugar.* It truly felt like we were slowly and painfully getting over a chemical dependency that we didn't even know we had.

We powered through the first week, and everything immediately got easier. The first benefit we noticed, and what we still consider to be the biggest benefit of a ketogenic diet, was that we had consistent energy levels throughout the day. This was most noticeable around 2 to 3 p.m., when everyone else at the office was dozing off or running for coffee refills. Our productivity increased, and life became more enjoyable.

We also found a freedom from food that we had never experienced before. We're both the type of people who, if you put something in front of us, eat the entire thing. A few weeks after starting keto, we actually found ourselves becoming full and not finishing everything on our plates. In time this led to less eating due to boredom and less snacking between meals.

Nothing else has had such a big impact on our daily sense of well-being as switching to a ketogenic diet and removing sugar. It was clear to us that there was something different about this diet and that we'd be sticking to it for a while.

While our diet changed, our love for cooking up creative recipes in the kitchen did not. In fact, we began coming up with low-carb replacements for all of our favorite high-carb foods. We started by making keto bread, biscuits, hash browns, and even pizza. You can come up with a suitable low-carb replacement for any food you might be craving. We're not going to lie to you and say keto bread tastes as good as Grandma's homemade rolls, but it will do the job. As we continued to learn more about low-carb ingredients and how they could be used to replicate sugar and flour, our creations improved.

We started a food blog, KetoConnect.net, and a YouTube channel to share our recipes, and people responded in droves. Over the course of the next year, we published hundreds of recipes and videos, until we had enough viewers to quit our jobs and pursue our passion full-time. We've since started a podcast called *Keto for Normies*, and we've authored a number of cookbooks and e-books. Our love for self-experimenting is as strong as ever, and we share all of the results on our YouTube channel. In the past we have done things like test our blood glucose response to different types of sweeteners to see which ones are most suitable for a keto diet. Matt has eaten 4,000 calories a day for twenty-one days to see how much weight he could gain on a keto diet. We've even done videos where we replicate the diets of well-known people, like Joe Rogan and Marilyn Monroe.

Our diet and our interests have progressed since we started KetoConnect. What started as a passion for cooking with a focus on health has turned into an overhauling of our entire lifestyle to try to live more in line with the way ancestral humans did—the way our bodies were designed to live. We enjoy exploring health and nutrition from an ancestral perspective and look for ways to combine the wisdom of primitive cultures with the conveniences of modern life. We love diving deeper and deeper into learning about nutrition, and we are honored to be able to share what we've learned so far. We hope this book helps you reclaim your health once and for all.

ABOUT THIS BOOK

This book, like so many others, is focused on helping you reclaim your health. What sets this book apart from the rest is that we'll be taking a practical approach. You don't go from donuts to bone broth overnight (and if you do, you'll probably be back in the donut line a few weeks later).

Most of us were raised on processed, habit-forming foods that make healthy eating impossible, and now we're told that it is a personal failing or a lack of willpower that keeps bringing us back to unhealthy foods. In a state of desperation, we purchase the first ten-day detox we come across, hoping for a miracle to help us break our unhealthy eating habits. Unsurprisingly, it never works.

This book is not a miracle cure either. There is no miracle cure. But there *are* techniques and principles that can make eating healthy possible, every day. This book is filled with proven techniques and concepts that will help you regain your health and vitality over time. There is one path to lifelong health, and they don't sell it in a bottle for three payments of $49.99. It's going to take some time and it is going to be uncomfortable at times, but if health and happiness are what we seek, it is essential that we return to a natural human diet.

However, this book will not give you an in-depth and comprehensive understanding of human nutrition. We are not doctors or nutritionists; we are simply people who have been on a quest for better health and happiness for the past five years. Our expertise is in making the intimidating world of nutrition more manageable for ordinary people, and that's what we aim to do with this book. If you're interested in learning more about nutrition and the science behind what to eat, there are tons of resources online.

Those resources will help you build a solid foundation of nutrition knowledge. That said, we hope that you'll question any claim about nutrition and think about it critically. So often we are all guilty of seeking out only the information that confirms our beliefs, without looking at what the other side has to say. Nutrition is an ever-evolving field, and there are very few topics that everyone agrees on. It's worth taking the time to figure out what works for you—what makes you feel your best.

Our goal with this book is to provide you with the ultimate resource for transitioning from your current diet, whatever that may be, to a sustainable ketogenic diet. Everyone starts at a different point, but no matter where you are at now, getting to a healthy diet is not only possible, but it's a fun and rewarding journey! No matter how discouraged you are from years of dieting, extreme calorie restriction, juice fasts, and ten-day detoxes, there is hope.

This book will take you on a fifty-day journey to fat adaptation. In those seven weeks, your body will start burning fat efficiently. You'll feel less hungry and experience fewer cravings, and many people also lose weight.

And if you're like us, you'll experience positive changes in your life outside of food. Before we started eating a ketogenic diet, we both came home from work and sat around watching TV and playing video games. Shortly after starting keto and beginning to experience a change in how we felt physically, we decided we wanted more out of other aspects of our lives as well. We began working on KetoConnect every possible moment that we weren't working at our day jobs. We would wake up at 5 a.m. just to test out new recipes and work on the website. As soon as we got home from work, we would take photographs of dishes while it was still light outside. Neither of us had ever been this motivated until we started keto.

You will be amazed at how different your life can be when you focus on improving one area at a time, and at how this improvement will compound in other areas of your life. Everyone has a different motivator: for some it is working their way up the corporate ladder; for others it is the achievement of running a marathon. Very rarely do these accomplishments happen in isolation, meaning you keep everything else in your life the same and just change one small part of it. We hope this book and the ketogenic diet are the catalysts that set you down the path to happiness and fulfillment. We hope keto encourages you to improve in other areas and get as much out of life as possible.

What Is Your Biggest Health Mistake?

Starting a ketogenic diet for the first time can be quite intimidating. It's easy to overanalyze everything and become stressed about whether you are doing things wrong. Learning from the mistakes of experts is a great way to avoid making the same mistakes yourself, and it can help you realize that mistakes are part of the process. No one gets everything right the first time.

In the last few years of running our food blog, YouTube channel, and podcast, we have had the privilege of speaking to and learning from some of the brightest minds in health and nutrition. We reached out to a handful of them and asked them what was the biggest mistake they made when they first began their journey toward a healthy and fulfilling life.

I honestly think that mistakes are where the best learning happens. One thing I wish I had done more of is taking documentation along the way, even just photos, but also bloodwork. It would be nice to have more baselines.

—AMBER O'HEARN,
cofounder of Ketotic.org

The biggest mistake I made on my health journey was undervaluing the importance of quality with foods. Growing up, I heard a lot of people around me following this "if it fits your macros" approach where they would eat whatever, whenever as long as it fit their macronutrient intake for the day. So when I first started a ketogenic diet, all I ate was a keto mousse that consisted of heavy cream, coconut manna, protein powder, and unsweetened cocoa powder. Needless to say, I felt horrible and quickly realized how important it was to get ample amounts of nutrients from things like avocados, vegetables, and quality meats, along with some occasional treats to appeal to that sweet tooth I still have.

—RYAN P. LOWERY,
coauthor of *The Ketogenic Bible*

One of my biggest mistakes was thinking I could out-exercise a bad diet!

I signed up for a marathon eight years ago for weight loss, and guess what happened? I gained weight! I was overtraining, and my high-intensity exercise routine pushed my body's stress response too far, which led to a cascade of biochemical responses that caused damage to my health. Too much cardio stimulates cortisol, and chronically high levels of cortisol increases your risk for a variety of health issues, including weight gain. Plus, cortisol makes you more resistant to insulin and increases blood glucose (at least temporarily). What goes up must come down, and when blood sugar falls, hunger kicks in. So if you are exercising to just eat more food (I'm not judging, I have done this!), you are making a huge mistake!

—MARIA EMMERICH,
author of *Keto: The Complete Guide to Success*
and founder of MariaMindBodyHealth.com

Not listening to the feedback of my body and staying in overdrive mode. It is so important to redirect at times of anxiety, chronic fatigue, hair loss, insomnia, brain fog, hormone shifts. Maybe it is more or less protein, fat, or carbs; maybe it is adjusting exercise, learning to say no, redirecting priorities, cutting out inflammatory foods, increasing strategic nutrient supplementation. When the body tells you things are off, you need to adjust and go into reconnect, recharge, bubble wrap mode.

—ALI MILLER, RD, LD, CDE,
author of *The Anti-Anxiety Diet*

If there's one thing I wish I'd realized sooner, it's how amazing my body really is—how resilient and powerful it can be. I feel like, if I'd known this from the very get-go, healthful changes would have been much easier to implement. Instead of pitting myself against my body, thinking that I needed to fight tooth and nail to get it to do what I wanted, I would have treated it with respect. My biggest health mistake was not making changes out of love for my body.

—LEANNE VOGEL,
author of *The Keto Diet*
and founder of HealthfulPursuit.com

My biggest health mistake, which I think many of us make, is that I tend to get sucked into the "I'm not there yet!" mindset. I remember as I lost over 100 pounds, I was constantly putting pressure on myself along the journey. For example, when I was down 70 pounds, I had a hard time celebrating that huge win because I wasn't at 100 pounds yet. What we all have to realize is that our big goal is just a horizon line that will keep moving out into the distance and motivating us to push forward. We will never truly be "there" because once we reach that goal we will set a new one, and that horizon line moves into the distance again. Just remember this: be inspired by that big goal on the horizon, but always compare your current position to where you started … and be proud!

—ADAM SCHAEUBLE,
coach at TransformationCoach.me

One of the biggest mistakes I made on my journey to health, and I made it more than once, was thinking that I had to lose weight to be healthy. It's been a struggle balancing autoimmune health issues, stress-induced health issues, and weight-loss goals. There were times when eating to heal my body induced effortless weight loss, but there were also times of long stalls and times of weight gain. I often saw these as signs that I was failing at my task of healing. So, in efforts to remedy it, I restricted calories, even when my body was already in a fragile and stressed state or when my thyroid function was already impaired. The little voice inside my head that was terrified of not reaching my goal weight or, even worse, gaining it all back, would talk me into that old mentality of restriction. Over and over again I caused my already depleted system more stress than it could handle, and it always backfired. What I've learned is that when we truly nourish our bodies, when we support detox pathways and our gut microbiome with diet, proper sleep, movement, and stress management, that is when we truly begin to heal. We need to have patience and let the homeostatic mechanisms of our bodies do the work. We already have all of the innate wisdom we need to be truly healthy inside—we just need to create the right environment to let our bodies do what they do best, keep us healthy!

—CRISTINA CURP, NTP,
author of *Made Whole*
and founder of TheCastawayKitchen.com

My biggest mistake was getting caught up in the idea that I needed to count calories (which was pushed in my dietetics training). Sadly, we now know that the calories-in-calories-out theory is incorrect and that the quality of food you eat (as well as macronutrient balance) plays a large role in our metabolism. I've found the combination of moderately low-carb real food and mindful eating to be a perfect match for maintaining my metabolic health, keeping my weight at a stable and healthy place, and helping me have a positive relationship with food.

—LILY NICHOLS, RDN, CDE,
author of *Real Food for Gestational Diabetes*
and *Real Food for Pregnancy*

The biggest mistake I made in my health journey was trying to out-exercise a bad diet. It's just the wrong way of approaching fitness, because you'll end up running like a hamster in a wheel. A much smarter and effective approach would be to make your diet so easy to stick to that you'll induce a mild caloric deficit by default. The key is to eat nutrient-dense foods that promote satiety while not making you overconsume calories. Then you can structure your meals on your requirements for physical activity. Just don't ever increase physical activity to meet your nutritional intake.

—SIIM LAND,
author of *Metabolic Autophagy*

The biggest mistake I made in the past was thinking there was a one-size-fits-all solution to being "healthy." The real answer is that there are many roads to success, but you have to find what will work for you. After college I weighed almost 300 pounds, and it was depressing. The idea of changing my lifestyle was scary, not only because I knew it would be difficult, but because it would be embarrassing if I failed … and I was already embarrassed enough by my weight. In retrospect, after losing 70 pounds on keto, the most important thing was finding a healthy lifestyle that was actually sustainable for me.

—JON HART,
founder and CEO of Keto Bars

The biggest mistake I made was not realizing early on how important it is to have the right mindset in addition to a healthy diet. Most of my life I struggled with weight, and after countless failed attempts to lose weight, I lost confidence in my ability to change. I learned about the growth vs. fixed mindset, and I realized that I had a lot of work to do with my mental health and low self-esteem. I started working on changing my mindset and started viewing my struggles and failures as simply opportunities to learn, grow, and improve. After losing 120 pounds with the ketogenic diet, I've realized that many of the changes I implemented were truly about mind over matter.

—SUZANNE RYAN,
author of *Simply Keto* and founder of KetoKarma.com

My biggest mistake was thinking I could bend the rules a little here and there—for instance, having a glass of wine and letting the kids have high-carb contraband in the house. I have found that having a healthy way of life has to be consistent. You make a decision, develop the habit—and stick to it. Some people may be able to bend the rules and return to form with no issue—great for them. My reality is more akin to giving up smoking. I cannot go off track without slipping back into bad habits. Everyone has to find out for themselves what the threshold for making an exception is. For me, it can only be very special occasions. So what happened this year when I was strictly true to my own advice again? I lost 10 pounds in four weeks, and I look and feel much better!

—IVOR CUMMINS,
coauthor of *Eat Rich, Live Long*
and founder of TheFatEmperor.com

My biggest health mistake was thinking that the only way I would be happy and successful in life was if I was as thin as possible. I had no desire to eat a nutrient-dense, high-quality diet, or put on muscle, both of which would have made me happy and healthy. I subsisted on low-fat, low-calorie products for years and damaged my metabolism to no end. I would eat small snacks all day and feed my mind with negative self-talk. If I could go back in time, I would tell myself, "The antithesis of life is depriving yourself to look a certain way." Life isn't all about calories, the number on the scale, or food, for that matter. To truly enjoy life and love yourself, you need to find things outside food that bring you happiness, such as friends and family, hobbies, or work. Remember, if you indulge on vacation, date night, or any given Tuesday, don't beat yourself up. Tomorrow is a new day, and you are still the amazing you.

—MEGHA BAROT,
coauthor of *Keto Made Easy*
and cofounder of KetoConnect.net

"Learn from the mistakes of others. You can't live long enough to make them all yourself." —ELEANOR ROOSEVELT

My biggest mistake was thinking only about short-term results and aesthetics. It took me a long time to realize that developing sustainable eating and exercise habits would be essential to my long-term health and happiness. We are wired to seek out short-term results through extreme tactics like ten-day diets, cleanses, and detoxes. By making slow and steady improvements to my diet over the past four years, I have built a truly sustainable lifestyle that I can stick to for the long run.

—MATTHEW GAEDKE,
coauthor of *Keto Made Easy*
and cofounder of KetoConnect.net

The biggest health mistake I've made in my dieting journey is not having a defined goal. Oftentimes, health goals compete against one another. For instance, it's not possible to optimize your muscle building if your goal is also to lose as much fat as possible. Finding a balance between your goals and cycling through them efficiently, in a healthy manner, is the best way to turn a diet into a truly sustainable lifestyle. My mistake was blurring the lines between my different performance and body composition goals. Define your goal and then embrace the environment that you need to be in to reach that goal. Making the most out of each of these different cycles allows you to be excited about the phase you're in. If you're excited about it and understand what you're doing and why, you're significantly more likely to stick with it and see results.

—ROBERT SIKES,
founder of KetoSavage.com

One of the biggest mistakes I've made is an overall underappreciation for my body's circadian rhythms. I would do research into the wee hours of the night and mask fatigue with caffeine. Consulting opportunities required me to travel frequently from the West to East Coasts and I'd take a red-eye. After five years of over seventy annual cross-country flights—and many circadian rhythm disturbances—my hair was graying and thinning, and my recovery from exercise was poor. All this, despite eating a low-carb, organic whole-foods diet. Circadian rhythm distribution is linked with serious diseases, including cancer, diabetes, obesity, and a range of disorders. With this research top of mind, at the end of 2017 I walked away from a lucrative consulting arrangement to be home more—grounded and living in more harmony with the seasons and rise and fall of the sun.

—MIKE MUTZEL,
founder of HighIntensityHealth.com
and author of *Belly Fat Effect*

Quite simply, being too dogmatic in my thinking. Early on in my journey to health, I thought I knew it all. I was twenty-five years old, a medical resident, ripped, with a six-pack and no overt health problems. However, despite the outward appearance, I felt horrible. I figured this was due to a lack of sleep and working over one hundred hours per week in a high-stress environment, and that the way I felt would get better once my life got better. I was eating based on the USDA dietary guidelines, so that couldn't be the issue. Well, as life got easier, I felt the same. Worse, my labs indicated that things under the hood were not looking too good. I figured this was a mistake or just due to stress. The dogmatic thinking that following the recommended guidelines would bring me back to health was very difficult to overcome. I carry this experience with me as I read about the latest, greatest iteration of a healthy diet and make sure to keep an open mind, do my research, and judge for myself what the evidence shows. The reality is we are not created equal and a one-size-fits-all approach does not work.

—DR. JOHN LIMANSKY,
physician and biohacker

PART 1:

The Keto Diet:

A PRACTICAL APPROACH

A keto diet is unlike any other diet because it teaches the body to rely on a different fuel source: fat!

Due to the recent (historically speaking) addition of refined sugar and grains to the human diet, nearly everyone these days has a carbohydrate-based metabolism. That didn't used to be the case. Throughout history people survived on a plethora of different diets, basically just eating whatever was abundant in the area at the time. They had metabolic flexibility—they could easily use either fat or carbs as their primary fuel, switching between the two on a day-by-day basis. They almost never consistently got a majority of calories from carbohydrates, as we do today. Now, on average, 55 percent of our daily calories come from carbohydrates.

Carbohydrates are metabolized quickly, providing the body with immediate energy. This can be useful in some situations, like before doing some heavy lifting or playing a basketball game. Most of us, however, do not make use of the energy provided by this fast-burning fuel source. After "carbing up," we sit at the computer or in front of the TV, and all of that unused energy is stored as body fat. And because carbs are quickly removed from the bloodstream, we constantly need to fuel up with more carbs, so we're hungry all the time.

Matt here. I remember what a typical day was like before I started eating keto:

6 A.M.	7 A.M.	12 P.M.

Drink a few cups of coffee on my drive to work (using caffeine to override my lack of natural energy).	Grab another cup of coffee and a couple of granola bars as I ease into the day. (What better way to start the workday than mindlessly eating while checking last night's football scores?)	Eat a sub, chips, and a soda for lunch. (This was my idea of a somewhat healthy lunch—hey, the chips were oven baked and the soda was diet!)
2 P.M.	4 P.M.	EVENING

The dreaded 2 p.m. crash: spend the next ninety minutes struggling to stay awake while drinking a few cups of coffee and snacking on whatever pastries someone had brought to work that day.	Grab a takeout dinner on the way home.	Watch TV while having a few more snacks before bed.

I hated the constant need to fuel up. I was never satisfied and I was always tired, especially after lunch.

You've probably gone through this kind of energy roller coaster and frequent eating yourself. While we as humans have the metabolic framework in place to use both fat and carbs as fuel, today most of us have only ever experienced a carbohydrate-based metabolism, and we are extremely limited in our ability to use fat as a source of energy.

Metabolizing fat requires different processes than metabolizing carbs does, and when we rely primarily on carbs, those processes get rusty. It takes time to brush off the cobwebs and develop the ability to efficiently use fat as a primary fuel source—in other words, to become fat adapted. And the way you become fat adapted is by eating a low-carb, high-fat ketogenic diet.

I never realized that what I ate at lunch was causing my midafternoon drowsiness until after I started eating keto. Three weeks after starting a keto diet, I finally put it together. At our monthly office lunch, we were served pasta, an office favorite. While it was tough to resist, I managed to stick to salad and chicken while everyone else was three servings deep in pasta. Then 2 p.m. rolled around, and everyone around me was yawning and talking about how sleepy they were. Me? I was still feeling alert and energetic.

That's when I finally figured out what should have been obvious. If your body isn't relying on a constant inflow of carbs for energy, you no longer have to deal with the daily energy roller coaster. Your blood sugar doesn't spike and crash, and your body is able to get fuel from the fat stored on your body, so your energy is smooth and steady all day long. You're no longer a slave to the next granola bar or the fourth cup of coffee. Life is completely different.

What does a typical day look like for me now?

6 A.M.	10 A.M.	1 P.M.
	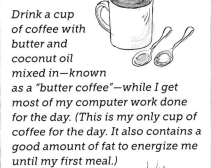	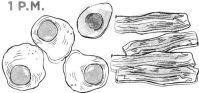
Hydrate with a large glass of water while taking the dog for a short walk. (This gets my body moving and connects me with nature.)	*Drink a cup of coffee with butter and coconut oil mixed in—known as a "butter coffee"—while I get most of my computer work done for the day. (This is my only cup of coffee for the day. It also contains a good amount of fat to energize me until my first meal.)*	*Eat my first meal, usually bacon, eggs, and avocado. (This is my new idea of a healthy lunch—three ingredients, compared to the fifty-plus I was having before.)*

2 P.M.	5 P.M.	EVENING

No crash! Instead of staring at the clock, waiting to end my workday, I actually am productive and get things done.	*Sit down to a dinner of steak, broccoli, and butter for my second and last meal of the day. (I focus on larger meals with less frequency instead of the standard three meals a day. Listening to my body has led me to this pattern of eating.)*	*Watch TV and have the occasional snack. (I'm still human! I enjoy relaxing with TV and a healthy snack at the end of the night, but it is no longer a necessity like it was when I was carb-dependent.)*

If you don't expend a lot of energy on high-intensity activities, you could probably benefit from some degree of fat adaptation. It can be beneficial for health and longevity, and because a healthy keto diet increases satiety and reduces the consumption of hyperpalatable foods, it makes it much easier to maintain a healthy body weight. Blood sugar stability is another benefit of keto. We all know the low-blood-sugar feeling that you get when you're on a high-carb diet and you haven't eaten anything in a few hours. It's that combination of hungry and irritable that the word *hangry* was invented to describe. On a keto diet there is no such thing as hangry. And if all that's not enough for you, here are some other proven benefits of a keto diet:

- Reduced inflammation
- Mental clarity
- Increased insulin sensitivity
- Improvement of some neurological conditions

Again, it takes time to become fat adapted, and the longer you eat a low-carb, high-fat ketogenic diet, the better your body becomes at metabolizing fat. The goal of this book is to help you establish a high degree of fat adaptation so that you can improve your eating habits in a sustainable, long-term way.

KETO: THE BASICS

The ketogenic diet is called "ketogenic" because it results in the production of ketones, molecules that are by-products of fat-burning. With the near elimination of carbohydrates on a ketogenic diet, the body shifts over to burning fat and using ketones instead of glucose (carbs). And just like that, you're "in ketosis."

The keto diet is not difficult or unnatural, but it is a dramatic departure from the way most of us eat these days. The diet is built around a certain ratio of macronutrients: carbohydrate intake is very low, healthy fats account for most of our daily calories, and protein intake is moderate, enough to maintain or build lean muscle mass.

In practical terms, this balance of macronutrients means focusing more on healthy fats—such as butter, coconut oil, and animal fats like lard and tallow—and avoiding carbohydrates, especially refined carbs like bread, pasta, and baked goods. There are lots of ways to eat a well-formulated keto diet, but you'll likely find that you get most of your carbs from vegetables, you eat a good amount of meat and eggs, and you add healthy fats to most of your meals.

MACRONUTRIENTS AND HOW TO TRACK THEM

Macronutrients, or "macros" for short, are the major nutrients that make up foods: fat, protein, and carbohydrates. Consuming these macros in certain proportions is critically important for a well-formulated ketogenic diet.

RATIO: 70/25/5

25% PROTEIN

70% FAT

5% CARBS

The chart above shows the easiest approach to the breakdown of macros on a ketogenic diet, a 70/25/5 ratio of fat, protein, and carbs. But it is just a starting point. Over time you may find that a different balance of macros is better for you.

The percentages here refer to the percentage of total daily calories. Here is an example of a 70/25/5 keto diet for someone eating 2,000 calories per day:

TOTAL CALORIES: 2,000

500 CALORIES FROM PROTEIN

1,400 CALORIES FROM FAT

100 CALORIES FROM CARBOHYDRATES

On nutrition labels, the amounts of fat, protein, and carbs are given in grams. (For example, you're probably familiar with protein bars advertising "30 grams of protein.") So it's best to translate your target macros from calories into grams, as opposed to always converting everything to calories.

FAT = 9 CALORIES PER GRAM   **PROTEIN = 4** CALORIES PER GRAM   **CARBOHYDRATE = 4** CALORIES PER GRAM

Now, looking back at that example of a 2,000-calorie keto diet, let's see what the macronutrient breakdown in grams would be:

TOTAL CALORIES: 2,000

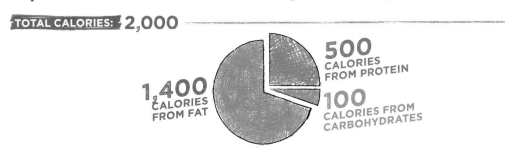

1,400 / 9 = 155.5
CALORIES FROM FAT — GRAMS OF FAT

500 / 4 = 125
CALORIES FROM PROTEIN — GRAMS OF PROTEIN

100 / 4 = 25
CALORIES FROM CARBOHYDRATES — GRAMS OF CARBOHYDRATE

If you like, you can use our online calculator to find your keto macros, personalized for your height, weight, and age: www.ketoconnect.net/calculator/. Remember, though, everyone is different. Calculators are just a starting point and cannot factor in all of the variables that have an impact on your metabolism and daily energy expenditure, such as your dieting or medical history. The values generated by the calculator are a great place to start, but it's up to you to continue making small tweaks until you find the macros that work best for you.

Once you know your target intake of each macronutrient, find a macro tracker and get familiar with it. Here are a few of the most popular:

- **Cronometer:** Great for tracking macros, and it also includes vitamin and mineral data on every food.

- **My Fitness Pal:** The oldest and most user-friendly tracking app. It has user-inputted data, so even if you are eating something uncommon, there will be an entry for it.

- **Lifesum:** Offers keto diet settings for easy setup and carb tracking.

- **Carb Manager:** A tracker made specifically for low-carb diets, with lots of low-carb recipes.

It's best to just pick one and stick with it so you get familiar with the interface. Most macro trackers have a website as well as an app. We personally use Cronometer because we like to see how our vitamins and minerals add up each day, but any of the hundreds of trackers out there will do the job.

All that's left is to input the foods you eat each day into the tracker to begin to form a picture of your daily intake. You can also configure the tracker with your daily macro goals, and then each day you can aim to hit those numbers. You're not going to be perfect on day one, so don't stress about it. Practice makes perfect, and in no time you will be an expert!

If you want to do it the old-fashioned way, you can even track everything on paper. Just put your target macros at the top of the page and list the macronutrients of the foods you eat at each meal. Total everything up at the end of the day and see how close you got to your targets.

Lazy Keto

While we strongly encourage you to track your food when starting a ketogenic diet, some people either hate tracking or have had bad experiences with it in the past. One helpful alternative to tracking everything is tracking only carbs. This is often referred to as "lazy keto." Eating a very low amount of carbs is the most important part of keto, and that alone can be enough for you to begin to experience benefits in satiety and food control. But most people who start with this approach eventually move on to tracking protein and fats as well in order to achieve even better results.

LOW CARB

Eating low-carb is the most important part of a keto diet, and at the beginning, it's the hardest. For someone just starting out on keto who wants to be in a state of ketosis, 20 grams of net carbs (total carbs minus fiber—more on that in a moment) per day is the upper limit. This can become more flexible the longer you eat keto, but starting out with a very-low-carb intake is essential. Limiting carb intake will cause your body to use up glycogen (stored carbohydrates) instead of carbs from food, and that ultimately creates the demand for a new source of energy: fat.

WHAT ARE NET CARBS?

Total carbs are just what they sound like: the total amount of carbohydrates you eat. Net carbs, on the other hand, are the amount of carbs that actually affect blood sugar levels. These are the only carbs that should be counted when you tally up your daily intake.

NET CARBS = TOTAL CARBS – FIBER

Fiber comes in two forms, soluble and insoluble. Insoluble fiber is completely indigestible, does not raise blood sugar, and does not trigger the release of insulin, as starches and sugars do. Soluble fiber is partially digestible, but it isn't absorbed the way other carbs are. Instead, it is fermented and produces short-chain fatty acids, which have been shown to improve gut health and stabilize blood sugar levels. For these reasons, it makes sense to subtract all fiber from total carbs when you're tracking your macros. Plus, counting net carbs encourages more vegetable consumption, which is always a good thing. For the purposes of tracking macros, the only value we care about are the net carbs.

Reading Labels

When it comes to packaged foods, not all countries have the same nutrition-labeling standards. The US and Canada list total carbs, while most other countries, including Mexico and all European countries, list "available carbohydrates," another name for net carbs. If you're outside the US and Canada, your nutrition labels likely already show net carbs, so you do not need to subtract fiber.

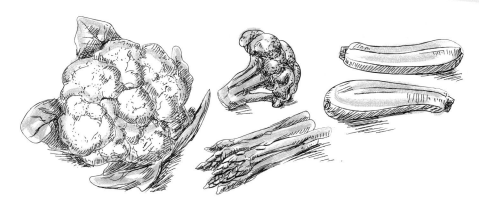

ARE THERE ANY OTHER CARBS WE CAN SUBTRACT?

There is one other group of carbohydrates that can be subtracted from your total carbs, but you have to be careful with this one. Sugar alcohols are alternatives to sugar that have fewer calories, and many of them don't raise blood sugar. The carb content from certain sugar alcohols can be subtracted from total carbs because they are undigested and not used for energy.

A Sweetener Experiment

We tested our blood sugar after consuming nine of the most popular sugar alcohols, natural sweeteners, and artificial sweeteners, and we had some surprising results. You can see the experiment and its results on our YouTube channel, www.youtube.com/c/ketoconnect.

Sugar alcohols have become increasingly popular in the last few decades—in fact, we use erythritol, one of the most common sugar alcohols, in a handful of recipes in this book. But not all sugar alcohols are created equal. Some, like maltitol, are just as bad as sugar when it comes to affecting blood sugar levels. As with everything surrounding your diet, there is genetic individuality in the response to sweeteners, so if you consume any sugar alcohols on a daily basis, it may be worth your while to test how your blood glucose and maybe even your ketone levels respond. But when it comes to tabulating your daily carb intake, you're usually safe subtracting the carbs that come from sugar alcohols.

THE SWEET STUFF

Going very-low-carb doesn't have to mean giving up all sweetness! There are low-carb sweeteners that you can use instead of sugar—though some low-carb sweeteners are better than others.

First, here are the sweeteners we recommend:

- **Stevia (natural sweetener, does not contain carbs):** Stevia is extracted from the leaves of a South American plant. It is 250–300 times as sweet as sugar and usually comes in liquid form. It has become increasingly popular in the last few decades and can be found in most grocery stores. Be careful, though, if you're buying stevia in powder form: check the ingredients label to see what other ingredients are included. Maltodextrin, dextrose, and fructose are commonly used as bulking agents in powdered stevia products and should be avoided. We recommend buying the liquid form to be safe.

- **Monk fruit (natural sweetener, does not contain carbs):** More expensive and less sweet than stevia, monk fruit is extracted from the luo han guo plant. It is 150–200 times as sweet as sugar. As with stevia, we recommend buying it in liquid form, and if you do buy it as a powder, check the ingredients! Monk fruit is not quite as sweet as stevia, but many people feel it does not have an aftertaste the way stevia does. If you can't handle the stevia aftertaste, this might be the one for you.

- **Erythritol (sugar alcohol, contains carbs that can be subtracted from total carbs):** Erythritol is the bulk sweetener we use exclusively. It is less expensive than other low-carb sweeteners and does not affect blood glucose levels. It occurs naturally in fruit and fermented foods, but packaged erythritol is usually derived from corn. Erythritol is 70 percent as sweet as sugar.

- **Allulose (rare sugar, contains carbs that can be subtracted from total carbs):** Rare sugars are a new category of keto-friendly sweeteners. Essentially, this class of sweeteners occurs in very small quantities in nature and has only recently made its way into our food. Allulose is the most popular of these and has found its way into a number of low-carb products. We've tested its impact on our blood sugar because we were skeptical (always be skeptical), and it had no impact whatsoever. Like erythritol, allulose is 70 percent as sweet as sugar, but we find it to be cost prohibitive and choose to go with erythritol instead.

All sweeteners not listed above should be approached with caution. There are a number of artificial sweeteners (such as aspartame, sucralose, acesulfame potassium, and saccharin) that do not affect blood glucose levels, but their impact on the body is not fully understood yet. While they are not going to knock you out of ketosis, they are definitely not part of a healthy diet and should be used sparingly, if at all.

Xylitol is a sugar alcohol that is commonly used in the keto community, but it is not ideal. It contains 2.4 calories per gram—in contrast, erythritol contains just 0.2 calories per gram. This means using xylitol in a cookie recipe will result in a cookie quite high in carbs. When tallying your daily carb intake, you should count half of the amount of carbs from xylitol. We see no reason to use xylitol when erythritol is cheaper and has fewer net carbs per serving.

Then there's the bad boy of the sugar alcohol family, maltitol. This sweetener is in just about every "sugar-free" candy bar you see at the grocery store. The reason it's in everything is that it's cheap to produce and tastes identical to sugar (maybe even better). The bad news is that maltitol is not at all keto-friendly. In our personal testing, we found it spiked our blood glucose almost as much as sugar did. Maltitol also has a long list of unwanted side effects when consumed in high amounts, like bloating and diarrhea. When you calculate your daily carb intake, it cannot be subtracted at all.

MODERATE PROTEIN

While carbohydrates are the major focus of a keto diet, protein is the most important macronutrient for your body. Protein is necessary to build and repair tissues and to maintain muscle mass, and it can even help reduce your appetite. It's also the easiest macro to meet on keto, especially when you're starting out. Most Americans already get around 20 to 25 percent of their daily calories from protein, so not much is going to change in that regard. It's likely that your sources of protein are going to be very different, though. Most people tend to favor lean cuts of meat, such as chicken breast, often fried in an assortment of harmful vegetable oils or eaten with buns made of refined white flour. On a ketogenic diet, you will be focusing on higher-fat meats, like beef, lamb, and dark-meat chicken, prepared with healthy fats and eaten without the high-carb bun.

While most people don't need to change their protein intake when they switch to keto, it's not uncommon to start to eat too much or too little protein. The most common response to removing carbs is to replace the missing carbs with protein, not fat. Forty years of low-fat propaganda is hard to shake off, and you likely still have lots of conventional wisdom about fat being bad for you in your head. It's important to truly embrace the idea that fat is good and necessary for your body to operate at its best. If you're afraid of fat when you start keto, chances are you'll be eating too much protein.

Of course, the opposite can also be true and you can start eating too little protein. This is usually prompted by an irrational fear of overdoing it on protein due to something called gluconeogenesis. Gluconeogenesis is a process by which your body derives glucose from non-carbohydrate substrates such as amino acids (protein). The fear stems from the idea that if you're eating too much protein, then your body will convert a lot of the excess into glucose, which will prevent your body from making the switch over to using ketones as a fuel source. This fear is largely unwarranted except in cases of extreme excess of protein intake.

Both of these pitfalls—eating too much or too little protein—are easily avoided by tracking your daily intake, but they can also be avoided by using a commonsense approach to your meals. If you're eating fatty cuts of meat, some vegetables, and a little bit of added fat, like butter or olive oil, you're probably doing just fine.

The appropriate amount of protein varies for each individual. The biggest factor is your lean body mass. Lean body mass is simply your total body weight minus your body fat. The greater your lean body mass, the more protein you need, so someone who is 200 pounds with very little body fat may need more protein than someone who is 250 pounds with a great deal of body fat.

Again, everyone is different, but as a general rule, daily protein intake should be between ½ pound and 1 pound of higher-fat cuts of meat. Megha, who weighs 125 pounds, eats around ½ pound of steak, chicken, or fish daily. Matt, who weighs 190 pounds, eats closer to 1 pound daily. As long as you're not wildly out of this range, you're probably doing a good job as far as your daily protein intake goes.

HIGH FAT

Fat is your body's new primary fuel source, so it's important to fuel up accordingly. Adding large amounts of fat to meals is something that most people are completely unfamiliar with—plus, everything at the grocery store is low-fat. So switching to a high-fat diet can take quite a bit of adjustment. But over the course of a few weeks, your energy levels will become tied to your fat intake, and this will make eating high amounts of fat second nature. Getting 70 percent or more of your daily calories from fat can be made easier by implementing a few of the tips in the box below.

As you're starting out on keto—and especially during the fifty days this guide covers—maintaining a high fat intake is extremely important. Once you have built up a strong fat adaptation, limiting fat can be a tactic for improved weight loss, but if you try limiting fat before that, you'll just turn a sustainable long-term way of eating into a restrictive diet.

The big takeaway is to embrace the high-fat aspect of this diet and everything that comes with it. Don't dwell on the fact that you can't eat blueberry muffins for breakfast. Instead, take advantage of all the delicious high-fat foods that are back on the menu, like bacon, butter, and eggs.

How to Get More Healthy Fats in Your Diet

1. START YOUR DAY WITH A TEA OR COFFEE WITH ADDED FATS. *Blending 1 tablespoon each of coconut oil and butter into your morning coffee is a good place to start.*

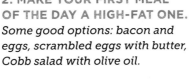

2. MAKE YOUR FIRST MEAL OF THE DAY A HIGH-FAT ONE. *Some good options: bacon and eggs, scrambled eggs with butter, Cobb salad with olive oil.*

3. HAVE FAT BOMBS IN THE FREEZER *for snacks, like Peanut Butter Pecan Fat Bombs (page 266).*

4. ADD FAT TO ALL OF YOUR VEGGIES. *Butter, olive oil, coconut oil, avocado oil, and animal fats like tallow are all great options.*

5. AVOID LEAN CUTS OF MEAT, *like chicken breast and ground turkey.*

6. COOK WITH HEALTHY FATS *like butter and coconut oil instead of nonstick cooking sprays.*

FREQUENTLY ASKED QUESTIONS

1. HOW DO I KNOW HOW MANY CALORIES I SHOULD EAT EACH DAY?

The easy answer to this question is to listen to your body and eat when you're hungry. Unfortunately, most of us were raised on processed foods, and that means that listening to your body will have you going to the McDonald's drive-through. The truth is, you can't listen to your body's hunger cues when you're starting out on keto because they are lying to you. But as you become fat adapted over the course of four to eight weeks, you will become much more in tune with your true hunger and will finally be able to eat a healthy diet intuitively.

The easiest way to figure out your daily caloric needs is to use a keto macro calculator (we have one on our website, but they're also available as apps). This tool will give you a rough estimate for how many calories someone of your height, weight, and muscle mass should consume on a keto diet. This is just an estimate, though! It's impossible for a calculator to factor in all the elements that determine how many calories you need each day, such as dieting history, medical conditions, and activity level.

Over the course of weeks and months, you will build a clearer picture of how your food intake affects your weight, mood, and energy levels. Experience will give you a far better picture of what you need to eat to feel your best than any calculator.

2. DO I NEED TO COUNT CALORIES?

If your goal is to lose weight, you need to be in a calorie deficit, no matter what kind of diet you're eating. That means you need to burn more calories than you take in from food. That doesn't mean that the best way to lose weight is to obsessively count calories forever. Taking a long-term approach is the key to losing weight in a healthy and sustainable way. That means eating foods that you know to be healthy.

At first you'll probably overeat on keto, simply because that's what most of us are used to. Overeating keto-friendly foods in the beginning is fine—the focus should be on breaking your dependence on carbs. After a while, you will naturally eat the right amount of food for your body's needs.

That said, on keto, counting calories is important because it helps you make sure that you're eating the right proportions of fat, protein, and carbs. We always recommend tracking your calorie intake and macros at first, and some people find tracking every day to be freeing and continue doing it forever. However, once you get a handle on what is in the foods you're eating, their macronutrient profiles, and how they make you feel, tracking everything is not necessary. You will begin to fall into a routine, and the key concepts of a keto diet will be ingrained in all of your food choices without your having to put much thought into them.

3. HOW MANY CARBS CAN I EAT PER DAY AND BE IN KETOSIS?

This varies from person to person, but the best rule for starting out is to consume no more than 20 grams of net carbs per day. Anything less than this is fine; some people even do zero grams of carbs.

The longer you are on a keto diet and the more active you are, the more carbs you can consume and still be in ketosis. After a while, ketosis becomes the default state for your body and is easy to maintain.

4. HOW LONG DOES IT TAKE TO GET INTO KETOSIS?

Typically between twenty-four and seventy-two hours, but everyone is different. The lower your carbohydrate consumption and the higher your activity level, the faster you will get into ketosis. Remember, though, fast and quick are not synonymous with long-term diet adherence. How long it takes to achieve ketosis should not be a big concern; the important thing is that you're developing the ability to use fat for fuel, which is a longer process.

5. CAN I HAVE ALCOHOL?

Alcohol is best avoided, but the occasional drink isn't going to cut into your progress too severely. When you drink alcohol, the liver's top priority is to process it, so it stops producing ketones until the alcohol is cleared from your system. With no new ketones being produced, you may have a very low ketone level until all of the alcohol is metabolized.

That said, if you do choose to drink, some options are more keto-friendly than others. The best alcohol choices for keto are zero-carb spirits such as whiskey, scotch, tequila, and vodka. Dry wines are also a good option at 3 to 7 grams of carbs per glass. Beers are the worst option, but if you're a die-hard beer drinker, there are some low-carb beers that contain less than 5 grams of carbs per bottle. Sadly, just about every craft beer (the good stuff) will have north of 10 grams of carbs per bottle, often upwards of 25 grams.

6. I THOUGHT FRUIT WAS HEALTHY. WHY ARE SOME FRUITS AVOIDED ON A KETO DIET?

While fruit does have some health benefits, they do not outweigh the tremendous amount of sugar fruit contains. Certain low-sugar fruits, such as blackberries, raspberries, and lemons, are fine in moderation, but most fruit should be avoided. Interestingly, today's fruits have been selectively bred to contain as much sugar as possible, so their nutritional profiles are very different than they were thousands of years ago.

People emphasize fruit consumption so much these days because it is better than sweet alternatives like cake, candy, and other processed foods, but fruit is by no means an essential part of our diets. The Inuit in Alaska and native Northern Europeans have thrived on low-fruit diets for thousands of years.

It's important to understand that a lot of what we think we know about nutrition today stems from correlative data—we know that there's an association between two things, but not that one causes the other. So yes, people who eat more fruit are healthier than those who eat less fruit. But people who eat more fruit are also more likely to exercise, less likely to smoke cigarettes, and less likely to eat processed foods. There are too many confounding factors to definitively say that fruit is what is causing these people to be healthier.

7. WHAT IS INTERMITTENT FASTING, AND DO I NEED TO DO IT?

Fasting has become very popular in the past decade due to the publication of more studies on the benefits of fasting and a greater emphasis on trying to replicate the eating patterns of early humans.

The most popular form of fasting is intermittent fasting, which is essentially fasting for a certain number of consecutive hours each day. The most common type of intermittent fasting is fasting for sixteen hours per day and eating all of your food in an eight-hour window. Here's what this often looks like: skip breakfast, eat lunch at noon, maybe have a small snack at 4 p.m., and then eat dinner around 7 p.m. You then don't eat again until noon the next day.

Intermittent fasting isn't required, but you may want to try experimenting with it at some point. Many people find that they are not hungry first thing in the morning, so it's natural for them to not eat until closer to lunchtime. Our recommendation is not to force it. As you become increasingly fat adapted, fasting will become easier, and sometimes you will just naturally fall into it.

The key, as always, is to figure out what's sustainable for you. A good rule of thumb is that if you've tried something a few times and don't think you can do it for the rest of your life, it probably isn't worth doing.

8. I'M NOT LOSING WEIGHT. WHAT AM I DOING WRONG?

You might not be doing anything wrong, but it doesn't hurt to double-check to be sure. If you're not already using a macro tracker (see page 26 for some examples), start. Plugging your food intake into a tracker for just a few days can verify that you're on track with your intake of fat, protein, and carbs. If you are, then you just need to stick to the plan and stop stepping on the scale every day. Weight loss can be deceptive. You could be losing inches without dropping pounds—in fact, this is usually the case if you're lifting weights and starting a keto diet at the same time.

Similarly, if you've been steadily losing weight and you hit an extended plateau, it can be a good idea to check back in and make sure you're hitting your macros. Weight loss is not linear, but the general trajectory should be downward. If you weigh yourself every day, start weighing in weekly or monthly to get a better sense of the overall trend.

And remember, weight loss is not really what you're after, anyway. What you really want is fat loss, and that takes time. So many of us have a history of yo-yo dieting and extreme calorie restriction that it can take some time to repair our metabolism and get to the point that we're burning fat effectively. You may not want to hear this, but if you start eating real food and gain weight, then you probably needed to gain that weight as a step toward good health.

Quick Reference FOOD GUIDE

Now that you know the parameters of the keto diet, within those confines you need to come up with *your* diet. So many people get stressed out about doing everything right as soon as they start eating keto. They force themselves to eat avocados just because they heard they were good for keto, even though they hate avocados. Pro tip: Don't eat things you hate. Make this diet your own. Learn as you go. Eat foods you love—we guarantee that plenty of them support a healthy keto diet!

The list at right will guide you in choosing what to eat. Each kind of food is grouped into three tiers:

COMPLETELY AVOID

These are foods you should avoid as much as you can. They're far from natural foods and are the worst for your health. Some, like vegetable oils, are low-carb and can fit into a keto diet in theory, but their negative health consequences put them on the avoid list.

EAT IN MODERATION

These foods are a perfectly acceptable part of a keto diet, but they shouldn't be staple foods. Use them as complements to your diet, which should be composed mainly of items from the next category.

BEST CHOICES

If your diet consists only of these foods, then you're doing a great job. Foods in this category should make up a large percentage of your diet.

Good Things Happen in Threes!

To make grocery shopping as simple as possible, on your first trip to the store, pick up three items from each of the main macro categories: fats, proteins, and carbs. Try to get as many of these items as possible from the "best choices" lists. This should simplify meal planning and provide you with enough variety for at least a few days. Be sure to throw in a few snacks from the "other" category as well.

What would we grab on our first shopping trip for a keto diet?

FATS	PROTEINS	CARBS	OTHER

FATS	PROTEINS	CARBS	OTHER
Butter	*Chicken wings*	*Broccoli*	*Brazil nuts*
Coconut oil	*Salmon*	*Brussels sprouts*	*Coffee*
Tallow	*Steak*	*Kimchi*	*Eggs*
			Pumpkin seeds

FATS

COMPLETELY AVOID

Margarine

Vegetable oils (canola, corn, cottonseed, rapeseed, soybean)

EAT IN MODERATION

Nut and seed oils (peanut, sesame, sunflower, walnut)

BEST CHOICES

Avocado

Avocado oil

Butter

Coconut

Coconut oil

Duck fat

Ghee

Lard

Mayonnaise (made without vegetable oils)

MCT oil

Olive oil

Tallow

PROTEINS

COMPLETELY AVOID

Processed meats with added sugar (bacon, ham, sausage—but these are fine without added sugar)

Soy foods and other plant-based protein replacements (seitan, tempeh, tofu)

EAT IN MODERATION

Lean meats (chicken breast, ground turkey, pork chops)

Processed meats (beef jerky, deli meats, pepperoni)

BEST CHOICES

Bone marrow and broth

Chicken thighs

Duck

Fish (all, but favor higher-fat species, like halibut, salmon, and sardines)

Ground beef (85% or less lean)

Lamb

Organ meats

Shellfish

Steak

CARBS

COMPLETELY AVOID

Grains (barley, corn, oats, quinoa, rice, wheat)

High-sugar fruits (apples, bananas, grapes, mango, pineapple, watermelon)

Legumes (kidney beans, lentils)

Starchy vegetables (potatoes, sweet potatoes)

EAT IN MODERATION

Higher-carb non-starchy vegetables (carrots, cucumbers, eggplant, green beans, jicama, onions, peas, peppers, radishes, tomatoes, zucchini)

Low-sugar fruits (blackberries, blueberries, lemons, limes, raspberries, strawberries)

BEST CHOICES

Fermented vegetables (fermented pickles, kimchi, sauerkraut)

Lower-carb non-starchy vegetables (asparagus, broccoli, Brussels sprouts, cabbage, cauliflower, celery, chard, collards, kale, lettuce, spinach)

Mushrooms

EGGS & DAIRY

COMPLETELY AVOID

Pasteurized milk (all types)

Foods made from low-fat and skim milk (cheese, cream cheese, kefir, sour cream, yogurt)

EAT IN MODERATION

Raw full-fat milk

Foods made from pasteurized full-fat milk (cheese, cream cheese, kefir, sour cream, yogurt)

BEST CHOICES

Butter (preferably grass-fed)

Cream

Eggs

Foods made from raw full-fat milk (cheese, cream cheese, kefir, sour cream, yogurt)

OTHER

EAT IN MODERATION

Coffee

Herbs & spices

Keto-friendly sweeteners (allulose, erythritol, monk fruit, stevia—see page 28)

Low-carb nuts (almonds, Brazil nuts, hazelnuts, macadamia nuts, pecans, walnuts)

Low-carb protein bars (Quest Bars, Keto Bars)

Low-carb seeds (chia, flax, hemp, pumpkin, sesame, sunflower)

Stevia-sweetened chocolate (at least 85% cacao)

Supplements (collagen powders, protein powders)

Tea

Unsweetened nondairy milks (almond, cashew, coconut, flax)

Shopping GUIDE

You can get everything you need for a keto diet at your local grocery store, but over the years we've found that it's best to seek out certain items at a few specialty grocery stores: either the item is only available at a particular store or it's extremely cheap at that store. The lists below indicate which foods we go out of our way to buy at Costco, Trader Joe's, or Whole Foods. As you can imagine, nothing on the Whole Foods list is there because it's extremely cheap, but they do have a lot of good stuff!

COSTCO

Some of our absolute favorite buys are the primal cuts of beef from Costco. These are 10- to 20-pound slabs of New York strip steak or rib eye, often for less than $6 per pound! Wild-caught sardines are great for a quick lunch when you don't have time to cook, and Costco has them for less than half the price of other grocery stores. Costco might also be the best place to stock up on bulk ingredients for baking. Almond flour, coconut flour, coconut oil, and grass-fed butter are all nicely priced.

- Almond butter
- Almond flour
- Almond milk
- Almonds
- Cheese crisps
- Chia seeds
- Coconut flour
- Coconut oil
- Coffee
- Ghee
- Grass-fed butter
- Guacamole
- Heavy whipping cream
- Hemp seeds
- Low-carb protein bars
- Macadamia nuts
- Mayonnaise (made with avocado or coconut oil)
- Olive oil
- Pecans
- Primal beef cuts (rib eye and New York strip)
- Raw-milk cheeses*
- Sardines
- Sausage
- Smoked salmon
- Walnuts

TRADER JOE'S

Trader Joe's has a lot of seasonal items that we absolutely love. When they have Halloumi cheese in stock, we buy up as much as we can carry. We slice it thin and fry it on the stovetop, then snack on it while marathoning TV shows. Trader Joe's also has a really good selection of high-quality frozen meats and seafood. And the nuts and seeds section has everything you could ever want at great prices.

- Almond flour
- Almonds
- Avocados
- Bacon
- Butter
- Chia seeds
- Chicken burgers
- Chopped kale
- Coconut aminos
- Coconut flour
- Flax seeds
- Frozen grass-fed meats
- Frozen organic veggies
- Halloumi cheese
- Hemp seeds
- Hot sauce
- Low-carb protein bars
- Macadamia nuts
- Mahi mahi burgers
- Organic lettuce
- Pecans
- Pimento cheese
- Precooked chicken for salads
- Salad dressings
- Salmon burgers
- Smoked and cured meats (pepperoni, salami, etc.)
- Smoked oysters
- Turkey burgers
- Walnuts

WHOLE FOODS

Whole Foods is the only place in our area where we can find bone marrow, so we go there to stock up for making homemade bone broth. You're not going to find many deals here, but there are some items that you can't find anywhere else. What's great about Whole Foods is that they source a lot of items from local businesses. So here in Georgia, for instance, they have amazing pecans, fermented coconut milk kefir, and steak and ground beef from cattle raised in the state. While we're there we usually get dinner from the hot bar, which has a bunch of keto-friendly options and lists all the ingredients above each dish.

- Beef bones (for marrow and bone broth)
- Butter
- Canned oysters and sardines
- Deli meats
- Eggs
- Fermented vegetables (fermented pickles, kimchi, sauerkraut)
- Frozen berries
- Frozen vegetables
- Halloumi cheese
- Hot bar items
- Kombucha
- Low-carb ice cream
- Low-carb protein bars
- Meat sticks and bars
- Mineral water
- Organ meats
- Organic produce
- Pork rinds
- Raw-milk cheeses*
- Stevia-sweetened chocolates (at least 85% cacao)
- Stevia-sweetened sodas
- Wild-caught seafood
- Wild game (bison, quail)
- Wild mushrooms

* Look for "unpasteurized milk" or "raw milk" on the ingredients list; French and Swiss cheeses are typically made with raw milk.

Healthy Go-To SNACKS

Snacks are a by-product of the way we eat today—always on the go, no time to sit down and eat a real meal. Many of us subsist on nothing but snacks until we get home at night and finally have time to eat some real food. While this is a habit you will want to break at some point, it will be easier to stop snacking after you have been on a keto diet for a few months. So while you're still getting used to this way of eating, it's important to stock up on keto-friendly snacks that you can turn to when you don't have time to prepare a meal. During the adaptation phase in particular, having healthy snacks on hand can be the key to success.

The list below suggests some keto-friendly snacks you may want to keep on hand.

Avocados

Beef jerky

Butter coffee*

Cheese

Deli meats

Fat bombs *(pages 266 and 272)***

Fresh coconut

Hard-boiled eggs

Low-Carb Graham Crackers *(page 300)***

Low-carb protein bars**

Mug cakes *(page 294)***

Nuts**

Olives

Pork rinds

Salmon Jerky *(page 258)*

Sardines

Seeds**

Stevia-sweetened chocolate *(at least 85% cacao)*

Store-bought low-carb cheese crisps

Store-bought or homemade low-carb crackers, such as flaxseed crackers*

Tuna

Unsweetened nut butters**

* Recipe available on KetoConnect.net

** LIMIT: These foods are highly palatable and easy to overconsume. For nuts, seeds, nut butters, and fat bombs, limit yourself to 1–2 servings per day. Low-carb protein bars are best as an occasional treat every few days.

272
Lemon Blueberry Cheesecake Fat Bombs

266
Peanut Butter Pecan Fat Bombs

300
Low-Carb Graham Crackers

294
Blueberry Mug Cake

258
Salmon Jerky

Our Favorite Ready-Made Snacks

4505 cracklins

4505 pork rinds

Applegate organic deli meats

Dang Bars

Doctor in the Kitchen Flackers

Eating Evolved Midnight Coconut chocolate bar

EPIC pork rinds

EPIC Venison Sea Salt and Pepper bar

Grillo's pickles

Keto Bars *(online only)*

Kite Hill almond milk yogurt

Lily's chocolate bars

Moon Cheese

Quest Bars

Quest Tortilla Style Protein Chips, nacho cheese flavor

Real Good Foods pizzas and enchiladas

Seasons canned sardines in olive oil

Smart Cakes *(online only)*

So Delicious ice cream

Wild Planet canned chicken

Wild Planet sardines in olive oil

Note:
When buying prepared foods at the store, please remember to check the labels for added sugars or other unhealthy additives.

Supplements

The beauty of any species-appropriate diet—the kind of diet that a species evolved to eat, whether that means grasses, as with cattle, or a wide range of plants and animals, as with humans—is that the diet is nutritionally complete. There's no need for nutritional supplements because the foods on the diet are naturally nutrient dense. There shouldn't be any glaring weaknesses that need to be filled with pills and potions.

That said, our food supply and way of life have changed drastically from those of our ancestors. Since we can't truly replicate the early human diet, there are a few supplements you may want to consider taking to compensate. Also, the transition to a ketogenic diet can increase your body's need for certain minerals, so these should be supplemented for the first few months while you adapt to this way of eating.

In addition to the supplements listed here, there are a number of supplement-like food items that can be consumed as part of your diet, such as MCT oil, whey protein, and collagen peptides.

MAGNESIUM

One of the most important minerals in our body, magnesium has become increasingly scarce in our food supply for a few reasons. First, magnesium is becoming depleted in the soil used for growing crops, which translates to less magnesium in the food supply. We're also simply eating fewer magnesium-containing foods, like leafy greens, nuts, and seeds. Finally, when starting a ketogenic diet your body holds on to less water because glycogen (stored carbohydrate) binds to water, so as glycogen is burned through, water is flushed out—and with it, lots of electrolytes, like magnesium. Over time, the need for supplemental magnesium may be reduced.

RECOMMENDED INTAKE:
400 mg magnesium glycinate daily

SODIUM

Sodium is one of the few minerals that is actually more abundant in our food supply than ever before because of the prevalence of packaged and processed foods. But on a healthy keto diet, those kinds of foods are generally avoided in favor of healthy whole foods, so intentionally consuming more sodium may be necessary. Over time, the need for sodium may be reduced.

RECOMMENDED INTAKE:
2 g to 4 g sea salt daily

COD LIVER OIL

No supplement can make up for a poor diet, but cod liver oil comes close. It's loaded with vitamin A, anti-inflammatory omega-3 fatty acids, and vitamin D_3, so if you are not eating much seafood or organ meats—good sources of all these nutrients—cod liver oil will help you cover your bases. Whenever a family member asks us for help with their diet but has trouble sticking with the changes we suggest, we tell them to prioritize cod liver oil. That way they're at least getting an adequate dose of essential nutrients that can be difficult to get in foods.

RECOMMENDED INTAKE:
About 1 teaspoon per day (check the label of the brand you are using; 10,000 IU of vitamin A daily from cod liver oil is adequate)

POTASSIUM

When you're first starting a keto diet, potassium is the most important electrolyte to pay attention to in order to mitigate keto flu symptoms (see page 50). Sodium and potassium have an ideal balance in your body that is likely out of whack due to the high sodium and low potassium in modern diets, and when you adapt to a keto diet and your electrolyte levels drop, it can exacerbate the need for potassium.

The best way to supplement is to use a salt substitute or low-sodium salt. These are composed of potassium chloride or a mixture of potassium chloride and sodium chloride, making them perfect as potassium supplements. There is some concern surrounding potassium supplementation—in high amounts, it has been linked to cardiac arrhythmias—so do your research on this topic and be sure not to overdo it. We routinely supplement up to 2 grams per day and eat potassium-rich foods like avocados and salmon. As with the other electrolytes, the need for supplementation will decrease over time.

RECOMMENDED INTAKE:
1 g to 2 g potassium from salt substitute daily

VITAMIN D_3

It's no secret that we don't spend nearly enough time outside these days. A 2011 study in *Nutrition Research* that examined 4,495 people found that over 40 percent were vitamin D deficient, and the darker your skin, the greater the likelihood of vitamin D deficiency. Supplementing with vitamin D is something that a lot of people could benefit from, especially those in colder climates and those who spend most of their time indoors. A study published in the *International Journal of Endocrinology* in 2017 showed that using vitamin K_2 in tandem with vitamin D_3 is more beneficial than just supplementing with D_3 on its own; we recommend liquid drops of vitamin D_3/K_2.

RECOMMENDED INTAKE:
1,000 IU to 4,000 IU (varies depending on the individual, but this range works for most people)

PART 2

50 Days to Fat Adaptation

The journey to fat adaptation is going to take determination, commitment, and the willingness to step outside your comfort zone. But by the end, you will have better control over your diet, better energy, and, hopefully, a newfound love for preparing delicious meals from whole ingredients.

We've created a plan for developing a strong fat adaptation over the course of fifty days—seven weeks, plus one day of celebration. As you journey on this path, the intensity will gradually be ramped up as you become more used to the keto diet and to tracking your food intake, and as you compile a handful of go-to meals that you enjoy. We will slowly scale back the amount of snacks and number of meals in a way that will feel natural. It's important to understand that huge changes do not happen overnight, or even over the course of fifty days. However, fifty days is more than enough time to lay the groundwork for a future of health and longevity.

The fifty days of the plan are broken up into seven one-week segments with specific focus areas. This setup is designed to help you avoid "paralysis by analysis." There's so much information out there about keto these days, with all the resources online and on TV, that it can be overwhelming. The weekly segments will help you focus on making a few small changes each week and gradually put everything together as you progress through the fifty days.

Making slow but steady progress also makes it much easier to stick with a new way of eating. We simply can't change our behaviors drastically from one day to the next and expect the changes to stick. Continual improvement is the name of the game. Start slow. Remain steady. You're going to mess up along the way, but that's okay. As long as you're doing better than you were last week, last month, last year, you're doing a good job. You do not need to immediately switch to only whole foods and cook everything from scratch. That might be a long-term goal, but it's not where you start on day one. Start with some healthier substitutions for the food you are currently eating. If you eat potato chips every day after work, that's a hard habit to break. Start by eating almonds or pork rinds instead, rather than trying not to snack at all. Make sensible changes that put you on the path of improvement.

Keep this in mind when you embark on this fifty-day journey. Rather than feeling pressured to adhere to the plan 100 percent as it is written, allow yourself to make some modifications in the name of long-term sustainability. Everyone reading this book is at a different place in their journey, so if the plan is too intimidating for you currently, try one of the following options:

- **THE TAKEOUT LIFE:** If you're one of the growing number of people who eat most meals away from home and have limited cooking skills, your best bet is going to be a slow transition. Before starting the fifty-day plan, take a few weeks to find a number of reliable keto-friendly takeout options (more info on takeout can be found on page 53). Make an effort to increase the number of home-cooked meals you prepare each week, and use meal prepping to your advantage. After a number of weeks you will be more equipped in the kitchen and you'll be ready to jump into the fifty-day plan!

- **THE SNACK-BASED DIET:** Do you rely on a constant flow of snacks to get you through the day? If so, you're not alone; most people these days do. Snacking is a hard habit to break. Before starting the fifty-day plan, it is a good idea to take a few weeks to try to cut back on the snacking and concentrate on fewer, larger meals. Snacks just keep you wanting more, never feeling truly satisfied. Start by switching completely to the keto-friendly snacks listed on page 40. Starting a completely new diet and forgoing a deeply ingrained habit like snacking at the same time can be very challenging. It's best to tackle these one by one and approach everything with a long-term outlook.

The weekly meal plans we present here can be followed to a T—we've made sure they have the right proportions of macronutrients for a 1,800-calorie diet (with some variation within about 200 calories)—but they're best used as a reference that you adjust to suit your needs and tastes. Some people don't like avocados or eggs; some people don't eat pork or beef. Maybe you live five minutes away from a local farm and get good deals on quality eggs and cheese, so you want to eat more of those. There is no one-size-fits-all plan, so feel free to stray from what we've suggested here. The most important tenets of the meal plan, which should be followed to achieve the desired results, are a low carb intake and the addition of healthy fats. As long as you're following those two guidelines, you will have success. If you want to change the plan to better suit your food preferences, just keep the carb count under 20 grams of net carbs daily and make sure to add fats!

10 THINGS TO KNOW BEFORE YOU START

Before we dive into the meal plan itself, let's talk about what you can expect and what actions and attitudes will prepare you for success. Understanding these ten principles will make life much easier as you transition to keto.

1. WHAT GETS MEASURED GETS MANAGED

We're definitely not in favor of *restricting* calories—the last thirty years of dieting culture in America are hard proof that it doesn't work in the long term—but *counting* calories, along with fat, protein, and carbohydrate, is an important and illuminating part of the process of transitioning to keto. The difference is that you're not counting calories to see how little you can eat each day. You're simply learning about what's in the food you eat and how it affects you.

We recommend using a tracking app that tells you the amount of fats, proteins, and carbohydrates in your food. Knowing these details is absolutely essential to taking charge of your health and optimizing your diet. How can you know what is causing you to doze off in your cubicle every afternoon around 2 p.m. if you don't know the nutritional contents of your lunch? Counting calories in this sense isn't a weight-loss tactic but part of taking an active role in your nutrition. It means you care enough about your food to make time to understand it.

A common pitfall of counting calories is the tendency to consume foods that are high in volume but low in calories, like popcorn and rice cakes. That's great for the overall calorie count but not so great for supplying your body with the nutrients it needs—and remember, the goal here is not to minimize calories. On a keto diet, you will be consuming foods that are both nutrient dense and calorie dense, so do not let the amount of calories determine your food choices. Humans have been seeking out the most calorie-dense foods for hundreds of thousands of years—don't stop now. These foods will keep you feeling full longer and prevent drops in energy levels after meals.

"What gets measured gets managed." —PETER DRUCKER

2. THE DIET ISN'T MAGIC

We've noticed a common theme when we talk to people who are trying to change the way they eat: they talk about their previous diets the way a plumber talks about wrenches, as if finding the exact right one will suddenly make everything work just right. Once they find the right diet, they'll drop a bunch of weight, have more energy—heck, they might even start horseback riding on the weekends because they found the magical diet that makes their lives awesome.

There's no such thing as a one-size-fits-all diet. Every body is different, and what works for one person may not work for you. That means that you need to take ownership of your food choices. There are millions of different ways to implement a ketogenic diet, and figuring out which one best suits you is your personal responsibility. Instead of "trying a diet," reframe this idea as "refining my diet." You're going to be eating food for the rest of your life, so it's a good idea to start figuring out which ones fuel you and give you energy, and which ones drain you.

Yes, we're providing a fifty-day meal plan, and we hope that it will be useful to you as you transition to keto. But if you are not getting the results you set out to achieve, make some changes! Tweak your diet and see what happens. Start building a database of what works for you. Over time, you'll figure out what foods help you feel your best.

At the same time, don't abandon keto completely after just a couple of weeks. Give it time. We have been experimenting with our health and fitness for the better part of the last decade, and we have found lots of things that work for us, as well as some that don't. We wouldn't have learned any of this if we'd hopped from diet to diet every few months when we hit a setback.

3. KETO IS THE ANTIDOTE TO THE STANDARD AMERICAN DIET

Some critics of keto claim that it is not a "natural diet." While it's true that most of our ancestors did not exclusively eat a low-carbohydrate diet, they all had a high degree of fat adaptation due to a lack of refined carbohydrates in the food supply. Plus, times of food scarcity were much more common, and in those times, they had to switch easily to fueling from the body's fat stores.

But all of that is actually beside the point. The reason adopting a ketogenic diet is the first step to reclaiming your health is not that it's the perfect human diet or the most natural diet. It's that keto is the best diet for breaking your reliance on the standard American diet and its abundance of processed, high-sugar foods. For most of us, eating healthy is extremely hard to do, if not impossible, when we are eating a diet high in carbohydrates.

This is because on a high-carb diet, the only thing your body knows how to do is burn carbs for energy. That means that when you try to lose body fat, which requires burning more calories than you take in, your energy levels crash. Your body has no idea how to burn fat for energy, whether dietary fat or stored body fat, so you feel terrible in the absence of carbs. This is why the ketogenic diet is so vital for losing body fat. You will slowly but surely improve your body's ability to utilize fat (that is, its fat adaptation), making it possible to eat a calorie deficit and not feel like a zombie!

Once you've completed this fifty-day plan and broken out of the standard American diet cycle, you can consider adding some healthy whole-food carbohydrates, or you can stick to a strict ketogenic diet. We have personally stuck to a ketogenic diet strictly for close to four years now and plan to for the foreseeable future. Occasionally, we experiment with different things, like eating 100 grams of carbohydrates after an intense workout, just to see if we can improve upon our progress. We think it's important to never abide by absolutes like "All carbs are bad" or "I'm doing a ketogenic diet for the rest of my life." Always leave the door open for new ideas that could improve upon your current diet. The important thing is that by improving your body's fat adaptation, you'll be back in control of your dietary decisions. You'll no longer be ruled by hunger and the constant need to fuel up with fast-burning carbs.

4. THE KETO FLU IS COMING

Most people experience the "keto flu" when they start out on keto. It typically begins around days 2 to 4 and can last a few days. Symptoms may include headaches, muscle soreness, fatigue, brain fog, insomnia, irritability, nausea, poor focus, and sugar cravings. The keto flu generally lasts for one to three days, up to a week at most.

Keto flu occurs because your body is no longer receiving dietary carbohydrates, which means it is holding on to less water. For each gram of glycogen (stored carbohydrate), your body holds on to 4 grams of water. As your carb intake drops, your body starts to burn through glycogen stores (a good thing—glycogen needs to drop in order for your body to get used to using fat for fuel). This causes a loss in water, and with the water, you also lose electrolytes. The good news is that that means keto flu symptoms can be greatly reduced or even prevented entirely by supplementing with electrolytes and drinking lots of water to stay hydrated. Read more about supplementing electrolytes on page 43.

MEGHA BAROT AND MATT GAEDKE

5. YOUR WEIGHT WILL FLUCTUATE

The scale is going to play tricks on you during this fifty-day process. Your body is going to be fluctuating in weight more than it ever has before, due in large part to your hydration levels and the volume of food you're eating (a keto diet tends to be more calorie dense than traditional diets, so the weight and volume of your daily food intake will be lower). While the scale may jump or drop 5 pounds from one day to the next, that does not mean those 5 pounds are body fat!

During your first two weeks on keto, you'll probably lose some water weight due to the lack of dietary carbohydrates and corresponding drop in glycogen, as noted earlier. While this can be encouraging, it's important to temper expectations and maintain a long-term mindset.

For the next few weeks, weight loss will be much slower because your body is working in a very inefficient fashion. It is used to running on carbs, but it is not receiving much through your diet. Ketones are being produced, but they're a new fuel source, and your body is still figuring out what to do with them. Some people get discouraged during this period of time: the scale doesn't move much, and it can seem like keto is just another fad diet that lets you lose a quick few pounds and then stops working. Stick with it! Once you break through this phase and become fat adapted, your weight-loss progress will pick up once again.

The amount of time it takes to become fully fat adapted varies greatly based on a number of factors, including age, dieting history, body fat percentage, and how strictly you stick to a ketogenic diet. But most people find that after about six weeks, they have established a good level of fat adaptation, are steadily losing weight and feeling more energized, and are free from carb cravings.

Just remember not to be influenced by the scale during this turbulent time for your body. If stepping on the scale every morning has a large impact on your emotions, it might be best just to stay off of it and focus on how you feel instead. Maintaining a long-term, holistic mindset can help keep your eyes on the prize!

6. YOU'LL PROBABLY HAVE TO DEAL WITH CRAVINGS

Cravings are an inevitable part of weaning yourself off the addictive high-sugar foods that have become staples of our diet. In the first few months of adapting to a ketogenic diet, you will likely encounter a strange phenomenon. You will sit down and eat an incredibly filling and nutritious meal, only to feel like something is missing afterward. Your body is full and nourished, but your mind is still hungry and searching for the rush of a sweet after-dinner treat.

The best approach to dealing with this is to eat keto-friendly foods until you are satisfied. Keep keto snacks in the house. Make fat bombs and keep them in the freezer. Find an awesome keto-friendly takeout option nearby. The most important part of the adaptation process is to stick to keto-friendly foods. Don't worry about how much you're eating—limiting calories by avoiding snacks (if weight loss is one of your goals) can come later, after you have broken your dependence on processed carbs and high-sugar foods.

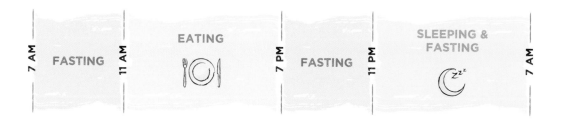

7. FASTING GOES HAND IN HAND WITH KETO

Intermittent fasting—cycling between eating and fasting over a set time period—has become increasingly popular over the last decade and has a number of proven benefits for health and longevity, the big ones being improvement to insulin sensitivity, lower inflammation, and improved cognition. The most popular intermittent fasting method is to eat in an eight-hour window every day, leaving sixteen hours (usually overnight) of fasting. This is known as a 16/8 eating pattern (see the chart above).

A keto diet and intermittent fasting often go hand in hand because fat adaptation reduces hunger and increases satiety, leading naturally to fewer meals. On keto, fasting is easier than you think, especially if you're rarely hungry when you wake up or you don't like eating later in the day. It can be as simple as skipping breakfast and having a larger lunch and dinner. Our fifty-day meal plan starts with the standard three meals per day and over time drops down to two meals per day. That usually fits very well with a 16/8 eating pattern; you can have two meals during your eight-hour eating window.

However, fasting should not feel forced and may take some time to get used to. If you get hungry and can't wait until your first meal of the day, just listen to your body and eat sooner.

The longer you eat a ketogenic diet, the easier fasting will become, but it's not for everyone. Both of us have been eating a ketogenic diet for nearly four years, and neither of us is a big fan of fasting. That is something that we've learned about ourselves through trial and error. Experiment with it for yourself and see what feels good.

8. MEAL PREPPING ISN'T OPTIONAL

Meal prep is an essential part of eating a healthy, whole-foods-based diet. Most of us don't have time to cook three meals a day from scratch—sometimes even just making dinner feels like too much. Cooking in bulk on the weekends is the best way to set yourself up for the week ahead.

The fifty-day meal plan incorporates weekly meal prep. Most days call for cooking one meal (dinner) from scratch, while the other meals are cooked ahead of time.

9. YOU CAN STILL HAVE TAKEOUT!

Even the strictest people enjoy ordering takeout and having a movie marathon every once in a while. But the stress of ordering out can be overwhelming when you are new to keto and you're trying not to inadvertently sabotage your progress. For this reason, it is a great idea to find a handful of local takeout spots that you can rely on for keto-friendly meals. Here are some of our favorite options:

1. **BBQ:** Ask if the rub they use has sugar in it and avoid the sauce.

2. **Buffalo wings:** Ask what oil they use for frying and whether the wings are breaded. Buffalo Wild Wings uses beef tallow and does not bread the wings. That's our favorite option.

3. **Hot bars and salad bars:** Some of the fancier grocery stores have hot bars with a variety of good keto options. Salad bars are also keto-friendly, with toppings from hard-boiled eggs and grilled chicken to cheese and crumbled bacon.

4. **Fast food and casual dining:** You can always ask for sauces and dressings on the side if you aren't sure about the sugar content. We like to swap vinegar and extra-virgin olive oil for salad dressings when possible; this helps us avoid dressings made with unhealthy oils (see the list on page 37), which most restaurants use. Also, don't be scared to ask for a side salad or veggies in place of fries! Here are some of our favorite fast-food options:

BUNLESS BURGERS: *The ultimate fail-safe option, which you can find at just about any burger joint. Most of them are used to this request because of the popularity of low-carb diets.*

CHICKEN WINGS: *We like to check that they are baked, smoked, or fried in healthy oils, and we make sure they are not breaded (they usually aren't).*

GRILLED CHICKEN: *Some fried chicken places offer a grilled option.*

SALAD BURRITO BOWLS: *Burrito bowls are popular these days, and they make great keto options if you replace the rice and beans with lettuce and vegetables.*

SALADS: *We love loaded Cobb and chicken Caesar salads.*

10. SUSTAINABILITY IS ALL THAT MATTERS

Many people are infatuated with the idea of dropping as much weight as possible in the shortest amount of time. We get the appeal, but don't fall into the trap of focusing on the scale and short-term weight loss. The only thing that matters is whether a diet is sustainable over the long term. Most people who lose weight end up gaining it back. What you really want is to improve your overall health—sustainable weight loss will follow. Shifting the focus to your health and working on developing a healthy diet that you can stick with will pay dividends in the long run.

What a ketogenic diet offers is inherent sustainability because it takes control away from the food companies selling hyperpalatable processed food and puts it back in your hands. It puts your body back on your team. Once you're fat adapted, you will no longer have to fight against your body on a daily basis just to see a lower number on the scale. This makes a ketogenic diet more sustainable than any other when approached with a healthy long-term mindset.

HOW TO USE
THE 50-DAY MEAL PLAN

With this meal plan, our goal is to outline a plan for eating a healthy, well-formulated ketogenic diet for fifty days. It's designed to reflect the way we actually eat and cook, including meal prep on the weekends, and to have lots of variety while still making good use of leftovers. If you find that so much variety is causing you more stress because you're cooking a lot of new-to-you dishes, it's perfectly fine to keep it simple in the kitchen and stick to a few meals that you enjoy.

On the other hand, if you are feeling restricted by the meal plan, it is okay to branch out. The point of the plan is to help you stick to keto-friendly foods for an extended period of time so that you can develop a high degree of fat adaptation, and you can do that with different dishes than the ones we've suggested here. It's best to eat foods you enjoy; just make sure your substitutions are similar in nutrition to the food you are replacing. A nutrition tracker, like those discussed on page 26, will help you know what foods are similar in nutrition to the one you're replacing. It's especially important to keep your eye on the carb count!

MACROS

During these fifty days, we recommend tracking your intake of fat, protein, and carbohydrate as percentages of your overall daily calories, as outlined on page 25. The meal plan gives the amount of calories, fat, protein, and carbohydrate for each meal and each day. But snacks are not accounted for in these totals. While we've suggested having a snack with certain meals with an eye to calories, the snack you choose will determine exactly how many calories and how much fat, protein, and carbohydrate it adds to your total. So when you look at your daily calories and macros, keep in mind that you'll need to add the figures from your snacks.

However, the plan will work if you simply eat to satiety rather than tracking your macros. If you go with this option, you'll just eat according to how you feel: if you are hungrier one day, eat more of the foods listed for that day; if you're less hungry, just eat less. This approach is less precise than tracking your macros, but because the recipes in the meal plan are low in carbs and high in healthy fats, it can still work, as long as you give your body the time it needs to become fat adapted.

SERVINGS

The meal plan is designed to feed one person. While the meal plan uses leftovers throughout the week, you'll find that you'll still have some leftovers from individual dishes. That's okay! These leftovers make great snacks, so feel free to eat them anytime a snack is listed in the meal plan. Just remember that snacks are intended to be added to your meals rather than eaten between meals.

The meal plan is based on a 1,800-calorie diet, so if you need more or fewer calories, you'll want to adjust it to suit you. For example, if you're on the small side, like someone who's five foot two and 110 pounds, you'll need fewer calories. You can adjust the plan to your requirements by removing some of the snacks and eating smaller portions. On the other hand, if you are a larger person, like someone who's six foot five and 290 pounds, you'll need more calories. You can adjust the plan by adding snacks, eating larger portions (maybe two servings of a dish instead of one), and even adding an additional meal to your day.

PLANNING AHEAD

Meal prep is an important part of the meal plan. For each week, the recipes to be made in advance—usually the most time-intensive recipes—are listed as "Meal Prep" in the meal plan. We find that prepping is best done the day before the start of the week or on the morning of day 1, the first day of the week—so generally either Sunday or Monday morning—to reduce the amount of time you spend cooking during the week.

A number of the meal prep recipes are what we call foundation recipes, which form the base of other meals later in the week. For example, week 4 lists Barbacoa (page 106) to be made ahead, and then during the week it's used for Barbacoa Breakfast Skillet (page 112) and Barbacoa Lettuce Wraps (page 108). Using foundation recipes keeps your meals varied while cutting down on your cooking time: you can get a number of meals during the week by cooking one recipe in advance.

We also include stand-alone recipes in the preparations column; these recipes are not used in different recipes throughout the week, but they store and reheat well, making them good make-ahead candidates. An example is the Herbed Ricotta Breakfast Casserole (page 140) used in week 3. Once made, it simply needs to be reheated throughout the week.

To give you more time for meal prep and grocery shopping, each week's day 7 is designed to be a reduced cooking day. On that day, the meal plan calls for mostly leftovers, takeout, or a combination of the two.

It can be hard to start making all your meals from scratch, so we've included takeout meals to give you an opportunity to slowly transition to more home cooking. If you are in a rush one night and don't have time to cook dinner, picking up takeout can be helpful—see page 53 for some helpful tips for choosing keto-friendly takeout. But you can always skip the takeout meals if you prefer to stick entirely to home-cooked meals.

Shopping Lists

The shopping lists include everything you'll need to make every dish in the meal plan. (Remember, though, that it's designed for one person eating around 1,800 calories a day, so you may need to adjust portions for your needs.) The lists are divided up by weeks, with one exception: pantry items—like coconut oil, chia seeds, and dried herbs and spices—are listed once for the full seven weeks. That's because you'll really only need to buy these items once. After the first week, you'll just need to shop for meat, eggs and dairy, and produce.

Tips for Successful Planning

USE QUICK, NO-RECIPE MEALS

When you're short on time, tired, or missing key ingredients for a planned meal, quick and easy no-recipe meals can be a lifesaver. Here are some of our favorites, all of which can be whipped up in less than 10 minutes:

- *Bacon and eggs*
- *Baked chicken and broccoli*
- *Butter coffee*
- *Caesar salad*
- *Charcuterie and cheese plate*
- *Cheese and meat roll-ups*
- *Chicken stir fry*
- *Cobb salad*
- *Egg salad*
- *Ham and cheese omelet*
- *Protein shake with heavy whipping cream*
- *Scrambled eggs*

LOOK AHEAD FOR CHANGES TO YOUR ROUTINE

On your meal prep day, before you start cooking or go grocery shopping, have a look ahead at that entire week of meals. Decide if you want to make any changes to the plan and prepare yourself for anything out of the ordinary in the week ahead, like happy hour at work, a child's birthday party, or a weekend vacation.

KEEP HEALTHY SNACKS ON HAND

Don't underestimate the power of having prepared food in the fridge. After a long day, it can be tempting to revert to the old habit of grabbing a shelf-stable packaged food from the pantry and settling into the couch for TV and snacks. Making or buying keto-friendly snacks ahead of time will give you something healthy to turn to when you're tired and don't have the energy to cook. See page 40 for some healthy snack suggestions.

NUMBER OF MEALS

Weeks 1 and 2 of the plan include three meals per day because this is the way most of us are used to eating, and until our bodies are fat adapted, we're likely to get hungry more often. But starting with week 3, the plan includes just two meals per day. The caloric intake is the same; only the number of meals changes—so you will not be eating less food, just fewer meals. In our experience, this style of eating comes naturally when you're on a keto diet and helps you feel more satisfied after meals, so you don't need a snack an hour later.

However, you can still eat as many meals as you like. If the meal plan calls for two meals but you would prefer to eat four, for instance, just divide the food across four mealtimes instead. While we encourage you to explore reducing the number of meals you eat, there's no rush and no need to force it—it's something you can do when you feel comfortable with it.

And if you find that you're often hungry throughout the day or after your last meal, go to page 40 for a list of healthy snacks you can turn to.

THE MEALS

It's hard for most of us to find the time to cook three meals from scratch each day. That's one reason to have a meal prep day, but it's also why we've included a lot of dishes that are easy to prepare without a recipe, such as bacon, scrambled eggs, steamed broccoli with butter, or a simple side salad dressed with oil and vinegar. Between meal prep, leftovers, and these easy no-recipe dishes, we hope that you'll find it very doable to cook more of your meals at home. (Though if it still feels like a lot, take a look at the suggestions for keto-friendly takeout on page 53.)

The 50-Day Meal Plan,
WEEK BY WEEK

Focus:
FOOD CHOICES;
HYDRATION AND ELECTROLYTES

This is probably going to be the most difficult week of your fifty-day journey. First, you're going to be saying goodbye to many of the items in your pantry, fridge, and freezer. Eliminating sugars, grains, processed carbohydrates, and refined vegetable oils means getting rid of things like breakfast cereals, breads, granola bars, pretzels, chips, pastries, protein bars, frozen meals, canola oil, and premade salad dressings. We know this sounds a bit extreme, but it's important to acknowledge that these things are not really food—they don't provide your body with real nourishment. If you keep items like these in your house, stopping yourself from eating them when you're bored or when you get home after a long day will drain you of your precious willpower.

If you share a home with people who aren't willing to eat keto, cleaning out the pantry and fridge can be a tougher process, and you may not be able to eliminate all of the problematic foods. In this situation, it is best to make changes to your diet without overhauling the pantry. It may take more determination on your part, but we've received countless emails from people who got their families on board with the keto diet after they did it by themselves for a few months and achieved some incredible results.

Starting around day 2 to day 4, you're likely to start feeling the effects of the "keto flu," like headaches and fatigue. The key to managing these symptoms is to stay hydrated and supplement with electrolytes. See page 50 for more on the keto flu.

Finding Support

The honest truth is that adapting to and sticking with the ketogenic diet can be difficult without a support system. If you do not have one in your day-to-day life, we encourage you to find a supportive keto community on social media. There are strong KetoConnect communities on YouTube and Instagram whose members share their journeys with one another: the struggle of sticking to their diet during the holidays, an awesome new recipe they just came up with, or what they think about a new nutrition article that just came out. The internet can also be a great place to turn to for accountability. Some people post all of their meals online, share progress pictures and weight updates, and discuss the successes and failures they have encountered along the way. Consistently sharing your journey can help build accountability, which is an important aspect of successfully changing habits.

EVERY WEEK, CHECK YOUR KITCHEN FOR THESE STAPLES

apple cider vinegar

avocado oil

bacon fat

baking powder

baking soda

blanched almond flour

cayenne pepper

chili powder

coconut flour

coconut oil

coffee or tea

Dijon mustard

dried oregano leaves

dried parsley

dried rosemary leaves

dried thyme leaves

extra-virgin olive oil

garam masala

garlic powder

ginger powder

granular erythritol

ground cinnamon

ground coriander

ground cumin

ground nutmeg

liquid stevia

mayonnaise

onion powder

paprika

red pepper flakes

soy sauce

toasted sesame oil

unseasoned rice wine vinegar

vanilla extract

vinegar

These items are used frequently, so it's best to make sure you always have them in your pantry or refrigerator.

WEEK 1 Shopping List

MEAT

bacon, *15 slices*

chicken, *1 whole (4½ pounds)*

chicken drumsticks, *6*

ground beef (90/10), *1 pound*

steak (fatty cut, such as rib eye), *6 ounces*

turkey deli meat, *3 thin slices*

SEAFOOD

salmon fillets, skin on, *4 (6 ounces each)*

EGGS AND DAIRY

butter, unsalted, *½ cup (1 stick) + 2 tablespoons*

cheddar cheese, *6 ounces*

cream cheese, *5 ounces*

eggs, *18 large*

heavy whipping cream, *1 cup + 1 tablespoon*

mozzarella cheese, *6 ounces*

Parmesan cheese, *3 ounces*

ricotta cheese, full-fat, *3½ cups*

PRODUCE

asparagus, *1 pound*

avocados, *2 large*

basil leaves, *1 bunch*

bell peppers, *6 medium*

blueberries, *½ ounce*

broccoli, *6 cups*

celery, *5 stalks*

cherry tomatoes, *10 ounces*

frozen spinach, *4 cups (about 14 ounces)*

garlic, *7 cloves*

ginger, *1 (1-inch) piece*

lemons, *3*

lime, *1*

oregano leaves, *3½ teaspoons*

red onion, *½ medium*

rosemary leaves, *1 tablespoon + 1½ teaspoons*

scallions, *8*

shallot, *1*

thyme leaves, *1½ teaspoons*

PANTRY

almond butter, *2 tablespoons*

almond milk, unsweetened, *¼ cup*

pork rinds, *1 ounce*

PLUS

8 snacks *(see page 40)*

1 takeout meal *(see page 53)*

The macros and calories are per meal, not per dish. The day's totals are in the blue row.

Meal Prep

98
Sweet Asian BBQ Spatchcocked Chicken

272
Lemon Blueberry Cheesecake Fat Bombs

DAY 01

MEAL 1

3 slices bacon | 3 eggs cooked in bacon fat

CALORIES	FAT	PROTEIN	CARBS	FIBER
422	33g	27g	2g	0g

MEAL 2

2 celery stalks with 2 tbsp almond butter, ½ avocado | Snack *(see page 40)*

CALORIES	FAT	PROTEIN	CARBS	FIBER
460	40g	17g	14g	9g

MEAL 3

102

272

Chicken and Ricotta Stuffed Peppers *(2 servings)* | Lemon Blueberry Cheesecake Fat Bombs *(2)*

CALORIES	FAT	PROTEIN	CARBS	FIBER
968	59g	80g	27g	9g

CALORIES: 1850 • FAT: 132g • PROTEIN: 124g • CARBS: 43g • FIBER: 17g

---

DAY 02

MEAL 1

Fatty tea/coffee with 1 tbsp butter + 1 tbsp coconut oil | Snack *(see page 40)*

CALORIES	FAT	PROTEIN	CARBS	FIBER
365	37g	9g	0g	0g

MEAL 2

104

Loaded Chicken Salad | **LEFTOVER** Lemon Blueberry Cheesecake Fat Bombs *(2)*

CALORIES	FAT	PROTEIN	CARBS	FIBER
694	56g	39g	6g	2g

MEAL 3

192

Italian Herbed Meatballs *(2 servings)* | 3 cups steamed broccoli with 1 tbsp butter

CALORIES	FAT	PROTEIN	CARBS	FIBER
727	44g	64g	21g	9g

CALORIES: 1786 • FAT: 137g • PROTEIN: 112g • CARBS: 27g • FIBER: 11g

---

DAY 03

MEAL 1

5 scrambled eggs cooked in 2 tbsp butter

CALORIES	FAT	PROTEIN	CARBS	FIBER
591	50g	32g	2g	0g

MEAL 2

LEFTOVER

Italian Herbed Meatballs *(2 servings)* | Snack *(see page 40)*

CALORIES	FAT	PROTEIN	CARBS	FIBER
627	39g	62g	3g	0g

MEAL 3

227

LEFTOVER

Bacon Garlic Asparagus, 6 oz steak (fatty cut) | Lemon Blueberry Cheesecake Fat Bomb *(1)*

CALORIES	FAT	PROTEIN	CARBS	FIBER
630	48g	41g	11g	3g

CALORIES: 1848 • FAT: 137g • PROTEIN: 135g • CARBS: 16g • FIBER: 3g

DAY 04

MEAL 1

Fatty tea/coffee with 1 tbsp butter + 1 tbsp coconut oil

Snack *(see page 40)*

CALORIES	FAT	PROTEIN	CARBS	FIBER
365	37g	9g	0g	0g

MEAL 2

Chopped Caprese Salad *(2 servings)* **226**

Snack *(see page 40)*

CALORIES	FAT	PROTEIN	CARBS	FIBER
538	48g	22g	3g	1g

MEAL 3

Chicken and Ricotta Stuffed Peppers *(2 servings)* **102**

Lemon Blueberry Cheesecake Fat Bombs *(2)* **LEFTOVER**

CALORIES	FAT	PROTEIN	CARBS	FIBER
968	59g	80g	27g	8g

CALORIES: 1871 • FAT: 144g • PROTEIN: 111g • CARBS: 30g • FIBER: 9g

DAY 05

MEAL 1

3 slices bacon

3 eggs cooked in bacon fat

CALORIES	FAT	PROTEIN	CARBS	FIBER
422	33g	27g	2g	0g

MEAL 2

Loaded Chicken Salad **LEFTOVER**

Lemon Blueberry Cheesecake Fat Bombs *(2)* **LEFTOVER**

CALORIES	FAT	PROTEIN	CARBS	FIBER
694	56g	39g	6g	2g

MEAL 3

Salmon Topped with Avocado Bruschetta **190**

3 cups steamed broccoli with 1 tbsp butter

CALORIES	FAT	PROTEIN	CARBS	FIBER
655	41g	52g	24g	11g

CALORIES: 1771 • FAT: 130g • PROTEIN: 118g • CARBS: 32g • FIBER: 13g

DAY 06

MEAL 1

5-Minute Breakfast Sandwich **162**

CALORIES	FAT	PROTEIN	CARBS	FIBER
502	34g	35g	11g	6g

MEAL 2

Salmon Topped with Avocado Bruschetta **LEFTOVER**

Snack *(see page 40)*

CALORIES	FAT	PROTEIN	CARBS	FIBER
602	40g	54g	6g	4g

MEAL 3

Lemony Roasted Drumsticks **202**

Lemon Blueberry Cheesecake Fat Bomb *(1)* **LEFTOVER**

CALORIES	FAT	PROTEIN	CARBS	FIBER
596	51g	32g	4.5g	0g

CALORIES: 1700 • FAT: 125g • PROTEIN: 121g • CARBS: 21.5g • FIBER: 10g

DAY 07

MEAL 1

Mini Breakfast Cakes *(2 servings)* **150**

CALORIES	FAT	PROTEIN	CARBS	FIBER
736	56g	42g	12g	4g

MEAL 2

Snack x2 *(see page 40)*

CALORIES	FAT	PROTEIN	CARBS	FIBER
384	24g	18g	0g	0g

MEAL 3

Takeout meal *(see page 53)*

CALORIES	FAT	PROTEIN	CARBS	FIBER
800	62g	50g	10g	5g

CALORIES: 1920 • FAT: 142g • PROTEIN: 110g • CARBS: 22g • FIBER: 9g

Today's diet culture can make it difficult to maintain a long-term outlook. Everything is a two-week transformation challenge or a ten-day detox. When you're excited about a new diet, it is tempting to hop on the scale every morning and allow the number to dictate your day. Down 2 pounds, you're flying high. Up 2 pounds, and keto is the worst diet you've ever tried. But remember, you're in this for the long haul! It's the long-term benefits of keto that you're after, not a quick weight loss and even quicker regain. If the scale has a large impact on your well-being, then it is best to just stay off it, at least until you are fat adapted and your weight has stopped fluctuating—which it will for a few weeks.

Chances are you dropped a couple of pounds the first week on keto. (But if you didn't, that's okay!) In these first few weeks, your decreased carbohydrate intake leads to a loss of water weight. While it's nice, it does not mean you are losing body fat yet. You're still laying the groundwork so that in the future, you'll have an easier time dropping body fat and maintaining a healthy weight. Once you've dropped all of the water weight, there may be a period when the scale doesn't move much. Don't be alarmed, the diet is still working; just stick with it and focus on staying consistent. It will pay off in the long run.

If weight loss isn't a primary goal of yours, then begin to keep tabs on the area of your life you are hoping to improve. If it's productivity, try keeping track of the amount of work you're getting done daily. If it's gym performance, keep a journal of your maximum lifts.

This week is about the time when carb cravings are at their worst. Excitement about keto and a clear sense of your motivation can take you through the first week without too many thoughts of carbs, but after that, visions of donuts and cake tend to come back with a vengeance. There are two approaches to dealing with these cravings:

1. Indulge in keto sweets and carb replacements.

2. Completely abstain from carb replacements and power through the cravings.

Of course, option 2 is the one that will truly break your reliance on carbohydrates, but the approach you take comes down to personal preference. If completely abstaining is not feasible for you, then you're better off including some keto treats to make the diet more sustainable. Remember, sustainability is the single most important factor of your diet. If you can't stick with it in the long term, then it's not going to give you the results you're looking for.

MEAT

bacon, *13 slices*

chicken thighs, boneless, skinless, *4*

chicken wings, *2 pounds*

pork tenderloin, *2 pounds*

steak (fatty cut, such as rib eye), *6 ounces*

SEAFOOD

sardines in olive oil, *1 tin*

EGGS AND DAIRY

butter, *1 cup (2 sticks) + 3 tablespoons*

cheddar cheese, *6 ounces*

cream cheese, *1 ounce (2 tablespoons)*

eggs, *31 large*

heavy whipping cream, *2 cups + 2 tablespoons*

mozzarella cheese, *5 ounces*

Parmesan cheese, *1 ounce*

PRODUCE

asparagus, *1 pound*

avocado, *1 large*

baby bella mushrooms, *3 ounces*

basil leaves, *2 to 3 tablespoons*

blueberries, *1 ounce*

broccoli, *6 cups*

carrot, *1 medium*

cauliflower, *1 medium head*

celery, *2 stalks*

cherry tomatoes, *5 ounces*

garlic, *7 cloves*

jalapeño peppers, *2 large*

lemon, *1*

mixed greens, *2 cups*

parsley, *2 tablespoons*

rosemary leaves, *1 tablespoon*

shallots, *2 medium + 1 small*

thyme, *4 sprigs*

white onion, *¼ medium*

yellow onion, *1 small*

PANTRY

almond butter, *2 tablespoons*

chicken broth, low-sodium, *2 cups*

unflavored beef gelatin powder, *2 teaspoons*

PLUS

8 snacks *(see page 40)*

1 takeout meal *(see page 53)*

Forget About Calories!

One additional piece of advice: during the first few weeks, don't worry about calories at all. Removing carbs from your diet and restricting calories at the same time is a recipe for disaster. The major focus at the start should be conquering your reliance on carbohydrates and processed foods. In a month or two, restricting calories is going to be a piece of cake. Don't stress about it right now.

WEEK 2 *Meal Plan*

The macros and calories are per meal, not per dish. The day's totals are in the blue row.

Meal Prep

114

Mustard-Rubbed Pork Tenderloin

DAY 08

MEAL 1

120

Omelet for Two *(2 servings)*

CALORIES	FAT	PROTEIN	CARBS	FIBER
926	74g	66g	4g	1g

MEAL 2

Celery stalk with 2 tbsp almond butter **Snack** *(see page 40)*

CALORIES	FAT	PROTEIN	CARBS	FIBER
347	29g	16g	8g	5g

MEAL 3

214

Indian Spiced Wings **Side salad** *(mixed greens with ½ tbsp olive oil + 1 tbsp vinegar)*

CALORIES	FAT	PROTEIN	CARBS	FIBER
673	46g	57g	7g	4g

CALORIES: 1946 • FAT: 149g • PROTEIN: 139g • CARBS: 19g • FIBER: 10g

---

DAY 09

MEAL 1

152

Jalapeño Popper Egg Bites *(4)*

CALORIES	FAT	PROTEIN	CARBS	FIBER
592	44g	44g	0g	0g

MEAL 2

1 tin sardines in olive oil **Snack** *(see page 40)*

CALORIES	FAT	PROTEIN	CARBS	FIBER
362	28g	29g	0g	0g

MEAL 3

116

Pork Tenderloin in Mushroom Cream Sauce *(2 servings)* **3 cups steamed broccoli with 1 tbsp butter**

CALORIES	FAT	PROTEIN	CARBS	FIBER
799	53g	54g	26g	9g

CALORIES: 1753 • FAT: 125g • PROTEIN: 127g • CARBS: 26g • FIBER: 9g

---

DAY 10

MEAL 1

LEFTOVER

Jalapeño Popper Egg Bites *(4)* **½ avocado**

CALORIES	FAT	PROTEIN	CARBS	FIBER
592	44g	44g	0g	0g

MEAL 2

Fatty tea/coffee with 1 tbsp butter + 1 tbsp coconut oil **Snack** *(see page 40)*

CALORIES	FAT	PROTEIN	CARBS	FIBER
114	11g	1g	6g	5g

MEAL 3

118   294

Pork Fried Rice *(2 servings)* **Blueberry Mug Cake**

CALORIES	FAT	PROTEIN	CARBS	FIBER
365	37g	62g	33g	14g

CALORIES: 1871 • FAT: 139g • PROTEIN: 116g • CARBS: 39g • FIBER: 19g

---

DAY 11

MEAL 1

5 scrambled eggs cooked in 2 tbsp butter, topped with 1 oz Parmesan cheese, grated

CALORIES	FAT	PROTEIN	CARBS	FIBER
710	58g	40g	2g	0g

MEAL 2

Fatty tea/coffee with 1 tbsp butter + 1 tbsp coconut oil

Snack *(see page 40)*

CALORIES	FAT	PROTEIN	CARBS	FIBER
365	37g	9g	0g	0g

MEAL 3

LEFTOVER · 288

Pork Fried Rice *(2 servings)*

Peanut Butter Cookies *(2)*

CALORIES	FAT	PROTEIN	CARBS	FIBER
698	42g	61g	32g	13g

CALORIES: 1773 • FAT: 137g • PROTEIN: 110g • CARBS: 34g • FIBER: 13g

---

DAY 12

MEAL 1

3 slices bacon · 3 eggs cooked in bacon fat · ½ avocado

CALORIES	FAT	PROTEIN	CARBS	FIBER
536	44g	28g	8g	5g

MEAL 2

226

Chopped Caprese Salad *(2 servings)*

Snack *(see page 40)*

CALORIES	FAT	PROTEIN	CARBS	FIBER
538	48g	22g	3g	1g

MEAL 3

227

Bacon Garlic Asparagus · 6 oz steak (fatty cut) · Peanut Butter Cookies *(2)*

LEFTOVER

CALORIES	FAT	PROTEIN	CARBS	FIBER
768	61g	50g	19g	7g

CALORIES: 1842 • FAT: 153g • PROTEIN: 100g • CARBS: 30g • FIBER: 13g

---

DAY 13

MEAL 1

166

Coconut Flour Pancakes *(2)* with 1 tbsp butter · 2 slices bacon

CALORIES	FAT	PROTEIN	CARBS	FIBER
751	67g	17g	16g	13g

MEAL 2

Snack *(see page 40)*

CALORIES	FAT	PROTEIN	CARBS	FIBER
142	12g	9g	0g	0g

MEAL 3

210 · LEFTOVER

One-Pan Chicken with Lemon-Garlic Cream Sauce, 3 cups steamed broccoli with 1 tbsp butter, Peanut Butter Cookies *(2)*

CALORIES	FAT	PROTEIN	CARBS	FIBER
885	70g	51g	32g	12g

CALORIES: 1778 • FAT: 149g • PROTEIN: 77g • CARBS: 48g • FIBER: 25g

---

DAY 14

MEAL 1

5 scrambled eggs cooked in 2 tbsp butter

CALORIES	FAT	PROTEIN	CARBS	FIBER
591	50g	32g	2g	0g

MEAL 2

Snack **x2** *(see page 40)*

CALORIES	FAT	PROTEIN	CARBS	FIBER
284	24g	18g	0g	0g

MEAL 3

Takeout meal *(see page 53)*

CALORIES	FAT	PROTEIN	CARBS	FIBER
800	62g	50g	10g	5g

CALORIES: 1775 • FAT: 136g • PROTEIN: 100g • CARBS: 12g • FIBER: 5g

50 Days to Fat Adaptation

Focus:
TWO SQUARE MEALS A DAY

That's not a typo! This week we're going to try two meals per day instead of the standard three. Let's be honest, though, no one really does three square meals these days. It's more like three meals, four snacks, and a dessert. There is nothing innate to human beings that necessitates three meals a day. It's a social construct that has only been around for a couple of hundred years. Cavemen did not eat three meals a day. Some days they didn't eat at all!

Two meals a day is not going to be for everyone, but it is worth giving it a try. Cooking three meals a day from scratch is not possible for most of us in the busy world we live in today. Cooking two meals is much more achievable. (And of course with meal prep on the weekend, you can get that down to just cooking dinner each night.)

It's counterintuitive, but many people actually feel less hungry when they eat just two meals a day (as long as they're still getting the same number of calories, of course). Eating two meals allows for larger, more satisfying meals that take your mind off of food until it's time for the next meal. Just remember that you won't just be cutting out one meal—you also need to add the calories you'd normally get from that meal to the other two meals. So if you used to spread 2,000 calories a day over three meals, for 667 calories per meal, now you'll eat two meals of 1,000 calories each, or one meal of 500 calories and another of 1,500 calories.

Listen to your body and eat in accordance with its needs. We personally eat a smaller meal in the morning, just before noon, and a large dinner. This fits our life-style because we are active in the mornings and just want something quick that won't weigh us down too much. Then, as we start winding down in the evening, we cook a large dinner and sit down to enjoy it at leisure. Remember that a big part of the reason this works is that we're fat adapted, so we don't have spikes and crashes of blood sugar and our bodies are fueled steadily all day.

Finding something that works for you is going to be better than trying to follow any strict advice we give you, but the action item here is to try eating more food, less often. If you are still getting hungry between meals, then it doesn't make sense to force it. This entire process should be easy and not feel forced at all. Have a snack or a small meal until your body is ready to switch to two meals per day. Using the meal plan for week 3, you can take parts of the two listed meals and eat them at times outside of your scheduled meals, and you can always have snacks from page 40 if you need to.

WEEK 3 Shopping List

MEAT

bacon, *14 slices*

chicken wings, *2 pounds*

ground beef (80/20), *2 pounds*

ground pork, *1 pound*

short ribs, *3½ pounds*

turkey deli meat, *3 thin slices*

EGGS AND DAIRY

butter, unsalted, *½ cup (1 stick) + 1 tablespoon*

eggs, *26 large*

heavy whipping cream, *2 cups + 1 tablespoon*

mozzarella cheese, *2 ounces*

Parmesan cheese, *3 ounces*

ricotta cheese, full-fat, *2¼ cups*

PRODUCE

avocados, *2 large*

basil leaves, *¼ cup finely chopped*

broccoli, *3 cups*

Brussels sprouts, *1½ pounds*

cherry tomatoes, *3 ounces*

garlic, *4 cloves*

green bell pepper, *1 small*

jalapeño peppers, *2 medium*

lemons, *2*

Roma tomato, *1 medium*

shallot, *1 large*

white onion, *1 small*

zucchini, *1 medium*

PANTRY

almond milk, unsweetened, *¼ cup*

cacao powder, *2 tablespoons*

chicken broth, *low-sodium, 5½ cups*

natural creamy almond butter, *½ cup*

poppy seeds, *2 tablespoons*

pumpkin puree (100% pure), *¼ cup*

tallow, *2 tablespoons*

unflavored collagen peptides, *70 grams*

Worcestershire sauce, *1 teaspoon*

PLUS

3 snacks *(see page 40)*

1 takeout meal *(see page 53)*

The macros and calories are per meal, not per dish.
The day's totals are in the blue row.

Meal Prep

Herbed Ricotta Breakfast Casserole — 140
Chili with Bacon — 206
Pumpkin Collagen Fudge — 264

DAY 15

MEAL 1

Herbed Ricotta Breakfast Casserole *(2 servings)*
Snack *(see page 40)*

CALORIES	FAT	PROTEIN	CARBS	FIBER
870	62g	49g	7g	0g

MEAL 2

Chili with Bacon topped with ½ avocado — 206
Pumpkin Collagen Fudge *(2)* — 264

CALORIES	FAT	PROTEIN	CARBS	FIBER
931	69g	43g	21g	13g

CALORIES: 1801 • FAT: 131g • PROTEIN: 92g • CARBS: 28g • FIBER: 13g

DAY 16

MEAL 1

LEFTOVER
Herbed Ricotta Breakfast Casserole *(2 servings)*
Mocha Egg Coffee — 146

CALORIES	FAT	PROTEIN	CARBS	FIBER
844	65g	57g	9g	1g

MEAL 2

LEFTOVER
Chili with Bacon topped with ½ avocado
LEFTOVER
Pumpkin Collagen Fudge *(2)*

CALORIES	FAT	PROTEIN	CARBS	FIBER
931	69g	43g	21g	13g

CALORIES: 1775 • FAT: 134g • PROTEIN: 100g • CARBS: 30g • FIBER: 14g

DAY 17

MEAL 1

Lemon Poppy Seed Waffles *(2 servings)* — 170
4 slices bacon

CALORIES	FAT	PROTEIN	CARBS	FIBER
740	61g	30g	18g	11g

MEAL 2

LEFTOVER
Chili with Bacon
3 cups steamed broccoli with 1 tbsp butter
LEFTOVER
Pumpkin Collagen Fudge *(2)*

CALORIES	FAT	PROTEIN	CARBS	FIBER
1012	70g	50g	33g	15g

CALORIES: 1752 • FAT: 131g • PROTEIN: 80g • CARBS: 51g • FIBER: 26g

DAY 18

MEAL 1

LEFTOVER

Herbed Ricotta
Breakfast Casserole
(2 servings)

Snack
(see page 40)

CALORIES	FAT	PROTEIN	CARBS	FIBER
870	62g	49g	7g	0g

MEAL 2

212

238

Oven-Braised
Short Ribs

Zucchini Basil
Muffins *(2)*

CALORIES	FAT	PROTEIN	CARBS	FIBER
928	75g	48g	15g	4g

CALORIES: 1798 • FAT: 137g • PROTEIN: 97g • CARBS: 22g • FIBER: 4g

DAY 19

MEAL 1

LEFTOVER

146

Herbed Ricotta
Breakfast Casserole
(2 servings)

Mocha Egg
Coffee

CALORIES	FAT	PROTEIN	CARBS	FIBER
844	65g	57g	9g	1g

MEAL 2

LEFTOVER

LEFTOVER

Oven-Braised
Short Ribs

Zucchini Basil
Muffins *(2)*

CALORIES	FAT	PROTEIN	CARBS	FIBER
928	75g	48g	15g	4g

CALORIES: 1772 • FAT: 140g • PROTEIN: 105g • CARBS: 24g • FIBER: 5g

DAY 20

MEAL 1

150

Mini Breakfast
Cakes *(2 servings)*

Snack
(see page 40)

CALORIES	FAT	PROTEIN	CARBS	FIBER
878	68g	51g	12g	4g

MEAL 2

214

222

Indian Spiced
Wings

Creamy Brussels
Sprouts with Bacon

CALORIES	FAT	PROTEIN	CARBS	FIBER
873	62g	63g	16g	6g

CALORIES: 1751 • FAT: 130g • PROTEIN: 114g • CARBS: 28g • FIBER: 10g

DAY 21

MEAL 1

162

5-Minute Breakfast
Sandwich

1 avocado

Fatty tea/coffee
with 1 tbsp butter +
1 tbsp coconut oil

CALORIES	FAT	PROTEIN	CARBS	FIBER
952	80g	38g	23g	15g

MEAL 2

Takeout meal
(see page 53)

CALORIES	FAT	PROTEIN	CARBS	FIBER
800	62g	50g	10g	5g

CALORIES: 1752 • FAT: 142g • PROTEIN: 88g • CARBS: 33g • FIBER: 20g

Focus:
BAD EATING HABITS; NOTICING HOW YOU FEEL

By now, nearly a month into eating keto, you're starting to feel the power of a ketogenic diet, so it's time to turn it up a notch by working on a bad eating habit and tracking how you feel.

Everyone has eating habits that are less than ideal. Even with everything we have learned about health and nutrition over the past few years, we still sit in front of the TV to eat dinner every night, which can lead to mindless eating and a lack of focus on our meal and each other. Old habits die hard. So this week, identify one of your poor eating habits and make an active effort to correct it. Only pick one! If you're having trouble identifying any, here's a list of the most common ones:

1. Eating in front of the TV or computer

2. Snacking in the car

3. Snacking after dinner

4. Not making time for meals and relying on snacks instead

5. Eating right before bed, which can disrupt sleep

6. Drinking coffee too late in the day

7. Eating only because you're bored

8. Not chewing your food enough, which prevents proper digestion

Just about every one of these habits has applied to us, and correcting them is still a work in progress. It's not realistic to think that you can correct lifelong bad habits over the course of a week, but beginning to identify them and making an effort to correct them will go a long way.

How do you feel? Get used to asking yourself this question often. Don't just assume the way you wake up every morning is how you're supposed to feel. Strive for more! A few years ago, we just assumed that passing out in your cubicle after lunch was normal. "All humans get tired at 2 p.m. every day, right?" Nope! So start rethinking everything. Why are you tired and ready for bed as soon as you get home from work? Why is it a struggle to get out of bed every morning? Why are you procrastinating on your chores? Once you start noticing these effects and looking for causes, you'll be shocked at the number of things you took for granted that are related to your diet, exercise, and sleep habits.

A good way to identify those causes is to check in with yourself frequently and write down how certain foods or habits impact your well-being. You can keep a journal or take notes on your phone, or whatever system works best for you. We find it best to track metrics that are easy to quantify so you can clearly see how they change. For example, if you're a writer or blogger, start tracking how many words you write each day and then see what else is happening on your most and least productive days—perhaps your word count is higher on days when you eat breakfast or when you go to bed early. Another example, one that's especially applicable here, is how well you're able to stick to your eating plan. To make this quantifiable, so you can see patterns more easily, you can rate each day on a scale of one to ten and then see what common factors apply to the days with the highest and lowest scores. For us, sleep is the biggest factor in sticking to a way of eating—the more and better sleep we get, the easier it is to eat right—but it took us years to make that connection.

Have fun discovering how your body works and learning how you can improve performance by tweaking your daily routine!

WEEK 4 Shopping List

MEAT

bacon, *7 slices*

chicken thighs, boneless, skinless, *4*

chuck roast, boneless, *3 pounds*

steak (fatty cut, such as rib eye), *8 ounces*

turkey deli meat, *6 thin slices*

EGGS AND DAIRY

butter, unsalted, *1¼ cups (2½ sticks) + 2 tablespoons*

cheddar cheese, *about 9 ounces*

eggs, *26 large*

heavy whipping cream, *½ cup + 2 tablespoons*

mozzarella cheese, *2 ounces*

sour cream, full-fat, *3 tablespoons*

PRODUCE

asparagus, *1 pound*

avocados, *2 large*

broccoli, *3 cups*

butter lettuce, *6 leaves*

button mushrooms, *1 pound*

coleslaw mix, *12 ounces*

garlic, *7 cloves*

jalapeño peppers, *2 large*

lemon, *1*

lime, *1*

parsley leaves, *3 tablespoons*

pico de gallo, *¼ cup + 2 tablespoons*

red onion, *1 small*

scallions, *4*

shallots, *2 small*

thyme leaves, *1 teaspoon*

yellow onion, *½ medium*

PANTRY

chicken broth, low-sodium, *3 cups*

chipotle peppers in adobo sauce, *1 (7-ounce) can*

dry white wine, *2 tablespoons*

golden flax meal, *2 tablespoons*

lard, *1 tablespoon*

tallow, *1 tablespoon*

xanthan gum, *½ teaspoon*

PLUS

4 snacks *(see page 40)*

1 takeout meal *(see page 53)*

The macros and calories are per meal, not per dish.
The day's totals are in the blue row.

Meal Prep

Barbacoa — 106

Sour Cream Biscuits — 154

DAY 22

MEAL 1

5 scrambled eggs cooked in 2 tbsp butter

Snack *(see page 40)*

CALORIES	FAT	PROTEIN	CARBS	FIBER
733	62g	41g	2g	0g

MEAL 2

Barbacoa Lettuce Wraps — 108

Sour Cream Biscuit *(1)* with 1 tbsp butter — 154

CALORIES	FAT	PROTEIN	CARBS	FIBER
1047	85g	54g	11g	3g

CALORIES: 1780 • FAT: 147g • PROTEIN: 95g • CARBS: 13g • FIBER: 3g

DAY 23

MEAL 1

Barbacoa Breakfast Skillet *(2 servings)* — 112

Snack *(see page 40)*

CALORIES	FAT	PROTEIN	CARBS	FIBER
972	76g	69g	2g	0g

MEAL 2

8 oz steak (fatty cut)

3 cups steamed broccoli with 1 tbsp butter

LEFTOVER
Sour Cream Biscuit *(1)* with 1 tbsp butter

CALORIES	FAT	PROTEIN	CARBS	FIBER
910	71g	57g	22g	9g

CALORIES: 1882 • FAT: 147g • PROTEIN: 126g • CARBS: 24g • FIBER: 9g

DAY 24

MEAL 1

3 slices bacon

3 eggs cooked in bacon fat

LEFTOVER
Sour Cream Biscuit *(1)* with 1 tbsp butter

CALORIES	FAT	PROTEIN	CARBS	FIBER
756	67g	34g	6g	2g

MEAL 2

Asian Cabbage Bowl *(2 servings)* — 110

Snack *(see page 40)*

CALORIES	FAT	PROTEIN	CARBS	FIBER
1042	80g	65g	16g	4g

CALORIES: 1798 • FAT: 147g • PROTEIN: 99g • CARBS: 22g • FIBER: 6g

DAY 25

MEAL 1

5-Minute Breakfast Sandwich **162**

½ avocado

Fatty tea/coffee with 1 tbsp butter + 1 tbsp coconut oil

CALORIES	FAT	PROTEIN	CARBS	FIBER
838	69g	37g	17g	10g

MEAL 2

Barbacoa Lettuce Wraps **LEFTOVER**

Sour Cream Biscuit *(1)* with 1 tbsp butter **LEFTOVER**

CALORIES	FAT	PROTEIN	CARBS	FIBER
1047	85g	54g	11g	3g

CALORIES: 1885 • FAT: 154g • PROTEIN: 91g • CARBS: 28g • FIBER: 13g

---

DAY 26

MEAL 1

Jalapeño Popper Egg Bites *(4)* **152**

Snack *(see page 40)*

CALORIES	FAT	PROTEIN	CARBS	FIBER
734	56g	53g	0g	0g

MEAL 2

One-Pan Chicken with Lemon-Garlic Cream Sauce *(2 servings)* **210**

2 cups steamed asparagus with 1 tbsp butter

CALORIES	FAT	PROTEIN	CARBS	FIBER
1051	78g	74g	17g	7g

CALORIES: 1785 • FAT: 134g • PROTEIN: 127g • CARBS: 17g • FIBER: 7g

---

DAY 27

MEAL 1

Jalapeño Popper Egg Bites *(4)* **LEFTOVER**

Snack *(see page 40)*

CALORIES	FAT	PROTEIN	CARBS	FIBER
734	56g	53g	0g	0g

MEAL 2

One-Pan Chicken with Lemon-Garlic Cream Sauce *(2 servings)* **LEFTOVER**

Buttered Mushrooms *(2 servings)* **236**

CALORIES	FAT	PROTEIN	CARBS	FIBER
1190	90g	77g	15g	5g

CALORIES: 1924 • FAT: 146g • PROTEIN: 130g • CARBS: 15g • FIBER: 5g

---

DAY 28

MEAL 1

5-Minute Breakfast Sandwich **162**

1 avocado

Fatty tea/coffee with 1 tbsp butter + 1 tbsp coconut oil

CALORIES	FAT	PROTEIN	CARBS	FIBER
952	80g	38g	23g	15g

MEAL 2

Takeout meal *(see page 53)*

CALORIES	FAT	PROTEIN	CARBS	FIBER
800	62g	50g	10g	5g

CALORIES: 1752 • FAT: 142g • PROTEIN: 88g • CARBS: 33g • FIBER: 20g

Focus: SLEEP

A good night's sleep is the cheapest supplement on the market. You will truly be amazed at how different life can be when you start to place an emphasis on sleep.

Sleep is what's called a "leading variable"—a factor that you can directly control. "Lagging variables" are factors we can't directly control, but they're affected by leading variables. So often we place all of our attention on lagging variables instead of leading variables. For example, deep down, most of us care about the number on the scale, and we set goals for ourselves like "Lose 20 pounds by the end of the month." But the number on the scale is a lagging variable. We can't control it directly; we have to adjust other factors that affect it. If you want to lose 20 pounds, you need to focus on lead-ing variables—the things you can control—with goals like "Stick to my eating plan for three weeks straight" or "Get eight hours of sleep every night for a month." When you start placing focus on the leading variables, your progress will begin to pick up.

Sleep is the ultimate leading variable. A proper night's sleep makes everything better: It's easier to stick to your eating plan the next day. You're more productive at work. You have the energy to get things done even after a long day at work. You wake up energized and ready to attack the day ahead.

For the past four years, we've tested tons of different diet and lifestyle factors to see how they affect us, and to our surprise, sleep was the single greatest factor. We cross-referenced notes on sleep quality, duration, and more with our food journals and activity logs, and the results were astonishing. Without fail, every time we decided to skip the gym, we'd had a night of subpar sleep. And after a night of poor sleep, we were much less likely to stick to our intended eating plan for the day. Improving the quality of our sleep helped us improve dramatically in other areas of life.

Now, how can you go about improving your sleep? The first and most obvious step is to make sure you're getting the right amount, between seven and eight hours a night. The largest sleep study ever conducted, published in the December 2018 issue of *Sleep*, found that consistently sleeping less than seven hours or more than eight hours had measurable negative effects on cognition and memory.

The next step is to wake up and go to bed at the same time every day. If possi-ble, these times should match your natural circadian rhythm, which means sleeping when it's dark out and being active during the day. If you have a habit of staying up all night playing video games (like Matt) and you want to align your sleep cycle with your circadian rhythm, there are some steps you can take:

GET SUN EXPOSURE IN THE MORNING: *Getting large amounts of sunlight as soon as the sun comes up is a great way to signal your body that the day is starting.*

EAT EARLIER IN THE DAY: *Cortisol, known as the stress hormone, rises in the morning and is a key signaler of your body's circadian rhythm. For some people, eating a meal high in fat and protein early in the day can reduce the level to which cortisol rises, allowing an easier transition to restfulness at night. Also, eating too close to bedtime will cut into your deep sleep and energy the next day. We've monitored our sleep using tracking devices, and whenever we eat close to bedtime, our sleep suffers. A good rule of thumb is to eat dinner at least three hours before bed.*

AVOID LIGHT EXPOSURE AT NIGHT: *The Netflix marathon might have to end early, but at least you'll have episodes left for tomorrow, right? Artificial light from phones, computers, and TVs signal our bodies that it is daylight, which throws off our circadian rhythm big-time. If you're unwilling to give up electronics in bed, these tools can limit your exposure to blue light, which has the biggest disruptive effect:*

- *F.lux, a computer app that removes blue light from your screens at night*
- *Phone apps that remove the blue light from screens at night*
- *Blue-light-blocking glasses*

LIMIT CAFFEINE: *Sorry, we know you might not like to hear this one, but it's important. How much caffeine are you drinking, and how close to bedtime? The half-life of caffeine is about six hours. That means if you consume 200 mg of caffeine at 6 p.m., there will be 100 mg in your system at midnight! Giving up caffeine is not necessary or realistic for most people, but setting a caffeine cutoff is essential for the restful night's sleep you deserve. Try limiting or completely eliminating caffeine consumption after 12 p.m.*

EXERCISE: *You will fall asleep faster and sleep more deeply if you exert yourself each day. It doesn't have to be a high-intensity workout, just some form of exercise. We've all had days where we just sit in front of the computer or TV and struggle to fall asleep at night. That's because we didn't expend any energy all day.*

So here's the challenge: Take this week to focus on your sleep. Identify some problem areas. Take stock of how sleep quality impacts other areas of your life. Assess your productivity, your mood, your adherence to your diet plan. Monitoring all this will give you the motivation to continue improving long after the week is over. It sounds simple, but most of us never try to figure out why we have an awesome day at work or wake up on the wrong side of the bed. How many of those days are the result of how we slept the night before?

WEEK 5 Shopping List

MEAT

bacon, *14 slices*

chicken wings, *2 pounds*

ground pork, *1 pound*

SEAFOOD

salmon fillets, skinless, *1½ pounds*

EGGS AND DAIRY

butter, unsalted, *½ cup (1 stick)*

eggs, *23 large*

heavy whipping cream, *3¼ cups*

mozzarella cheese, *1 ounce*

Parmesan cheese, *2 ounces*

ricotta cheese, full-fat, *1½ cups*

PRODUCE

avocados, *2 medium*

Brussels sprouts, *1½ pounds*

celery, *4 stalks*

cherry tomatoes, *15*

chives, *2 tablespoons minced*

cucumbers, *2 small*

garlic, *4 cloves*

ginger, *1 (1-inch) piece*

lemons, *2*

mixed greens, *12 cups*

red bell pepper, *½ medium*

red onions, *2 small*

PANTRY

almond milk, unsweetened, *1½ cups*

chia seeds, *½ cup + 2 tablespoons*

hemp hearts, *½ cup + 2 tablespoons*

low-carb crackers, *for serving*

natural peanut butter, *¼ cup*

pecans, raw, *½ cup*

sesame seeds, *3 tablespoons*

Sriracha sauce, *½ teaspoon*

sun-dried tomatoes in olive oil, *2 ounces*

vanilla-flavored protein powder, *75 grams*

xanthan gum, *¼ teaspoon*

PLUS

7 snacks *(see page 40)*

1 takeout meal *(see page 53)*

The macros and calories are per meal, not per dish. The day's totals are in the blue row.

Meal Prep

Overnight Protein "Oats"
138

Soy-Glazed Salmon
122

Supreme Pizza Breakfast Casserole
136

Peanut Butter Pecan Fat Bombs
266

DAY 29

MEAL 1

Overnight Protein "Oats"
138

Supreme Pizza Breakfast Casserole *(2 servings)*
136

CALORIES	FAT	PROTEIN	CARBS	FIBER
868	54g	79g	19g	11g

MEAL 2

Mixed Greens Salad with Salmon and Sesame Dressing
126

Snack *(see page 40)*

Peanut Butter Pecan Fat Bombs *(2)*
266

CALORIES	FAT	PROTEIN	CARBS	FIBER
897	74g	43g	14g	4g

CALORIES: 1756 • FAT: 128g • PROTEIN: 122g • CARBS: 33g • FIBER: 15g

DAY 30

MEAL 1

LEFTOVER
Overnight Protein "Oats"

LEFTOVER
Supreme Pizza Breakfast Casserole

Fatty tea/coffee with 1 tbsp butter + 1 tbsp coconut oil

CALORIES	FAT	PROTEIN	CARBS	FIBER
822	63g	51g	16g	11g

MEAL 2

Mixed Greens Salad with Salmon and Sesame Dressing
126

Snack *(see page 40)*

LEFTOVER
Peanut Butter Pecan Fat Bombs *(2)*

CALORIES	FAT	PROTEIN	CARBS	FIBER
897	74g	43g	14g	4g

CALORIES: 1719 • FAT: 137g • PROTEIN: 94g • CARBS: 30g • FIBER: 15g

DAY 31

MEAL 1

LEFTOVER
Overnight Protein "Oats"

LEFTOVER
Supreme Pizza Breakfast Casserole *(2 servings)*

CALORIES	FAT	PROTEIN	CARBS	FIBER
868	54g	79g	19g	11g

MEAL 2

Salmon Salad *(2 servings)*
124

Snack *(see page 40)*

LEFTOVER
Peanut Butter Pecan Fat Bombs *(2)*

CALORIES	FAT	PROTEIN	CARBS	FIBER
960	82g	46g	7g	3g

CALORIES: 1828 • FAT: 136g • PROTEIN: 125g • CARBS: 26g • FIBER: 14g

DAY 32

MEAL 1

LEFTOVER

Overnight Protein "Oats" | 3 slices bacon | 3 eggs cooked in bacon fat | ½ avocado

CALORIES	FAT	PROTEIN	CARBS	FIBER
872	66g	51g	21g	15g

MEAL 2

LEFTOVER

Salmon Salad *(2 servings)* | Snack **x2** *(see page 40)*

CALORIES	FAT	PROTEIN	CARBS	FIBER
900	74g	52g	3g	1g

CALORIES: 1772 • FAT: 140g • PROTEIN: 103g • CARBS: 24g • FIBER: 16g

---

DAY 33

MEAL 1

LEFTOVER   **LEFTOVER**

Overnight Protein "Oats" | Supreme Pizza Breakfast Casserole *(2 servings)*

CALORIES	FAT	PROTEIN	CARBS	FIBER
868	54g	79g	19g	11g

MEAL 2

126   **LEFTOVER**

Mixed Greens Salad with Salmon and Sesame Dressing | Snack *(see page 40)* | Peanut Butter Pecan Fat Bombs *(2)*

CALORIES	FAT	PROTEIN	CARBS	FIBER
897	74g	43g	14g	4g

CALORIES: 1756 • FAT: 128g • PROTEIN: 122g • CARBS: 33g • FIBER: 15g

---

DAY 34

MEAL 1

166

Coconut Flour Pan-cakes *(2)* with 1 tbsp butter | 2 slices bacon

CALORIES	FAT	PROTEIN	CARBS	FIBER
751	67g	17g	16g	13g

MEAL 2

214   222   **LEFTOVER**

Indian Spiced Wings | Creamy Brussels Sprouts with Bacon | Peanut Butter Pecan Fat Bombs *(2)*

CALORIES	FAT	PROTEIN	CARBS	FIBER
1075	82g	66g	20g	8g

CALORIES: 1826 • FAT: 149g • PROTEIN: 83g • CARBS: 36g • FIBER: 21g

---

DAY 35

MEAL 1

150

Mini Breakfast Cakes *(2 servings)* | 4 slices bacon | Snack *(see page 40)*

CALORIES	FAT	PROTEIN	CARBS	FIBER
1028	79g	62g	12g	4g

MEAL 2

Takeout meal *(see page 53)*

CALORIES	FAT	PROTEIN	CARBS	FIBER
800	62g	50g	10g	5g

CALORIES: 1828 • FAT: 141g • PROTEIN: 112g • CARBS: 22g • FIBER: 9g

WEEK 6

Focus: ADD NUTRIENT DENSITY TO YOUR DIET

Micronutrients—vitamins and minerals—are what determine whether a food is healthy or not. They are vital to human growth and development, disease prevention, and overall health.

A healthy diet can really be reduced down to two components: high amounts of good things, like micronutrients, and the absence of bad things, like carcinogens, refined sugars, and artificial ingredients.

There is so much bad stuff in our modern food supply that most diets focus on how to exclude it. Even a keto diet is mostly known for the removal of carbohydrates. But making sure you're getting plenty of the good stuff is just as important. So it's time to talk superfoods! These are especially nutrient-dense foods that you'll benefit from including in your meals.

Below are superfoods we recommend most highly. They're not quite the superfoods you're used to hearing about—the foods highest in essential vitamins and minerals are not exotic berries. They are foods that people have valued for thousands of years and that are proven to make us strong and healthy.

ORGAN MEATS: *The most nutrient-dense foods on the planet, organ meats like liver and kidneys were prized throughout human history—up until the last fifty years or so. Our palates have been changed so much by the modern food supply that many of us find organ meats unappetizing. It can be a challenge to start eating them, but give it a shot. Eat beef, lamb, or bison liver for the best nutrient bang for your buck—they have the most vitamin A of any food source. If you find the taste unappetizing, start with liverwurst, which is cooked and seasoned so you won't even know you are eating an organ meat. Cod liver oil is also a great option: it can be taken in capsule form, and its nutrient profile is similar to liver's. If you have trouble finding organ meats in your local stores, there are a number of places to order from online.*

FATTY FISH AND SHELLFISH: *In addition to containing lots of trace minerals, seafood is high in omega-3 fatty acids, which are severely lacking in the standard American diet. Almost all seafood is a healthful addition to our diets, with the exception of lean, farm-raised white fish, like tilapia and cod.*

FERMENTED RAW DAIRY: *Raw-milk cheese is becoming widely available across the US and is a great option for adding nutrient density to your diet. It does not go through the pasteurization process, so the beneficial bacteria and enzymes of the cheese are preserved. Other forms of raw dairy are not available in many areas of the United States but can often be found at local farmers markets or from local farmers.*

BONE BROTH AND BONE MARROW: *While bone broth is popping up in grocery stores everywhere, bone marrow can be a bit harder to find. Both options are a great way to add healthy fats, gelatin, and collagen to your diet. The standard American diet is shockingly devoid of collagen and gelatin, which people used to eat in much higher amounts when the whole animal was eaten.*

FERMENTED VEGETABLES: *Fermentation helps preserve food as well as providing gut-friendly probiotics. The best options for a ketogenic diet are sauerkraut and kimchi.*

More Nutrients = Less Overeating

One thing to pay attention to when you eat particularly nutrient-dense foods is your satiety levels. We strongly believe that hunger is largely dictated by the amount of nutrients in your diet—your body doesn't send the signal that you're full until it gets the nutrients it needs. On a standard American diet, which is full of foods devoid of nutrients, it's extremely easy to overeat because it's hard to get that signal. But when you focus on eating nutrient-dense foods, you'll get that signal much sooner. You don't have to eat as much to get all the nutrients you need.

This week, make it a point to include one or two new-to-you nutrient-dense foods in your diet. You don't need to completely overhaul your diet and start buying exotic meats—just add one of these items to your diet every week and see how you feel.

In fact, we've designated one dinner this week as a "Superfood Challenge Meal." Make a special effort to make this a nutrient-dense meal with at least one of the superfoods listed at left. For inspiration, here are some of our favorite nutrient-dense meals:

Beef liver with garlic and onions, served with bacon and steamed asparagus and butter

Raw-milk cheese, smoked oysters, and kimchi (no cooking required!)

Beef short ribs slow cooked in bone broth, served with steamed broccoli and butter

Grilled salmon, served with grilled eggplant and olive oil

WEEK 6 Shopping List

MEAT
bacon, *6 slices*

brisket, *4 pounds*

chicken wings, *2 pounds*

EGGS AND DAIRY
butter, unsalted, *1 cup (2 sticks) + 2 tablespoons*

cheddar cheese, *8 ounces*

Cotija cheese, *6 ounces*

eggs, *22 large*

heavy whipping cream, *1 cup + 2 tablespoons*

Parmesan cheese, *3 ounces*

PRODUCE
avocado, *1 large*

basil leaves, *¼ cup*

broccoli, *6 cups*

garlic, *3 cloves*

green beans, *1 pound*

lemon, *1*

poblano peppers, *1½ pounds*

purple cabbage, *about ⅔ pound*

zucchini, *1 medium*

PANTRY
almond milk, unsweetened, *¼ cup + 2 tablespoons*

low-carb BBQ sauce, *2 tablespoons*

pickles

PLUS
9 snacks *(see page 40)*

1 takeout meal *(see page 53)*

Superfood Challenge Meal *(see above)*

WEEK 6 *Meal Plan*

The macros and calories are per meal, not per dish. The day's totals are in the blue row.

Meal Prep

Spice-Rubbed Brisket* `128`

Chile Rellenos Casserole `142`

Zucchini Basil Muffins `238`

* This recipe makes 4 pounds of brisket, but for the meals this week, you'll only need 10 ounces. You can always make half the brisket recipe if you like, and it freezes well, so you can use the rest later.

DAY 36

MEAL 1

Brisket Breakfast Skillet `132`

Fatty tea/coffee with 1 tbsp butter + 1 tbsp coconut oil

Snack *(see page 40)*

CALORIES	FAT	PROTEIN	CARBS	FIBER
963	85g	43g	6g	2g

MEAL 2

Chile Rellenos Casserole *(2 servings)*

3 cups steamed broccoli with 1 tbsp butter

Snack *(see page 40)*

CALORIES	FAT	PROTEIN	CARBS	FIBER
875	67g	49g	27g	11g

CALORIES: 1838 • FAT: 152g • PROTEIN: 92g • CARBS: 33g • FIBER: 13g

---

DAY 37

MEAL 1

LEFTOVER
Chile Rellenos Casserole *(2 servings)*

Fatty tea/coffee with 1 tbsp butter + 1 tbsp coconut oil

Snack *(see page 40)*

CALORIES	FAT	PROTEIN	CARBS	FIBER
910	79g	41g	9g	4g

MEAL 2

Brisket Sandwich `130`

Zucchini Basil Muffins *(2)* with 1 tbsp butter `238`

CALORIES	FAT	PROTEIN	CARBS	FIBER
825	57g	38g	19g	9g

CALORIES: 1735 • FAT: 136g • PROTEIN: 79g • CARBS: 28g • FIBER: 13g

---

DAY 38

MEAL 1

5 scrambled eggs cooked in 2 tbsp butter, topped with 1 oz Parmesan cheese, grated

Snack *(see page 40)*

CALORIES	FAT	PROTEIN	CARBS	FIBER
852	70g	49g	2g	0g

MEAL 2

LEFTOVER
Brisket Sandwich

LEFTOVER
Zucchini Basil Muffins *(2)* with 1 tbsp butter

Snack *(see page 40)*

CALORIES	FAT	PROTEIN	CARBS	FIBER
967	69g	47g	19g	9g

CALORIES: 1819 • FAT: 139g • PROTEIN: 96g • CARBS: 21g • FIBER: 9g

---

DAY 39

MEAL 1

  132

Brisket Breakfast Skillet

Fatty tea/coffee with 1 tbsp butter + 1 tbsp coconut oil

Snack *(see page 40)*

CALORIES	FAT	PROTEIN	CARBS	FIBER
963	85g	43g	6g	2g

MEAL 2

LEFTOVER

Chile Rellenos Casserole *(2 servings)*

3 cups steamed broccoli with 1 tbsp butter

Snack *(see page 40)*

CALORIES	FAT	PROTEIN	CARBS	FIBER
875	67g	49g	27g	11g

CALORIES: 1838 • FAT: 152g • PROTEIN: 92g • CARBS: 33g • FIBER: 13g

DAY 40

MEAL 1

LEFTOVER

Chile Rellenos Casserole *(2 servings)*

Fatty tea/coffee with 1 tbsp butter + 1 tbsp coconut oil

Snack *(see page 40)*

CALORIES	FAT	PROTEIN	CARBS	FIBER
910	79g	41g	9g	4g

MEAL 2

  214 250

Indian Spiced Wings

Garlic Green Beans *(2 servings)*

CALORIES	FAT	PROTEIN	CARBS	FIBER
873	63g	58g	20g	8g

CALORIES: 1783 • FAT: 142g • PROTEIN: 99g • CARBS: 29g • FIBER: 12g

DAY 41

MEAL 1

   147

Dutch Baby for Two *(2 servings)*

4 slices bacon

½ avocado

CALORIES	FAT	PROTEIN	CARBS	FIBER
792	68g	33g	14g	8g

MEAL 2

Superfood Challenge Meal *(see page 81)*

CALORIES	FAT	PROTEIN	CARBS	FIBER
--	--	--	--	--

CALORIES: 792 • FAT: 68g • PROTEIN: 33g • CARBS: 14g • FIBER: 8g

DAY 42

MEAL 1

  166

Coconut Flour Pancakes *(2)* **with 1 tbsp butter**

2 slices bacon, ½ avocado

Snack *(see page 40)*

CALORIES	FAT	PROTEIN	CARBS	FIBER
1007	90g	27g	22g	18g

MEAL 2

Takeout meal *(see page 53)*

CALORIES	FAT	PROTEIN	CARBS	FIBER
800	62g	50g	10g	5g

CALORIES: 1807 • FAT: 152g • PROTEIN: 77g • CARBS: 32g • FIBER: 23g

Focus:
PUTTING IT ALL TOGETHER

This is it—your last week on the plan! This is a good week to review what you've learned about yourself and what way of eating works for you, from the number of meals per day you prefer to how much sleep you need to the kinds of meals you prefer.

Look back over any notes you made during the previous weeks (or think back over these weeks) and see if any patterns jump out at you. Did you sleep better on days you worked out—and were you more likely to work out after you got a good night's sleep? Were there situations that made it hard for you to stick to keto, such as a work happy hour or a get-together with friends? (Planning ahead and bringing keto-friendly snacks can make those situations easier.) And how are you feeling now that you've been on keto for nearly two months? Are you more energized and no longer having that 2 p.m. slump? Are you less hungry and experiencing fewer cravings?

And looking at the broader picture, has keto been a catalyst to help you make other positive changes in your life? Maybe you're finally training to run that marathon or have the energy to go to the gym after work. Or maybe you're feeling more confident about your ability to change your life, and that's allowed you to start thinking about going back to school or looking for a new job. It's amazing how taking charge of one part of your life can lead you to make other changes.

Finally, do you feel like keto is sustainable for you over the long term? And if not, what would help make it more sustainable? Maybe you feel like you need to eat a little more carbs some days, particularly before or after workouts, or maybe you're still struggling with finding time to cook (meal prep is key, but no-cook meals can also be very useful—see page 57).

Think of this week as your time to look ahead to how you're going to continue eating keto after the plan ends. Build a database of tools and tactics that work for you. It's time to start looking forward to life after these fifty days and what you're going to do to maintain these changes. Remember, the most important aspect of any diet is its sustainability. Take this last week to come up with a sustainable plan that you can stick with indefinitely. It doesn't need to be perfect right now—you just need to keep making gradual improvements.

WEEK 7 Shopping List

MEAT

bacon, *15 slices*

chicken, *1 whole (4½ pounds)*

pork ribs, *3 pounds*

turkey deli meat, *3 thin slices*

EGGS AND DAIRY

butter, unsalted, *1 cup (2 sticks) + 1 tablespoon*

cheddar cheese, *10 ounces*

eggs, *32 large*

heavy whipping cream, *2 cups + 1 tablespoon*

mozzarella cheese, *1 slice*

PRODUCE

avocados, *5 medium*

broccoli, *7 cups*

carrot, *1 medium*

celery, *3 stalks*

garlic, *4 cloves*

ginger, *1 (1-inch) piece*

jalapeño peppers, *2 large*

lime, *1*

red onion, *½ medium*

rosemary leaves, *¾ teaspoon*

scallions, *2*

thyme leaves, *1½ teaspoons*

PANTRY

almond milk, unsweetened, *2 tablespoons*

chicken broth, low-sodium, *4 cups*

cocoa powder, *1 cup*

shredded coconut, unsweetened, *½ cup*

PLUS

3 snacks *(see page 40)*

1 takeout meal *(see page 53)*

The macros and calories are per meal, not per dish. The day's totals are in the blue row.

Meal Prep

98
Sweet Asian BBQ Spatchcocked Chicken

284
Chocolate Avocado Cookies

DAY 43

MEAL 1

5 scrambled eggs cooked in 2 tbsp butter

Snack *(see page 40)*

½ avocado

CALORIES	FAT	PROTEIN	CARBS	FIBER
847	73g	42g	8g	5g

MEAL 2

100
Chicken Pot Pie Soup *(2 servings)*

284
Chocolate Avocado Cookies *(2)*

CALORIES	FAT	PROTEIN	CARBS	FIBER
894	59g	67g	22g	10g

CALORIES: 1741 • FAT: 132g • PROTEIN: 109g • CARBS: 30g • FIBER: 15g

---

DAY 44

MEAL 1

162
5-Minute Breakfast Sandwich

½ avocado

Fatty tea/coffee with 1 tbsp butter + 1 tbsp coconut oil

CALORIES	FAT	PROTEIN	CARBS	FIBER
838	69g	37g	17g	10g

MEAL 2

104
Loaded Chicken Salad

LEFTOVER
Chocolate Avocado Cookies *(2)*

Snack *(see page 40)*

CALORIES	FAT	PROTEIN	CARBS	FIBER
964	74g	63g	15g	10g

CALORIES: 1802 • FAT: 143g • PROTEIN: 100g • CARBS: 32g • FIBER: 20g

---

DAY 45

MEAL 1

4 slices bacon, ½ avocado

4 eggs cooked in bacon fat

Fatty tea/coffee with 1 tbsp butter + 1 tbsp coconut oil

CALORIES	FAT	PROTEIN	CARBS	FIBER
866	78g	37g	8g	5g

MEAL 2

LEFTOVER
Chicken Pot Pie Soup *(2 servings)*

LEFTOVER
Chocolate Avocado Cookies *(2)*

CALORIES	FAT	PROTEIN	CARBS	FIBER
894	59g	67g	22g	10g

CALORIES: 1760 • FAT: 137g • PROTEIN: 104g • CARBS: 30g • FIBER: 15g

DAY 46

MEAL 1

5 scrambled eggs cooked in 2 tbsp butter, topped with 1 oz Parmesan cheese, grated

Fatty tea/coffee with 1 tbsp butter + 1 tbsp coconut oil

CALORIES	FAT	PROTEIN	CARBS	FIBER
940	83g	40g	2g	0g

MEAL 2

Chicken Pot Pie Soup *(2 servings)* LEFTOVER

Chocolate Avocado Cookies *(2)* LEFTOVER

CALORIES	FAT	PROTEIN	CARBS	FIBER
894	59g	67g	22g	10g

CALORIES: 1834 • FAT: 142g • PROTEIN: 107g • CARBS: 24g • FIBER: 10g

---

DAY 47

MEAL 1

Cinnamon Morning Muffins *(2)* with 1 tbsp butter — 144

Jalapeño Popper Egg Bites *(4)* — 152

CALORIES	FAT	PROTEIN	CARBS	FIBER
982	82g	53g	6g	3g

MEAL 2

Dry-Rubbed Ribs — 196

3 cups steamed broccoli with 1 tbsp butter

Chocolate Avocado Cookies *(2)* LEFTOVER

CALORIES	FAT	PROTEIN	CARBS	FIBER
849	65g	46g	31g	15g

CALORIES: 1831 • FAT: 147g • PROTEIN: 99g • CARBS: 37g • FIBER: 18g

---

DAY 48

MEAL 1

Cinnamon Morning Muffins *(2)* with 1 tbsp butter LEFTOVER

Jalapeño Popper Egg Bites *(4)* LEFTOVER

CALORIES	FAT	PROTEIN	CARBS	FIBER
982	82g	53g	6g	3g

MEAL 2

Dry-Rubbed Ribs LEFTOVER

3 cups steamed broccoli with 1 tbsp butter

Chocolate Avocado Cookies *(2)* LEFTOVER

CALORIES	FAT	PROTEIN	CARBS	FIBER
849	65g	46g	31g	15g

CALORIES: 1831 • FAT: 147g • PROTEIN: 99g • CARBS: 37g • FIBER: 18g

---

DAY 49

MEAL 1

Coconut Flour Pancakes *(2)* with 1 tbsp butter — 166

2 slices bacon, ½ avocado

Snack *(see page 40)*

CALORIES	FAT	PROTEIN	CARBS	FIBER
1007	90g	27g	22g	18g

MEAL 2

Takeout meal *(see page 53)*

CALORIES	FAT	PROTEIN	CARBS	FIBER
800	62g	50g	10g	5g

CALORIES: 1807 • FAT: 152g • PROTEIN: 77g • CARBS: 32g • FIBER: 23g

DAY 50

You did it! Sticking to an eating plan for fifty days is not easy, and you wouldn't be human if you didn't have any slipups. Instead of focusing on those or stressing over how you can improve in the future, take this day to appreciate what you've done. It's easy to be critical of ourselves all the time, but you've accomplished something that's not easy. Acknowledge the fact that you care about your health and have finished a fifty-day challenge to better your life.

For this last day on the plan, pick your favorite meals from those you've had so far and enjoy them! And remember, just because the fifty-day plan is done doesn't mean that you should go back to processed, high-carb foods. Your hard work has already had impressive health benefits, from stabilizing your blood sugar to reducing inflammation, but stick with keto to keep those improvements going. They'll have compounding results for you down the road. While the first fifty days are where you see the most dramatic changes, your body will continue to improve its ability to use fat for fuel the longer you eat a ketogenic diet.

DAY 50

MEAL 1

Your favorite breakfast
from the previous 49 days

MEAL 2

Your favorite dinner
from the previous 49 days

DESSERT

Any dessert from the Desserts
& Sweet Snacks chapter
*(our favorite is Pecan Snowball
Cookies, page 296)*

PART 3:
The Recipes

In our first cookbook, *Keto Made Easy*, we focused on giving you keto-friendly versions of your favorite recipes, from childhood comfort foods to holiday staples to delicious takeout dishes. The goal was to help you stick to the keto diet for the long haul while satisfying all your cravings.

The recipes in this book will also help make keto sustainable for the long term, but our goals have shifted to center on feeding the entire family, meal prepping for the week, and making easy-to-prepare everyday meals. When you're wondering how to plan weekly menus so you're eating healthy food without spending all day in the kitchen, these recipes, along with the meal plans on pages 59 to 88, are designed to meet your needs.

Of course, they're also delicious and filling! From our Cheddar and Sausage Scones (page 148) for breakfast to our Sweet Asian BBQ Spatchcocked Chicken (page 98) for meal prep, you'll be satisfied all day long. There are even several never-before-seen dessert recipes, like our triple-layer Carrot Cake (page 280) and Chocolate Pecan Pound Cake (page 286), that will make the entire family happy.

 ## MEAL PREP RECIPES

If you've read through the seven-week meal plan, you already know that meal prepping is the practice of making meals in bulk, often on the weekend. Meal prepping ensures that you have meals in the fridge and ready to eat throughout the week, so you do a lot less cooking on workdays and school days. Meal prepping is our biggest tip for achieving success with any new diet or lifestyle change.

The Meal Prep recipes chapter contains two kinds of recipes, both of which make meal prep for the week ahead a breeze. First there are the foundation recipes, like Barbacoa (page 106) and Sweet Asian BBQ Spatchcocked Chicken (page 98), which make large amounts and are used in other meals throughout the week. And then there are the recipes that use a foundation recipe as an ingredient. For instance, Barbacoa Lettuce Wraps (page 108) uses Barbacoa (page 106) as a main ingredient. Once you've made the barbacoa on your meal prep day, the wraps are a quick and easy meal. And because the foundation recipes make a lot of servings, they can be used in several meals throughout the week. One batch of Barbacoa (page 106), for instance, will make Barbacoa Lettuce Wraps (page 108), Asian Cabbage Bowl (page 110), and Barbacoa Breakfast Skillet (page 112).

We've grouped the foundation recipes and the recipes that use them together in the Meal Prep chapter so that you can easily see how to use them in your meal prep. And the meal plans on pages 59 to 88 have lots of examples of how to use these recipes to make meal planning super easy.

QUICK REFERENCE ICONS

Each recipe in the book features icons that give you at-a-glance information about allergens and food restrictions. The six icons tell you whether the recipe is:

 DAIRY-FREE

 EGG-FREE

 NUT-FREE

 VEGETARIAN

 GREAT FOR LEFTOVERS: *Like the foundation recipes in the Meal Prep chapter, these recipes are excellent to make ahead and then eat throughout the week (though they're not used as ingredients in other recipes). They tend to make more servings and reheat very well.*

 FOOLPROOF: *These recipes are the easiest to make and require very little experience in the kitchen.*

NUTRITIONAL INFORMATION

For each recipe, we've listed the total calories and grams of fat, protein, carbohydrate, fiber, and sugar alcohol, where applicable. Because fiber and sugar alcohols do not impact blood glucose levels in most people, if you're counting net carbs (which we recommend), you'll need to subtract these from the recipe's total carb count.

It is important to note that nutrition can vary from brand to brand. The information provided is based on what we use at home, and we have included a list of our most commonly used brands of store-bought products on page 94.

In each recipe, when a garnish is marked as "optional" or an ingredient is "for serving," the nutritional values of those ingredients are not included in the nutritional information at the bottom of each recipe.

Nutrition
CALORIES: 308   FAT: 25g   PROTEIN: 17g   CARBS: 1.5g   FIBER: 0.5g

NOTES ON INGREDIENTS

BBQ SAUCE: *Look for a brand that's low in sugar. We like G Hughes.*

NUT BUTTERS: *In our recipes, we use natural nut butters, which are unsweetened and unsalted—the only ingredient is nuts. Many grocery stores now have "grind your own" nut butter stations, but you can also find brands that use only nuts—just check the ingredients label.*

SWEETENERS: *We use erythritol as a sweetener in our recipes. It's non-nutritive, meaning it doesn't have any calories or nutrients, so it's great for low-carb baking. Erythritol is available in granulated and powdered forms; the recipe will indicate which should be used. We prefer Swerve brand, which measures cup for cup like sugar.*

TOMATO SAUCE: *Make sure your store-bought tomato sauce is as low in sugar as possible. Rao's brand marinara sauce is our favorite.*

Our Favorite Brands

apple cider vinegar: Bragg

baking chocolate: Baker's

chicken broth (organic, free-range): Imagine

chocolate chips (sugar-free): Lily's

coconut cream and coconut milk: Thai Kitchen

flavored protein powder: NutraBio Classic Whey in chocolate peanut butter, Quest in cinnamon crunch

low-carb BBQ sauce: G Hughes

marinara/tomato sauce: Rao's Homemade

mayonnaise: Primal Kitchen Avocado Oil Mayonnaise

Our Favorite KITCHEN GADGETS

CAST-IRON SKILLETS: We use our cast-iron skillets almost every day. While they take a little upkeep, they are well worth it in the end. They are very reasonably priced and easily found online. The brand we always purchase is Lodge. They are the only skillets you will ever need to use again! You don't have to worry about getting nonstick chemicals in your food, and they are great for transferring casseroles and meats from the stovetop to the oven.

HIGH-POWERED BLENDER: We use our Vitamix blender every day without fail. Although it's on the pricier side and any blender will work great, we both like to have our morning butter coffee/tea, so blending is a must! The Vitamix is a powerhouse and can be used to make soups, nut butters, and more.

SOUS VIDE: We mainly use our Joule sous vide to make hard-boiled eggs in bulk, and boy do we go through hard-boiled eggs! With the sous vide, they turn out perfect every time because you can hold the water at a specific temperature. We also love to use it for meats. It cooks steaks to the perfect temperature all the way through, so all you need to do is give it a quick sear on both sides and you'll never have an overcooked steak again. And we've even made ribs in it, slow cooked for six hours, and they turned out delicious and tender.

MULTICOOKER (INSTANT POT): We use our Instant Pot on a weekly basis to make homemade bone broth (recipe on KetoConnect.net). It takes three hours total and comes out perfect every time. We also use it to cook fresh vegetables and raw meat in minutes. We've used it to make yogurts and soups, and we love the slow cooker function for bone-in meats!

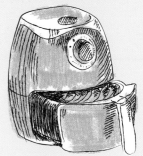

AIR FRYER: The air fryer is the newest addition to our home, and while it's a little clunky, we've found we use it at least four times a week. Megha loves to use it to make meatballs and chicken wings, while Matt finds it's great for a quick, minimal-cleanup steak. It allows us to have lunch or dinner done in under fifteen minutes on busy days!

Meal Prep

✕ SWEET ASIAN BBQ SPATCHCOCKED CHICKEN

MAKES 4 servings   **PREP TIME:** 15 minutes   **COOK TIME:** 45 minutes

Our favorite way to roast a chicken in the oven is by spatchcocking it! It always turns out juicier, cooks through faster, and is a lot easier to cut up and serve to family and friends. While it's great for eating on its own or with a side of veggies, we often use leftover spatchcocked chicken to make **CHICKEN POT PIE SOUP** (page 100), **CHICKEN AND RICOTTA STUFFED PEPPERS** (page 102), and Megha's favorite, **LOADED CHICKEN SALAD** (page 104). They are all great recipes to prep on the weekend and take to work for lunch all week long!

SAUCE:

¼ cup soy sauce or coconut aminos

2 tablespoons avocado oil

Juice of 1 lime

1 teaspoon unseasoned rice wine vinegar

½ teaspoon toasted sesame oil

½ teaspoon garam masala

1 (1-inch) piece fresh ginger, grated

2 teaspoons minced garlic

2 scallions, minced

⅛ teaspoon liquid stevia

1 (4½-pound) whole chicken

tips:

One 4½-pound roasted chicken will yield 1 pound of cooked and shredded white meat (about 2 cups) and 1 pound of cooked and shredded dark meat (about 2 cups).

Most of the Asian flavor from the spatchcocked chicken is in the skin, so there will no issue with the change in flavor profiles when you use the meat for other recipes!

1. Preheat the oven to 475°F. Grease a baking rack with coconut oil spray and set it on a rimmed baking sheet.

2. Place all the sauce ingredients except the stevia in a small saucepan. Cook over medium-high heat for 5 to 7 minutes, until slightly reduced, whisking every couple of minutes.

3. Remove the sauce from the heat, then add the stevia and whisk to combine.

4. Pat the chicken dry with paper towels and place it breast side down on a cutting board with the wings and neck facing you. Using kitchen shears, cut through the ribs right next to the spine along both sides, then remove the spine. Open the rib cage and use a heavy knife to score down the sternum. Pop out the breastbone and flatten the chicken.

5. Separate the skin from the chicken using your fingers. Rub the entire chicken under and on top of the skin with the reduced sauce.

6. Place the chicken on the baking rack skin side up, with the breasts in the center of the rack and the legs closest to the bottom (the long end). Bake for 15 minutes.

7. Turn the oven temperature down to 400°F and bake for an additional 25 minutes, until the skin is crispy and the meat is fully cooked through. When done, a thermometer inserted in a thigh will register 165°F.

8. Serve immediately or store in the refrigerator for use later in the week. Store in an airtight container in the fridge for up to 1 week.

Nutrition (combination white and dark meat)

| CALORIES: 402 | FAT: 27g | PROTEIN: 41g | CARBS: 1.5g | FIBER: 0.5g |

SWEET ASIAN BBQ SPATCHCOCKED CHICKEN

CHICKEN POT PIE SOUP

MAKES 6 servings   **PREP TIME:** 10 minutes   **COOK TIME:** 25 minutes

This soup is the perfect meal for a cold winter day. It's creamy, hearty, and ideal for meal prepping, for lunches all week long!

1½ tablespoons extra-virgin olive oil or coconut oil

2 teaspoons minced garlic

¾ cup roughly chopped broccoli florets

¾ cup roughly chopped carrots

1½ teaspoons fresh thyme leaves, or ½ teaspoon dried thyme leaves

¾ teaspoon fresh rosemary leaves, or ¼ teaspoon dried rosemary leaves

¾ teaspoon finely ground Himalayan pink salt

½ teaspoon ground black pepper

1¼ pounds cooked and shredded Sweet Asian BBQ Spatchcocked Chicken (page 98), white or dark meat (about 2½ cups)

4 cups low-sodium chicken broth

1 cup heavy whipping cream

¼ heaping teaspoon xanthan gum (optional)

1. Heat the oil in a stockpot over medium-high heat.

2. Once hot, add the garlic, broccoli, and carrots and sauté for 5 to 7 minutes, until the veggies are tender.

3. Add the thyme, rosemary, salt, and pepper and sauté for an additional 1 to 2 minutes, until fragrant.

4. Add the shredded chicken to the pot along with the chicken broth and cream. Bring the soup to a simmer, stirring frequently. Reduce the heat to medium-low and simmer for 10 minutes, or until slightly thickened.

5. If you prefer an even thicker soup, whisk in the xanthan gum and simmer for 2 to 3 minutes, until the soup has thickened further.

6. Serve immediately. Store leftovers in an airtight container in the fridge for up to 5 days.

Nutrition

CALORIES: 350   FAT: 21g   PROTEIN: 31g   CARBS: 5.5g   FIBER: 1g

CHICKEN AND RICOTTA STUFFED PEPPERS

MAKES 3 servings   **PREP TIME:** 10 minutes   **COOK TIME:** 25 minutes

Stuffed peppers are one of those super-easy fill-and-bake recipes, but they usually are high in carbs from all the rice. Here we've transformed the traditional high-carb version into an equally delicious low-carb option! Meat, veggies, and cheese are all you need, but if you're feeling a little wild, you can throw in some cauliflower rice.

7 ounces cooked and shredded Sweet Asian BBQ Spatchcocked Chicken (page 98) thigh and/or leg meat (about 1 cup)

2 cups frozen spinach (about 7 ounces), defrosted and drained

1 cup full-fat ricotta cheese

¼ cup grated Parmesan cheese, plus more for garnish if desired

3 tablespoons chopped scallions

½ teaspoon finely ground Himalayan pink salt

½ teaspoon ground black pepper

3 medium bell peppers (any color), halved, seeds and membranes removed

1. Preheat the oven to 425°F.

2. Put all the ingredients except the peppers in a large mixing bowl. Combine using a rubber spatula until fully incorporated.

3. Spoon the chicken mixture into each bell pepper half and place the peppers on a rimmed baking sheet.

4. Bake for 22 to 25 minutes, until the filling is heated through and the peppers are tender with a slight bite.

5. If desired, garnish with additional grated Parmesan and serve immediately.

6. Store in an airtight container in the fridge for up to 5 days.

Nutrition (per pepper)
CALORIES: 380   FAT: 18g   PROTEIN: 40g   CARBS: 12.4g   FIBER: 4g

SWEET ASIAN BBQ SPATCHCOCKED CHICKEN
LOADED CHICKEN SALAD

MAKES 6 servings   **PREP TIME:** 15 minutes, plus 1 hour to chill

Chicken salad is one of Megha's all-time favorite foods. She ate it every day in college and loved that it was loaded with nuts, veggies, and grapes. She has taken her love for higher-carb chicken salad and applied it to this low-carb version, which is still loaded and even more delicious!

½ cup mayonnaise

½ teaspoon finely ground Himalayan pink salt

¼ teaspoon ground black pepper

1 pound cooked and chopped Sweet Asian BBQ Spatchcocked Chicken (page 98) breast (about 2¼ cups)

5 slices bacon, cooked and roughly chopped

3 medium celery stalks, chopped

½ medium red onion, diced

1½ cups cubed cheddar cheese (about 6 ounces)

1 cup diced avocado (about 5 ounces)

Store-bought sugar-free BBQ sauce of choice (optional)

1. Put the mayo, salt, and pepper in a large mixing bowl and combine using a spoon.

2. Fold in the remaining ingredients until everything is well incorporated and covered in mayonnaise.

3. If desired, mix in some BBQ sauce to taste for a sweet kick. Refrigerate for 1 hour before serving.

4. Store in an airtight container in the fridge for up to 5 days.

Nutrition
CALORIES: **486**   FAT: **33g**   PROTEIN: **39.5g**   CARBS: **4g**   FIBER: **2g**

 # BARBACOA

MAKES 4 servings   **PREP TIME:** 10 minutes   **COOK TIME:** 3 hours

One of our favorite foods to meal prep for the week is a big hunk of meat! Meal-prepped meat is great for eating on its own or with a side of veggies, for adding to salads or casseroles, or for using as the protein component in so many recipes. In this book, we use leftover barbacoa to make **BARBACOA LETTUCE WRAPS** (page 108), **ASIAN CABBAGE BOWL** (page 110), and **BARBACOA BREAKFAST SKILLET** (page 112). Having several days' worth of meat prepared ahead of time will help you stay on track all week long.

1 tablespoon lard or avocado oil

1 small red onion, chopped

2 teaspoons minced garlic

1 tablespoon ground cumin

1 teaspoon paprika

1 teaspoon finely ground Himalayan pink salt

½ teaspoon ground black pepper

3 pounds boneless chuck roast, cut into 6 large chunks

2 cups low-sodium chicken broth

2 canned chipotle peppers

Juice of 1 lime

2 tablespoons apple cider vinegar

2 teaspoons adobo sauce (from the can of chipotles)

FOR GARNISH (OPTIONAL):

Fresh cilantro leaves

1. Preheat the oven to 325°F.

2. Heat the lard over medium-high heat in a Dutch oven or other large oven-safe pot with a lid.

3. Add the onion and garlic and sauté for 2 to 3 minutes, until fragrant and the onion is tender.

4. Add the cumin, paprika, salt, and pepper and combine using a spoon. Turn off the heat and add the remaining ingredients, stirring to combine.

5. Cover with the lid and bake for 3 hours, or until the meat is tender and can easily be shredded using two forks.

6. Remove the roast from the oven and shred the meat using two forks. Serve immediately, garnished with cilantro, if desired, or store in the refrigerator for use later in the week.

7. Store in an airtight container in the fridge for up to 1 week.

Nutrition

CALORIES: 550   FAT: 8g   PROTEIN: 24g   CARBS: 5g   FIBER: 0g

BARBACOA LETTUCE WRAPS

MAKES 3 servings (2 wraps per serving)   **PREP TIME:** 10 minutes

A lot of us miss using bread as a transport for delicious meats, cheeses, and spreads but hate that bread is high in carbs and filled with empty calories. You can easily solve this problem by using lettuce wraps as your low-carb vehicle. Lettuce wraps are so fresh and less filling than bread, so you can double up on the fillings!

6 butter lettuce leaves

18 ounces cooked and shredded Barbacoa (page 106) (about 2¼ cups)

¾ cup shredded cheddar cheese (about 3 ounces)

¼ cup plus 2 tablespoons pico de gallo

FOR GARNISH (OPTIONAL):

Full-fat sour cream

Fresh cilantro leaves

tip:
Feel free to use cabbage leaves instead of butter lettuce for sturdier wraps. Once filled, they will also keep longer in the fridge!

1. Wash and dry the lettuce leaves with paper towels and lay them flat on a plate.

2. Fill each leaf with 3 ounces of barbacoa, 2 tablespoons of cheese, and 1 tablespoon of pico de gallo.

3. If desired, top with sour cream and cilantro. Serve immediately.

4. If storing the lettuce wraps filled, store in an airtight container in the fridge for up to 2 days; any longer than that and the lettuce leaves will begin to wilt. If you store the ingredients separately, the lettuce will last longer, up to 5 days, and the meat will last for up to 1 week.

Nutrition
CALORIES: **713**   FAT: **51g**   PROTEIN: **47g**   CARBS: **6.8g**   FIBER: **0.8g**

BARBACOA

ASIAN CABBAGE BOWL

MAKES 4 servings   **PREP TIME:** 10 minutes   **COOK TIME:** 10 minutes

When we are looking to change up the flavors for dinner and practice our chopstick-handling skills, we make an Asian Cabbage Bowl with whatever meat we have left over in the fridge. It transforms something simple and filling, like barbacoa, into a flavorful, satisfying dinner!

1 tablespoon tallow or coconut oil

1 small shallot, chopped

1 large clove garlic, minced

12 ounces cooked and shredded Barbacoa (page 106) (about 1½ cups)

2 tablespoons soy sauce or coconut aminos

1½ teaspoons toasted sesame oil

1 teaspoon ginger powder

1 teaspoon unseasoned rice wine vinegar

2 scallions, chopped

12 ounces coleslaw mix or shredded green and purple cabbage

FOR SERVING (OPTIONAL):

Lime wedges

FOR GARNISH (OPTIONAL):

Sliced scallions

Sesame seeds (black and/or white)

Peanuts (raw or roasted), chopped

1. Heat a large skillet over medium-high heat.

2. Heat the tallow in the skillet, then add the shallot and garlic and sauté for 1 minute, until fragrant. Add all the remaining ingredients except the cabbage and lime wedges and combine using a spoon.

3. Sauté for 2 to 4 minutes, until the meat is heated through and fragrant. Add the cabbage and stir to combine. Sauté for 3 to 5 minutes, until the cabbage is tender.

4. Serve immediately with lime wedges. If desired, top with scallions, sesame seeds, and chopped peanuts.

5. Store in an airtight container in the fridge for up to 5 days.

note: *The flavors of the barbacoa pair well with the flavors in this recipe, which makes for a great fusion dish!*

Nutrition
CALORIES: 450   FAT: 34g   PROTEIN: 28g   CARBS: 8g   FIBER: 2g

BARBACOA BREAKFAST SKILLET

MAKES 5 servings   **PREP TIME:** 10 minutes   **COOK TIME:** 20 minutes

While eggs for breakfast can get awfully boring, they are one of the most filling and nutritious foods. Why not combine satisfying eggs and delicious barbacoa to make the perfect breakfast skillet—and amp up the flavors with some fresh pico de gallo and cilantro?

12 ounces cooked and shredded Barbacoa (page 106) (about 1½ cups)

5 large eggs

½ cup shredded cheddar cheese (about 2 ounces)

2 scallions, chopped

½ teaspoon finely ground Himalayan pink salt

¼ teaspoon ground black pepper

FOR GARNISH (OPTIONAL):

Pico de gallo

Fresh cilantro leaves

1. Preheat the oven to 425°F.

2. Heat a 9-inch oven-safe skillet over medium-high heat. Sauté the barbacoa in the hot skillet for 2 to 3 minutes, until crispy.

3. Spread the barbacoa over the entire bottom of the pan in an even layer and make 5 small divots throughout the meat.

4. Crack an egg into each divot. Top with the cheddar cheese, scallions, salt, and pepper.

5. Bake for 15 minutes, until the egg whites are cooked through and the yolks are slightly runny.

6. If desired, top with pico de gallo and cilantro. Serve immediately.

7. Store in an airtight container in the fridge for up to 3 days.

Nutrition

CALORIES: 415   FAT: 32g   PROTEIN: 30g   CARBS: 1g   FIBER: 0g

✗ MUSTARD-RUBBED PORK TENDERLOIN

MAKES 4 servings   **PREP TIME:** 10 minutes, plus 10 minutes to rest   **COOK TIME:** 40 minutes

When you're cooking a larger piece of meat such as pork tenderloin, it's important to let it rest before slicing and serving. This will allow the juices to settle in the center of the meat. If you slice it too early, you risk the meat drying out. No one likes dry meat! As with the barbacoa recipe, we use leftover pork tenderloin to make other recipes during the week, saving meal prep time. In this book, we use the meat from this recipe to make **PORK TENDERLOIN IN CREAM SAUCE** (page 116), **PORK FRIED RICE** (page 118), and **OMELET FOR TWO** (page 120).

2 pounds pork tenderloin

MUSTARD RUB:

2 tablespoons Dijon mustard

1 tablespoon extra-virgin olive oil

1 teaspoon minced garlic

1 teaspoon paprika

1 teaspoon finely ground Himalayan pink salt

½ teaspoon ground black pepper

FOR GARNISH (OPTIONAL):

Dried parsley

1. Preheat the oven to 350°F. Grease a baking rack with coconut oil spray and place it in a rimmed baking sheet.

2. Pat the pork tenderloin dry and place it on a cutting board.

3. In a small bowl, combine the ingredients for the rub to form a paste. Rub the entire pork tenderloin with the paste and place the pork on the greased baking rack.

4. Bake for 35 to 40 minutes, until the internal temperature reaches 150°F. Allow to rest for 10 minutes prior to slicing.

5. Garnish with dried parsley, if desired. Serve immediately or store in the refrigerator for use later in the week.

6. Store in an airtight container in the fridge for up to 5 days.

Nutrition
CALORIES: **422**   FAT: **16.6g**   PROTEIN: **64g**   CARBS: **0.6g**   FIBER: **0g**

PORK TENDERLOIN IN MUSHROOM CREAM SAUCE

MAKES 4 servings **PREP TIME:** 10 minutes **COOK TIME:** 15 minutes

Add a light cream sauce to anything and you've automatically made it the tastiest thing in the room! This mushroom cream sauce recipe uses fresh shallots, garlic, and rosemary to create a simple yet flavorful sauce for leftover pork.

2 tablespoons unsalted butter

1 medium shallot, chopped

2 teaspoons minced garlic

3 ounces baby bella mushrooms, sliced

1 tablespoon fresh rosemary leaves, minced

½ cup heavy whipping cream

¼ cup low-sodium chicken broth

1 tablespoon Dijon mustard

¼ teaspoon finely ground Himalayan pink salt

¼ teaspoon ground black pepper

¼ teaspoon xanthan gum

⅔ pound cooked Mustard-Rubbed Pork Tenderloin (page 114) (⅓ batch), cut into ½-inch-thick slices

1. Heat a large skillet over medium heat.

2. Melt the butter in the pan, then add the shallot and garlic and sauté for 2 to 3 minutes, until fragrant.

3. Add the mushrooms and rosemary and cook until all the juices from the mushrooms have released and evaporated, about 5 minutes.

4. Add the cream, broth, mustard, salt, and pepper and combine using a spoon.

5. Turn the heat up to medium-high and add the xanthan gum. Stir frequently until the sauce has thickened, 1 to 2 minutes.

6. Turn the heat down to medium and add the slices of cooked pork loin to the cream sauce. Cook for 3 to 5 minutes, until the pork is heated through, and serve immediately.

7. Store in an airtight container in the fridge for up to 5 days.

Nutrition
CALORIES: 302   FAT: 20g   PROTEIN: 23g   CARBS: 4g   FIBER: 1g

PORK FRIED RICE

MAKES 4 servings **PREP TIME:** 10 minutes **COOK TIME:** 10 minutes

Cauliflower is the perfect low-carb rice replacement, and trust us, you won't taste the difference. It's filling and even more delicious, and it won't leave you feeling like you need to take a nap! We like to serve our pork fried rice with a side of Sriracha and soy sauce for some extra flavor.

1 medium head cauliflower, cored and cut into florets

1 tablespoon unsalted butter

1 small yellow onion, diced

2 teaspoons minced garlic

½ cup diced carrots

⅔ pound cooked Mustard-Rubbed Pork Tenderloin (page 114) (⅓ batch), cubed

3 tablespoons soy sauce or coconut aminos

1½ teaspoons toasted sesame oil

1 teaspoon unseasoned rice wine vinegar

1 teaspoon ginger powder

FOR GARNISH (OPTIONAL):

Sliced scallions

1. Place the cauliflower florets in a food processor and process until the pieces are the size of grains of rice. Set the riced cauliflower aside.

2. Heat a large skillet over medium heat.

3. Melt the butter in the pan, then add the onion, garlic, carrots, and pork and sauté for 3 to 5 minutes, until the onion and carrots are tender and the pork is crispy.

4. Add the riced cauliflower along with the remaining ingredients and combine using a spoon. Cover with a lid and cook for 3 to 5 minutes, until the cauliflower is tender.

5. Top with sliced scallions, if desired, and serve immediately.

6. Store in an airtight container in the fridge for up to 5 days.

Nutrition

CALORIES: **228**   FAT: **9g**   PROTEIN: **26g**   CARBS: **11g**   FIBER: **4g**

OMELET FOR TWO

MAKES 2 servings **PREP TIME:** 5 minutes **COOK TIME:** 10 minutes

You can't go wrong with the classic ham-and-cheese combo, especially in breakfast form! We've amped it up a little by swapping out the ham deli meat for some hearty pork tenderloin. Feel free to swap in a different cheese. Megha's favorite is Gruyère!

2 tablespoons unsalted butter, divided

3 ounces cooked Mustard-Rubbed Pork Tenderloin (page 114), cut into large chunks

¼ medium white onion, diced

4 sprigs fresh thyme

4 large eggs

2 tablespoons heavy whipping cream

½ teaspoon finely ground Himalayan pink salt

¼ teaspoon ground black pepper

¼ cup plus 2 tablespoons shredded cheddar cheese

1. Heat a 9-inch skillet over medium-high heat. Melt 1 tablespoon of the butter in the pan, then add the pork, onion, and thyme. Sauté for 3 to 5 minutes, until the onion is tender. Remove from the skillet and set aside.

2. Lower the heat under the skillet to medium. Melt the remaining 1 tablespoon of butter in the pan, spreading it around the pan using a rubber spatula.

3. In a medium-sized mixing bowl, whisk together the eggs, cream, salt, and pepper, then pour the mixture into the hot skillet.

4. As the eggs begin to set around the edge of skillet, gently push the cooked portions toward the center of the pan with the spatula. Tilt and rotate the skillet to allow the uncooked egg to flow into the empty spaces.

5. When the eggs are almost set on the surface but still look moist, cover half of the omelet with the pork mixture and top with the cheese. Slip the spatula under the unfilled side and fold it over onto the filled half.

6. Cook for 1 more minute, then slide the omelet onto a plate. Serve immediately.

Nutrition

CALORIES: 480   FAT: 37g   PROTEIN: 34g   CARBS: 1.8g   FIBER: 0.25g

✕ SOY-GLAZED SALMON

MAKES 4 servings   **PREP TIME:** 10 minutes   **COOK TIME:** 25 minutes

This is one of our favorite recipes to meal prep in bulk. We love the combination of Asian flavors and hearty salmon, and salmon's high omega-3 content. When Matt used to work a desk job, he would often pack a lunch of salmon and Brazil nuts. We know, it's an odd combination! This salmon is a great recipe to prepare for the week ahead and then transform into new dishes for a change in flavors. We often use it to make **SALMON SALAD** (page 124) and **MIXED GREENS SALAD WITH SALMON AND SESAME DRESSING** (page 126).

1½ pounds skinless salmon fillets

¼ cup soy sauce or coconut aminos

1½ tablespoons unseasoned rice wine vinegar

1 tablespoon minced garlic

2 teaspoons grated fresh ginger

½ teaspoon Sriracha sauce

¼ teaspoon xanthan gum

⅛ teaspoon liquid stevia

FOR GARNISH (OPTIONAL):

Minced fresh chives

Sesame seeds (black and/or white)

DIPPING SAUCE (OPTIONAL):

Mayonnaise

Sriracha sauce

1. Preheat the oven to 425°F. Grease a baking rack with coconut oil spray and set it on a rimmed baking sheet.

2. Gently pat the salmon fillets dry using paper towels and place them on the baking rack with some space between them. Set aside.

3. In a small saucepan over medium heat, simmer the soy sauce, rice wine vinegar, garlic, ginger, and Sriracha sauce, stirring frequently, until the sauce has slightly reduced, about 5 minutes.

4. Whisk in the xanthan gum and stevia and simmer until the sauce thickens, 1 to 2 minutes. Remove from the heat.

5. Spoon the sauce over each piece of salmon and spread using a basting brush or spoon, so the entire fillet is covered.

6. Bake for 15 minutes for well-done salmon, or until the desired doneness is reached. (The exact timing will depend on the thickness of the fillets.) If desired, garnish with chives and/or sesame seeds and combine some mayo and Sriracha to make a dipping sauce.

7. Serve immediately or store in the refrigerator for use later in the week.

8. Store in an airtight container in the fridge for up to 5 days.

Nutrition

CALORIES: 321   FAT: 13.8g   PROTEIN: 44.5g   CARBS: 0.8g   FIBER: 0g

SALMON SALAD

MAKES 4 servings   **PREP TIME:** 10 minutes, plus 1 hour to chill

Chicken salad, egg salad, tuna salad, and, yes, salmon salad! You may not have known that it's possible to turn cooked salmon into something even more delicious. Salmon salad is the perfect high-fat, high-protein snack or meal at any time of day. We think the fresh chives really take it to the next level!

⅓ cup mayonnaise

Juice of ½ lemon

2 tablespoons minced fresh chives, plus sliced chives for garnish if desired

½ teaspoon finely ground Himalayan pink salt

¼ teaspoon ground black pepper

¾ pound Soy-Glazed Salmon (page 122) (½ batch), flaked into small pieces

4 stalks celery, chopped

¼ small red onion, diced

FOR SERVING (OPTIONAL):

Low-carb crackers

1. Combine the mayo, lemon juice, chives, salt, and pepper in a medium-sized mixing bowl using a spoon.

2. Add the salmon, celery, and red onion and stir until everything is coated in the mayo mixture. Garnish with sliced chives and serve with low-carb crackers, if desired.

3. Refrigerate for 1 hour prior to serving. Store in an airtight container in the fridge for up to 5 days.

Nutrition

CALORIES: 308   FAT: 25g   PROTEIN: 17g   CARBS: 1.5g   FIBER: 0.5g

MIXED GREENS SALAD WITH SALMON AND SESAME DRESSING

MAKES 1 serving   **PREP TIME:** 10 minutes

Matt created the perfect dressing for this salad. It's high in fat and big on flavor, with a slightly sweet profile that goes perfectly with the soy-glazed salmon. And best of all, it will keep in the fridge for up to three months. We love to make it in bulk and use it for stir-fries and salads like this one, as well as for topping steamed veggies. The quantity of dressing made here is more than you'll need for this salad, but we're sure you will find other uses for it!

DRESSING:

(Makes about ½ cup)

¼ cup avocado oil

2 tablespoons toasted sesame oil

2 tablespoons unseasoned rice wine vinegar

1 tablespoon soy sauce or coconut aminos

⅛ teaspoon liquid stevia

1 tablespoon sesame seeds

SALAD:

4 cups mixed greens

¼ pound Soy-Glazed Salmon (page 122) (⅙ batch), flaked into small pieces

½ medium avocado, thinly sliced

½ small cucumber, thinly sliced

¼ small red onion, thinly sliced

5 cherry tomatoes, halved

1. Place all the dressing ingredients in a bottle or mason jar, seal the lid, and shake vigorously. Set aside.

2. Place the mixed greens in a large bowl. Top with the salmon, avocado, cucumber, red onion, and cherry tomatoes.

3. Shake the dressing again and then drizzle over the salad. Serve immediately.

Nutrition (with about 2 tablespoons of dressing)
CALORIES: **553**   FAT: **41.5g**   PROTEIN: **31g**   CARBS: **10g**   FIBER: **1.5g**

✗ SPICE-RUBBED BRISKET

MAKES 12 servings   **PREP TIME:** 10 minutes, plus 25 minutes to rest   **COOK TIME:** 2½ hours

Brisket is hard to get right the first time. Honestly, it took us three tries to find the perfect cooking temperature, spice rub, and internal temperature at which it's tender yet not falling apart, but we finally nailed it! If you don't have a grill or smoker, you can make your brisket in the oven, and it will be just as delicious. It goes without saying that having a large portion of delicious meat already prepared will help greatly with your meal prep. We like to use the leftovers to make a **BRISKET SANDWICH** (page 130) with a super-easy microwave bread, as well as a satisfying **BRISKET BREAKFAST SKILLET** (page 132).

1 (4-pound) brisket

3 tablespoons finely ground Himalayan pink salt

¼ cup plus 1 tablespoon paprika

2 tablespoons garlic powder

2 tablespoons onion powder

1 tablespoon dried parsley

1 tablespoon ground black pepper

2 teaspoons cayenne pepper

2 teaspoons ground cumin

1 teaspoon chili powder

1 teaspoon ground coriander

FOR SERVING (OPTIONAL):

Low-carb BBQ sauce

1. Preheat the oven to 300°F.

2. Pat the brisket dry using paper towels and set aside. Place the salt and spices in a small bowl and combine using a spoon. Distribute the spice mixture over the entire brisket, rubbing it in using your hands. There may be some seasoning left over.

3. Place the seasoned brisket in a large casserole dish and cover with foil. Place in the oven and cook until the internal temperature reaches 190°F, 2 to 2½ hours.

4. Remove the brisket from the oven and allow it to rest for 10 minutes prior to removing the foil. Transfer it to a cutting board and allow it to rest for another 15 minutes before slicing.

5. Serve immediately, with barbecue sauce, if desired, or store in an airtight container in the fridge for use later in the week. It will keep for up to 5 days.

tips:

Feel free to use your favorite sugar-free store-bought BBQ rub for this recipe!

This recipe is easy to scale up or down. Just remember that the baking time is 30 to 40 minutes per pound.

Nutrition

CALORIES: 512   FAT: 39g   PROTEIN: 36g   CARBS: 2.6g   FIBER: 1g

BRISKET SANDWICH

MAKES 2 servings   **PREP TIME:** 5 minutes   **COOK TIME:** 2½ minutes

The star of this recipe is the easy and versatile microwave bread. You can use it for a turkey sandwich or toast it up and serve it with some eggs and bacon—but we love to make a brisket sandwich with leftover brisket. This yummy sandwich takes less than ten minutes to make and comes out perfect every time!

BREAD:

2 large eggs

2 tablespoons heavy whipping cream

2 tablespoons unsalted butter, melted but not hot

2 tablespoons water

¼ cup coconut flour

½ teaspoon baking powder

½ teaspoon finely ground Himalayan pink salt

FILLING:

4 ounces Spice-Rubbed Brisket (page 128), sliced or shredded, warmed

⅓ cup shredded purple cabbage

2 tablespoons low-carb BBQ sauce

FOR SERVING:

Your favorite pickles

Special equipment: 6-inch square ramekin

tip:
If you like, you can cook down the cabbage a little or make a simple coleslaw using some mayo and seasonings.

1. Grease a 6-inch square ramekin with coconut oil spray.

2. Put all the bread ingredients in a small bowl and combine using a fork until no lumps remain. Pour the batter into the ramekin and microwave on high for 2 minutes 30 seconds, until the bread is fully cooked through. (When cooked through, a toothpick will come out clean when inserted in the middle.)

3. Carefully remove the ramekin from the microwave and allow to cool before removing the bread. Cut the cooled bread into 4 slices and place on a plate.

4. Divide the sliced or shredded brisket between 2 slices of bread. Top with equal portions of the shredded cabbage and BBQ sauce.

5. Serve with your favorite pickles and enjoy!

Nutrition
CALORIES: 524   FAT: 42.4g   PROTEIN: 25g   CARBS: 9g   FIBER: 5g

BRISKET BREAKFAST SKILLET

MAKES 1 serving   **PREP TIME:** 5 minutes   **COOK TIME:** 10 minutes

We hear it all the time: breakfast is the most important meal of the day. Is it true? Who knows! What we do know, though, is that breakfast can be extra delicious if you add brisket to it, as we've done in this recipe! The cabbage can be omitted, but it adds a nice crunch and texture to this breakfast skillet.

2 tablespoons coconut oil, divided

½ teaspoon minced garlic

1 cup shredded purple cabbage

Finely ground Himalayan pink salt and ground black pepper

3 ounces Spice-Rubbed Brisket (page 128), chopped

1 large egg

FOR GARNISH (OPTIONAL):

Grated Parmesan cheese

1. Heat a medium-sized skillet over medium-high heat. Melt 1 tablespoon of the coconut oil in the pan, then add the minced garlic and shredded cabbage and season heavily with salt and pepper.

2. Sauté for 5 to 7 minutes, until the cabbage is cooked down and tender. Add the chopped brisket and continue to cook until the meat is heated through.

3. Heat a small skillet over medium-high heat. Melt the remaining tablespoon of coconut oil in the pan, then crack the egg in the pan and fry until cooked to your liking.

4. Place the fried egg on top of the cabbage and meat and season to taste with additional salt and pepper. Garnish with grated Parmesan, if desired, and serve immediately.

Nutrition

CALORIES: 598   FAT: 48g   PROTEIN: 33.6g   CARBS: 5.7g   FIBER: 2g

Breakfast & Brunch

SUPREME PIZZA BREAKFAST CASSEROLE

MAKES 8 servings   **PREP TIME:** 10 minutes   **COOK TIME:** 40 minutes

This breakfast casserole reminds us of late nights when we stayed out drinking and then found ourselves at a pizza shop. We always got two slices, one plain cheese and one supreme, and the supreme pizza slice was, by far, tastier and more filling. So when creating this casserole, we used the flavors of a supreme pizza for a low-carb, healthy alternative. Now you too can relive your pizza-eating days!

1 pound ground pork

1 dozen large eggs

¼ cup heavy whipping cream

1 teaspoon finely ground Himalayan pink salt

1 teaspoon dried rosemary leaves

1 teaspoon dried thyme leaves

1 teaspoon red pepper flakes

½ teaspoon dried oregano leaves

½ teaspoon garlic powder

½ teaspoon ground black pepper

2 ounces sun-dried tomatoes (packed in olive oil), chopped

½ cup diced red bell peppers

⅓ cup diced red onions

¼ cup grated Parmesan cheese, plus more for garnish if desired

1. Preheat the oven to 350°F and grease a 9 by 13-inch baking pan with coconut oil spray.

2. Brown the ground pork in a large skillet over medium-high heat, using a wooden spoon to break it apart as it cooks.

3. Crack the eggs into a large mixing bowl, then add the cream and whisk to combine. Add the salt and seasonings and whisk once more. Set aside.

4. Put the cooked pork, sun-dried tomatoes, bell peppers, and red onions in the prepared baking pan, stir, and spread into an even layer using a rubber spatula.

5. Pour the egg mixture over the top and sprinkle with the Parmesan cheese. Bake for 30 to 35 minutes, until the egg in the center is cooked through and no longer jiggly and the edges are starting to brown.

6. Slice and serve. Garnish with additional grated Parmesan cheese, if desired.

7. Store in an airtight container in the fridge for up to 5 days.

Nutrition
CALORIES: 345   FAT: 25g   PROTEIN: 26g   CARBS: 4g   FIBER: 0.8g

OVERNIGHT PROTEIN "OATS"

MAKES 5 servings   **PREP TIME:** 5 minutes, plus 30 minutes to chill

Oatmeal is one of those foods that we loved to eat growing up. Throw in some fresh berries, nut butter, and ground cinnamon, and you were eating dessert for breakfast! We shouldn't have to give up dessert for breakfast just because we are low-carb, so we created this overnight "oats" recipe, which you can make in bulk and store in separate containers for a quick grab-and-go breakfast dessert. We call this dish "overnight" because we like to make it the night before so our mornings are easier, but the truth is, it only needs to chill for half an hour in the fridge to get the perfect oatmeal texture.

1¼ cups unsweetened almond milk

½ cup plus 2 tablespoons chia seeds

½ cup plus 2 tablespoons hemp hearts

2½ scoops (75g) vanilla-flavored protein powder

¼ cup heavy whipping cream

¼ teaspoon finely ground Himalayan pink salt

FOR GARNISH:

Raspberries or other fresh berries of choice

Sliced almonds or other nuts of choice

1. Put the ingredients in a large bowl and combine using a whisk or spoon until smooth.

2. If you're meal prepping for the week ahead, divide the mixture evenly between five 8-ounce mason jars for five daily servings.

3. Chill in the refrigerator for at least 30 minutes prior to serving. Serve cold, straight out of the fridge, or microwave on high for 20 to 30 seconds before serving.

4. Garnish each serving with fresh berries and nuts.

5. Store (ungarnished) in an airtight container(s) in the fridge for up to 10 days.

note: *We have adapted this recipe, previously published in Keto Made Easy (our first cookbook), so it can be made ahead of time and eaten throughout the week. Since this is one of those recipes that will last a while in your fridge, it's great for meal prep.*

tip:
Change up the protein powder and toppings depending on what you're craving. Megha loves chocolate-flavored protein powder and crushed pecans in hers!

Nutrition (not including garnishes)
CALORIES: 379   FAT: 26g   PROTEIN: 27g   CARBS: 10g   FIBER: 7.8g

HERBED RICOTTA BREAKFAST CASSEROLE

MAKES 8 servings **PREP TIME:** 5 minutes **COOK TIME:** 50 minutes

Sometimes you just want to make something simple but filling enough to last you till dinner. Casseroles are the perfect option in that case because they take five minutes to throw together and the oven does all the real work. Eggs are high in nutrients and extremely filling, so all you have to do is add your favorite seasonings and toppings and eat up!

12 large eggs

¼ cup heavy whipping cream

1 pound ground pork

1 teaspoon finely ground Himalayan pink salt

½ teaspoon ground black pepper

½ teaspoon dried parsley

½ teaspoon dried thyme leaves

½ teaspoon garlic powder

½ teaspoon onion powder

¾ cup full-fat ricotta cheese

¾ cup grape tomatoes (about 3 ounces), halved

1. Preheat the oven to 350°F and grease a 9 by 13-inch baking pan with coconut oil spray.

2. Crack the eggs into a large mixing bowl. Add the cream and whisk to combine. Set aside.

3. Cook the ground pork in a large skillet over medium-high heat, using a wooden spoon to break it apart as it cooks. When it's partially cooked, stir in the salt, pepper, parsley, thyme, garlic powder, and onion powder.

4. When the pork is fully cooked, transfer it to the prepared baking pan and spread into an even layer using a rubber spatula. Pour the egg mixture over the meat. Dollop the ricotta cheese on top, then add the cherry tomatoes.

5. Bake for 35 to 40 minutes, until the egg in the center is fully cooked through and no longer jiggly and the edges are starting to brown.

6. Slice into 8 pieces and serve immediately.

7. Store in an airtight container in the fridge for up to 5 days.

Nutrition

CALORIES: 364   FAT: 30g   PROTEIN: 20g   CARBS: 3.5g   FIBER: 0g

CHILE RELLENOS CASSEROLE

MAKES 8 servings   **PREP TIME:** 15 minutes   **COOK TIME:** 50 minutes

If you've ever put salsa on your eggs in the morning, then you're definitely on board with Mexican food for breakfast. This chile rellenos casserole is a fun spin on the traditional stuffed-peppers version! Swap out some of the poblano peppers for jalapeño peppers if you really need to wake yourself up.

2 tablespoons extra-virgin olive oil, for the pan

1½ pounds poblano peppers

4 large eggs

½ teaspoon finely ground Himalayan pink salt

½ teaspoon ground black pepper

2 cups shredded cheddar cheese (about 8 ounces)

6 ounces Cotija cheese, crumbled (about 1½ cups), plus more for garnish if desired

1. Preheat the oven to 425°F and grease a 9 by 13-inch baking pan with the olive oil.

2. Place the poblano peppers on a rimmed baking sheet and roast in the oven until the skin is blistered, about 5 minutes. Remove the baking sheet from the oven and immediately cover the peppers with foil for 5 minutes to steam them. Once steamed, remove the foil and allow the peppers to cool completely.

3. Once the peppers are cool, peel their skins off, slice them in half lengthwise, and seed them. Set aside.

4. Whisk the eggs, salt, and pepper in a medium-sized mixing bowl and set aside.

5. Make the casserole: Layer half of the peppers in the bottom of the prepared baking pan and top with half of the cheddar cheese and half of the Cotija cheese. Repeat the layers using the remaining peppers and cheese, then top with the whisked eggs.

6. Cover the pan with foil and bake for 40 minutes, until fully cooked through and the eggs are set. Carefully remove the foil and serve immediately. Garnish with crumbled Cotija cheese, if desired.

7. Store in an airtight container in the fridge for up to 5 days.

Nutrition

CALORIES: 269   FAT: 21.3g   PROTEIN: 16g   CARBS: 4.3g   FIBER: 1.9g

CINNAMON MORNING MUFFINS

MAKES 8 muffins   **PREP TIME:** 5 minutes   **COOK TIME:** 25 minutes

Getting out from under the covers and braving the chilly morning air requires some encouragement, like the sound of coffee brewing in the kitchen or your alarm going off for the fifth time. But if you're especially lucky, the smell of warm cinnamon muffins wakes you up!

1 cup blanched almond flour

2 teaspoons baking powder

1 teaspoon ground cinnamon

¼ teaspoon finely ground Himalayan pink salt

¼ cup (½ stick) unsalted butter

¼ cup granular erythritol

2 tablespoons unsweetened almond milk

2 large eggs

1 teaspoon vanilla extract

¼ teaspoon liquid stevia

tip:
Matt loves to eat two of these muffins alongside his coffee in the morning, sliced in half and smeared with butter!

1. Preheat the oven to 350°F and grease 8 wells of a standard-size 12-well muffin tin with coconut oil spray.

2. In a medium-sized mixing bowl, whisk together the almond flour, baking powder, cinnamon, and salt; set aside.

3. Place the butter in a large microwave-safe bowl and microwave until melted but not hot. Add the remaining ingredients and whisk to combine.

4. Add the dry mixture to the wet mixture and whisk until fully incorporated. Evenly divide the mixture among the 8 greased muffin wells, filling each about three-quarters full.

5. Bake for 22 to 25 minutes, until a toothpick comes out clean when inserted in the middle of a muffin.

6. Allow to cool for 15 minutes prior to handling.

7. Store in an airtight container in the fridge for up to 10 days.

Nutrition (per muffin)
CALORIES: **144**   FAT: **13g**   PROTEIN: **4.5g**   CARBS: **3g**   FIBER: **1.5g**   SUGAR ALCOHOLS: **6g**

MOCHA EGG COFFEE

MAKES 1 serving   **PREP TIME:** 2 minutes

Megha used to work at Starbucks, so she knows a thing or two about making a good mocha. This recipe is a creamy blend that both coffee addicts and chocoholics will enjoy. Adding the egg not only ups the nutrition of this coffee but will keep you full till dinner!

8 ounces hot brewed coffee

1 tablespoon cocoa powder

1 scoop (10g) unflavored collagen peptides

½ scant teaspoon liquid stevia

1 large egg

TOPPING (OPTIONAL):

Cocoa powder

1. Put all the ingredients in a blender in the order listed. As soon as you add the egg, immediately blend the coffee for 10 to 15 seconds to ensure the egg doesn't curdle and the coffee incorporates uniformly.

2. Pour into a large mug. If desired, top with whipped cream and cocoa powder.

note: *This recipe calls for consuming a raw egg, which we are comfortable doing. If you are concerned, feel free to use a pasteurized egg.*

Nutrition

CALORIES: 116   FAT: 5g   PROTEIN: 16.5g   CARBS: 1.5g   FIBER: 1g

DUTCH BABY FOR TWO

MAKES 2 servings   **PREP TIME:** 5 minutes   **COOK TIME:** 15 minutes

The topping of colorful berries and powdered sweetener makes this the perfect brunch to bring to your mom on Mother's Day or to share with your spouse on Valentine's Day. Show them how sweet you really are!

1 tablespoon unsalted butter, for the pan

¼ cup plus 2 tablespoons blanched almond flour

2 tablespoons granular erythritol

¼ teaspoon finely ground Himalayan pink salt

2 large eggs

¼ cup plus 2 tablespoons unsweetened almond milk

¼ teaspoon vanilla extract

FOR GARNISH (OPTIONAL):

Fresh berries

Powdered erythritol

1. Preheat the oven to 400°F.

2. Melt the butter in a small (5- or 6-inch) oven-safe skillet over low heat.

3. In a small mixing bowl, whisk together the almond flour, granular erythritol, salt, eggs, almond milk, and vanilla extract until smooth. Pour the mixture into the skillet and transfer to the oven. Bake for 15 minutes, until the Dutch baby is fully cooked through (a toothpick will come out clean when inserted in the center).

4. Transfer the Dutch baby to a plate. If desired, top with fresh berries and powdered erythritol prior to serving.

Nutrition
CALORIES: 264 FAT: 23g PROTEIN: 10.5g CARBS: 3.8g FIBER: 1.3g SUGAR ALCOHOLS: 12g

CHEDDAR AND SAUSAGE SCONES

MAKES 8 scones   **PREP TIME:** 10 minutes, plus 10 minutes to rest
COOK TIME: 45 minutes

If you're hosting company this weekend, don't worry about dirtying every pan in the kitchen just to make pancakes, eggs, and bacon for breakfast. Easily fill up everyone's tummies with a batch of these hearty scones instead. To save yourself some time on the morning you make them, have your sausage cooked ahead of time. Having a large batch of sausage cooked ahead is one of our favorite meal-prepping tricks.

6 ounces bulk/ground sausage of choice

¾ cup coconut flour

½ teaspoon baking powder

¼ teaspoon finely ground Himalayan pink salt

4 large eggs

¼ cup (½ stick) unsalted butter, melted but not hot

1½ cups shredded cheddar cheese (about 6 ounces)

FOR GARNISH (OPTIONAL):

Chopped fresh parsley

1. Preheat the oven to 350°F and line a baking sheet with parchment paper.

2. Cook the sausage in a medium-sized skillet over medium-high heat until no longer pink, using a spoon to break it apart into crumbles as it cooks. Remove the sausage from the pan and set aside.

3. Put the coconut flour, baking powder, and salt in a medium-sized bowl and mix with a fork.

4. Put the eggs and melted butter in a large bowl and combine using a hand mixer. Add the dry ingredients in two parts and combine using a hand mixer until smooth.

5. Fold in the cheese and cooked sausage with a rubber spatula until evenly distributed.

6. Form the dough into a 1-inch-thick circle on the lined baking sheet. Cut the dough into 8 wedges and separate slightly.

7. Bake for 35 minutes, or until the edges are lightly browned.

8. Allow to cool on the pan for 10 minutes. Serve garnished with fresh parsley, if desired.

9. Store in an airtight container in the fridge for up to 1 week.

Nutrition (per scone)
CALORIES: 277   FAT: 23g   PROTEIN: 14g   CARBS: 9g   FIBER: 6g

MINI BREAKFAST CAKES
WITH LEMON WHIPPED CREAM

MAKES 16 mini cakes (4 per serving)   **PREP TIME:** 15 minutes   **COOK TIME:** 20 minutes

Fuel the day with some fun and food. Any recipe that calls for whipped cream and uses the word *mini* makes for a kid-friendly kitchen! Get them mixing and licking the bowls.

MINI CAKES:

1½ cups full-fat ricotta cheese

⅔ cup blanched almond flour

¼ cup unsweetened almond milk

4 large eggs

2 teaspoons baking powder

¼ teaspoon finely ground Himalayan pink salt

½ teaspoon liquid stevia

LEMON WHIPPED CREAM:

1 cup heavy whipping cream

2 teaspoons grated lemon zest, plus more for garnish

1 tablespoon lemon juice

¼ teaspoon liquid stevia

1. Preheat the oven to 350°F and grease 16 wells of a mini muffin tin with coconut oil spray.

2. Put all the cake ingredients in a large mixing bowl and combine using a hand mixer until the batter is smooth.

3. Evenly distribute the batter among the greased muffin wells, filling each about one-third full. Bake for 20 minutes, or until a toothpick inserted in the middle of a cake comes out clean. Set aside to cool while you make the whipped cream.

4. In a medium-sized bowl, whip the cream using a hand mixer until soft peaks form.

5. Add the lemon zest, lemon juice, and stevia and mix once more. Transfer to a small serving bowl, garnish with additional lemon zest, and serve alongside the cooled cakes.

6. Store the breakfast cakes and whipped cream in separate airtight containers in the fridge; the cakes will keep for up to 5 days, the whipped cream for up to 2 weeks.

Nutrition (without whipped cream)
CALORIES: 368 FAT: 28g PROTEIN: 21g CARBS: 6g FIBER: 2g SUGAR ALCOHOLS: 0g

JALAPEÑO POPPER EGG BITES

MAKES 8 bites   **PREP TIME:** 10 minutes   **COOK TIME:** 40 minutes

Make a batch of these egg bites on Sunday afternoon and you'll have a delicious grab-and-go breakfast in your hands every morning of the week.

4 slices bacon, roughly chopped

1½ large jalapeño peppers, finely diced

8 large eggs

1 cup shredded cheddar cheese (about 4 ounces)

8 jalapeño slices, for topping

FOR GARNISH (OPTIONAL):

Crumbled Cotija cheese

tip:

For a quick lunch while working at her desk, Megha loves to eat these egg bites topped with a dollop of sour cream.

1. Preheat the oven to 350°F and grease 8 wells of a standard-size 12-well muffin tin with coconut oil spray.

2. Heat a medium-sized skillet over medium-high heat. Put the chopped bacon in the pan and cook. When it is 80 percent cooked through, add the jalapeños and continue to cook until the bacon is crispy and the jalapeños are soft.

3. Remove from the heat and set aside.

4. Crack an egg into each greased muffin well and scramble slightly using a fork, then top each egg with 2 tablespoons of cheddar cheese. Top the cheese and eggs with the bacon-and-jalapeño mixture, dividing it evenly among the cups. Place a jalapeño slice on top of each cup.

5. Bake for 30 minutes, or until the eggs are cooked through and a toothpick inserted in the center of a bite comes out clean. Allow to cool in the pan for 10 minutes prior to flipping or popping out of the muffin tin. Serve garnished with crumbled Cotija cheese, if desired.

6. Store in an airtight container in the fridge for up to 5 days.

Nutrition (per bite)
CALORIES: **148**   FAT: **11g**   PROTEIN: **11g**   CARBS: **0g**   FIBER: **0g**

SOUR CREAM BISCUITS

MAKES 6 biscuits   **PREP TIME:** 10 minutes   **COOK TIME:** 12 minutes

These don't get as fluffy as traditional biscuits, but they'll satisfy your biscuit craving all the same. Try serving them with keto-friendly jam and a slice of cheddar cheese. The sweet jam and the sharp cheese are the perfect complement to the hearty biscuit. And of course, there's always butter.

1 cup blanched almond flour

2 tablespoons golden flax meal

1 teaspoon baking powder

½ teaspoon xanthan gum

½ teaspoon finely ground Himalayan pink salt

2 tablespoons unsalted butter, melted but not hot

1 large egg white

3 tablespoons full-fat sour cream

1. Preheat the oven to 400°F and line a baking sheet with parchment paper.

2. Put the almond flour, flax meal, baking powder, xanthan gum, and salt in a medium-sized mixing bowl and combine using a spoon. Set aside.

3. In a large mixing bowl, whisk together the melted butter, egg white, and sour cream. Add the dry ingredients to the wet mixture and whisk until it has a doughlike consistency.

4. Form the dough into 6 evenly sized balls and place them on the lined baking sheet. Slightly flatten them.

5. Bake for 10 to 12 minutes, until the biscuits have firmed up and browned and a toothpick inserted in the middle of a biscuit comes out clean. Allow to cool on the pan prior to handling.

6. Store in an airtight container or zip-top bag in the fridge for up to 1 week.

note: *This is Megha's favorite recipe in the entire book. Be sure to give it a try and let us know what you think by tagging us on Instagram—@keto.connect*

Nutrition (per biscuit)
CALORIES: 232   FAT: 22g   PROTEIN: 7g   CARBS: 4g   FIBER: 2.3g

RASPBERRY CRUMBLE CHEESECAKE

MAKES one 9-inch cheesecake (8 servings)   **PREP TIME:** 15 minutes   **COOK TIME:** 45 minutes

If you like to start your day with something sweet, then this recipe is perfect for you. It is full of rich fats and layers of flavors to keep you satisfied all morning.

BOTTOM LAYER:

1 cup full-fat ricotta cheese

4 large eggs

½ cup coconut flour

¼ cup granular erythritol

1½ teaspoons baking powder

¼ teaspoon finely ground Himalayan pink salt

¼ teaspoon liquid stevia

MIDDLE LAYER:

4 ounces cream cheese (½ cup), room temperature

2 tablespoons powdered erythritol

1 large egg

½ teaspoon vanilla extract

TOP LAYER:

⅓ cup coconut flour

¼ cup granular erythritol

1 teaspoon ground cinnamon

¼ cup (½ stick) cold unsalted butter, diced

2 ounces fresh raspberries, halved

1. Preheat the oven to 350°F and grease a 9-inch springform pan with coconut oil spray.

2. Make the bottom layer: In a large mixing bowl, whisk together the ricotta and eggs until combined. Add the remaining ingredients for the bottom layer and whisk until fully combined. Transfer the mixture to the greased pan.

3. Make the middle layer: Whisk together all the ingredients in a small mixing bowl until combined, then pour over the bottom layer in the pan.

4. Make the top layer: Place the coconut flour, erythritol, and cinnamon in a small mixing bowl and combine using a spoon. Add the butter and combine using your fingertips until it has a sandy consistency.

5. Place the halved raspberries over the middle layer in the cake pan. Top the raspberries with the cinnamon crumble.

6. Bake for 45 minutes, or until the cake is fully cooked through (a toothpick will come out clean when inserted in the center) and the cinnamon crumble has browned.

7. Allow to cool in the pan for 15 minutes, then run a knife around the edge to loosen the cheesecake and remove the rim of the springform pan. Cut into 8 slices and serve.

8. Store in an airtight container in the fridge for up to 1 week.

Nutrition

CALORIES: **234** FAT: **20g** PROTEIN: **11g** CARBS: **10.4g** FIBER: **6.5g** SUGAR ALCOHOLS: **15g**

MEGHA'S FAMOUS SMOOTHIE BOWL

MAKES 1 serving   **PREP TIME:** 5 minutes

Who doesn't love a frosty bowl of creamy goodness? Since ice cream for breakfast isn't optimal, Megha has found a workaround. Rich in protein and fat, this smoothie bowl is a delicious way to fuel the day.

2½ ounces frozen kale or spinach

½ cup unsweetened almond milk

2 tablespoons heavy whipping cream

5 or 6 ice cubes

¾ scoop (22g) flavored protein powder (see Tip)

¼ teaspoon finely ground Himalayan pink salt

¼ teaspoon xanthan gum

2 tablespoons sliced almonds, for the top

Put all the ingredients except the almonds in a blender and blend until smooth and thick, 30 to 45 seconds. Pour into a bowl, top with the sliced almonds, and enjoy immediately.

tip:
You can use whatever flavor of protein powder you prefer. Megha loves chocolate-flavored protein powder!

Nutrition
CALORIES: 298   FAT: 19g   PROTEIN: 24.5g   CARBS: 7.5g   FIBER: 3g

GOAT CHEESE SHAKSHUKA

MAKES 6 servings   **PREP TIME:** 10 minutes   **COOK TIME:** 40 minutes

This is one of those Instagrammable recipes. The yellow egg yolks pop against the vibrant red of the tomatoes in this dish. Snap a photo before digging in and show your followers how you do brunch!

2 tablespoons extra-virgin olive oil

1 small green bell pepper, thinly sliced

½ medium white onion, thinly sliced

1 teaspoon finely ground Himalayan pink salt

1 tablespoon ground cumin

1 tablespoon paprika

½ teaspoon ground black pepper

⅛ teaspoon cayenne pepper

1 (14-ounce) can diced tomatoes

4 ounces fresh (soft) goat cheese, crumbled, divided

6 large eggs

FOR GARNISH (OPTIONAL):

Chopped fresh parsley

1. Preheat the oven to 375°F and heat a large cast-iron skillet over medium heat.

2. Pour the olive oil into the hot pan, then add the bell pepper and onion. Cook until the veggies are very tender and the onions have browned and slightly caramelized, about 20 minutes, stirring with a wooden spoon every couple of minutes.

3. Add the salt and spices and stir to combine. Once the spices are fragrant, add the tomatoes and allow to cook down for 7 minutes.

4. Mix in three-quarters of the crumbled goat cheese, then make 6 small divots in the mixture. Carefully crack an egg into each divot, then top with the remaining goat cheese.

5. Bake for 8 to 10 minutes, until the egg whites are cooked through. (If you don't like runny yolks, bake for another 5 minutes.)

6. Garnish with fresh parsley, if desired, and serve immediately.

7. Store in an airtight container in the fridge for up to 3 days.

Nutrition
CALORIES: 198   FAT: 15g   PROTEIN: 8g   CARBS: 3.5g   FIBER: 1g

5-MINUTE BREAKFAST SANDWICH

MAKES 1 serving **PREP TIME:** 2 minutes **COOK TIME:** 8 minutes

Matt considers himself a breakfast sandwich connoisseur, so coming up with the perfect low-carb sandwich was no easy task. After several rounds of trial and error, he landed on something he's incredibly proud of.

BREAD:

1 tablespoon unsalted butter

2 tablespoons coconut flour

1 large egg

1 tablespoon heavy whipping cream

1 tablespoon water

¼ teaspoon baking powder

¼ teaspoon finely ground Himalayan pink salt

SANDWICH FILLINGS:

1 large egg

3 thin slices turkey deli meat

1 slice mozzarella cheese

1. Make the bread: Place the butter in a microwave-safe 8-ounce round or square ramekin. Melt the butter in the microwave, then add the remaining ingredients and thoroughly mix using a fork. Microwave on high for 60 to 90 seconds, until cooked through (a toothpick will come out clean when inserted in the middle).

2. Allow the bread to cool in the ramekin while you make the sandwich fillings. Once cool, carefully flip the bread out of the ramekin.

3. Make the fillings: While the bread is cooling, heat a small skillet over medium-high heat and grease the pan with coconut oil spray.

4. Grease a mason jar lid ring with coconut oil spray and place it in the hot skillet. Crack the egg into the ring and cook until the white is fully cooked through, 2 to 3 minutes. Flip and cook for an additional minute.

5. Remove the egg and lid ring from the skillet and place the egg on a plate. Fold the turkey slices into triangles and set in the hot skillet. Cook for about a minute on each side, until slightly browned and heated through. Transfer to the plate with the egg.

6. Slice the cooled bread in half horizontally and place the egg and turkey on one half. Place the slice of cheese on top and, if desired, place in the oven on broil to melt the cheese. Top with the second piece of bread and serve immediately.

Nutrition

CALORIES: 502   FAT: 34g   PROTEIN: 35g   CARBS: 11g   FIBER: 6g

POPCORN CHICKEN

MAKES 6 servings **PREP TIME:** 15 minutes **COOK TIME:** 25 minutes

Unfortunately, popcorn chicken gets put in the same category as chicken tenders and chicken nuggets, but these guys deserve a category all on their own. There's just something so special about these crispy bite-sized morsels of chicken. These pair well with a stack of Coconut Flour Pancakes (page 166) and sugar-free maple syrup!

POPCORN CHICKEN:

1 pound boneless, skinless chicken thighs, cubed

2 large eggs

2 tablespoons heavy whipping cream

¾ cup ground pork rinds

½ cup grated Parmesan cheese (about 1½ ounces)

1 teaspoon finely ground Himalayan pink salt

1 teaspoon garlic powder

½ teaspoon chili powder

½ teaspoon ground black pepper

DIPPING SAUCE:

½ cup mayonnaise

¼ cup reduced-sugar ketchup

1 teaspoon ground black pepper

½ teaspoon garlic powder

¼ teaspoon Worcestershire sauce

Sliced fresh chives, for garnish (optional)

1. Preheat the oven to 350°F. Grease a baking rack with coconut oil spray and set it in a rimmed baking sheet.

2. Set up three bowls for your breading station. Place the cubed chicken in the first bowl. Place the eggs and cream in the second bowl and whisk to combine. Place the ground pork rinds, Parmesan cheese, salt, and spices in the third bowl and stir to combine for the breading mixture.

3. Working in small batches, transfer the cubed chicken to the egg wash, allow the excess egg to drip off, and then dredge it in the breading, ensuring the chicken is fully coated. Place the breaded chicken pieces on the greased baking rack.

4. Bake for 22 to 25 minutes, until the chicken is crispy and cooked through.

5. While the chicken is baking, make the dipping sauce: Put all the ingredients in a small bowl and stir to combine. If desired, garnish with sliced chives. Refrigerate the sauce until you are ready to serve the chicken.

6. Once the chicken is done baking, transfer it to a large plate and serve immediately with the dipping sauce on the side.

7. Store the chicken and dipping sauce in separate airtight containers in the fridge; the chicken will keep for up to 1 week, the sauce for up to 2 weeks.

Nutrition

| CALORIES: 342 | FAT: 27g | PROTEIN: 25g | CARBS: 1.5g | FIBER: 0g |

COCONUT FLOUR PANCAKES

MAKES 5 medium pancakes   **PREP TIME:** 5 minutes   **COOK TIME:** 10 minutes

Are you a savory or sweet person in the morning? Either you're ordering the eggs and bacon special or you're eyeing the largest stack of pancakes on the menu. If you're into sticky stacks of whipped cream–covered cakes, then you're going to love this guilt-free recipe.

1 tablespoon coconut oil or ghee, for the pan

4 large eggs

1 cup heavy whipping cream

2 teaspoons vanilla extract

½ teaspoon liquid stevia

½ cup coconut flour

¾ teaspoon baking soda

¼ teaspoon finely ground Himalayan pink salt

TOPPINGS (OPTIONAL):

Butter

Fresh berries

1. Heat the oil in a large skillet over medium-high heat.

2. Place all the ingredients in a large mixing bowl and combine using a hand mixer until fully incorporated. The batter will be thick.

3. Using a ¼-cup measuring cup, scoop the batter onto the hot skillet and use the back of a spoon to spread it to about a ¼-inch thickness. Repeat once or twice, depending on how many pancakes fit in your pan. Cook the pancakes for 2 to 3 minutes, until bubbles start to form on the surface of the pancakes, then flip and cook for an additional 30 seconds.

4. Transfer the pancakes to a baking rack and repeat with the remaining batter. Serve immediately with butter and/or berries, if desired.

5. Store in an airtight container or zip-top bag in the fridge for up to 5 days.

Nutrition (per pancake)
CALORIES: 287   FAT: 24.4g   PROTEIN: 6.4g   CARBS: 8g   FIBER: 6.4g

SOUTHERN GRITS

MAKES 2 servings **PREP TIME:** 5 minutes, plus 10 minutes to thicken **COOK TIME:** 10 minutes

Matt was never a fan of traditional high-carb grits. When his friends would order a side of grits and butter, he would get extra bacon or fruit. Things have taken a sudden turn since starting low-carb. He now loves grits, and the secret is ground chia seeds and lots of cheese!

1 cup low-sodium chicken or beef broth

2 tablespoons chia seeds

¼ cup heavy whipping cream

½ teaspoon garlic powder

¼ teaspoon finely ground Himalayan pink salt

¼ teaspoon ground black pepper

½ cup grated Parmesan cheese (about 1½ ounces)

2 tablespoons unsalted butter

FOR GARNISH (OPTIONAL):
Sliced fresh chives

1. In a small heavy saucepan, simmer the broth over medium heat until reduced by half.

2. While the broth reduces, pulse the chia seeds in a clean coffee or spice grinder until ground; set aside.

3. Remove the pan with the reduced broth from the heat. Add the ground chia seeds, cream, garlic powder, salt, and pepper and whisk to combine.

4. Let the mixture sit for 5 to 10 minutes to allow it to thicken.

5. Add the Parmesan cheese and butter and whisk to combine. If the mixture is no longer hot, return the pan to the stovetop over low heat until the cheese and butter have melted.

6. Serve immediately, garnished with fresh chives, if desired.

Nutrition
CALORIES: 350   FAT: 23g   PROTEIN: 10g   CARBS: 7g   FIBER: 4g

LEMON POPPY SEED WAFFLES

MAKES 4 small waffles (2 per serving) **PREP TIME:** 10 minutes
COOK TIME: 12 minutes

All of Megha's dreams came true when we finally got a waffle iron. She's always coming up with new ways to make her waffles even better. These lemon poppy seed waffles are unexpected and delightful. Note: We've made the recipe relatively small because we think these waffles are best when made fresh!

3 large eggs

¼ cup (½ stick) unsalted butter, melted but not hot

Grated zest of 1 lemon

Juice of 1 lemon

2 tablespoons poppy seeds

¼ teaspoon liquid stevia

½ cup blanched almond flour

¼ cup coconut flour

1 teaspoon baking powder

¼ teaspoon finely ground Himalayan pink salt

1. Preheat a waffle iron to the medium setting.

2. Put the eggs, melted butter, lemon zest and juice, poppy seeds, and stevia in a medium-sized mixing bowl and whisk to combine.

3. In another medium-sized bowl, whisk together the flours, baking powder, and salt, then add the dry mixture to the egg mixture and whisk until fully incorporated.

4. Once the waffle iron is ready, grease it with coconut oil spray. Using a ⅓-cup measuring cup, scoop the batter into the center of the iron. Gently close the lid and allow to cook for 2 to 3 minutes, until steam has stopped coming out of the iron. Set the waffle on a plate and repeat with the remaining batter.

5. Store in a zip-top bag in the fridge for up to 3 days.

tip:
To dress up these waffles for brunch, we like to top them with whipped cream and grated lemon zest.

Nutrition (per serving)
CALORIES: 590   FAT: 50g   PROTEIN: 19g   CARBS: 17.5g   FIBER: 11g

ALMOND BUTTER PROTEIN LOAF

MAKES one 8 by 4-inch loaf (10 slices)   **PREP TIME:** 10 minutes   **COOK TIME:** 20 minutes

This lightly sweetened loaf is higher in protein, so we recommend eating it with butter or nut butter or alongside a fattier breakfast or other meal. Having the correct balance of protein and fat will keep you feeling full for much longer and sustain your energy.

½ cup coconut flour

2 scoops (60g) vanilla-flavored protein powder

2 tablespoons granular erythritol

½ teaspoon baking powder

¼ teaspoon baking soda

¼ teaspoon finely ground Himalayan pink salt

½ cup full-fat sour cream

2 large eggs

2 tablespoons natural almond butter

1 teaspoon vanilla extract

tip:
We often enjoy a slice of this loaf spread with almond butter for the perfect high-fat, high-protein afternoon snack!

1. Preheat the oven to 350°F and grease an 8 by 4-inch loaf pan with coconut oil spray.

2. In a medium-sized mixing bowl, whisk the coconut flour, protein powder, erythritol, baking powder, baking soda, and salt until blended.

3. In a large mixing bowl, whisk together the sour cream and eggs until incorporated, then add the almond butter and vanilla extract and whisk to combine.

4. Add the dry ingredients to the wet mixture in two batches as you combine using a spoon. Once fully incorporated, transfer the batter to the greased loaf pan and spread evenly using a rubber spatula.

5. Bake for 20 minutes, or until slightly browned on top and a toothpick comes out clean when inserted in the center. Allow to cool for 10 minutes before flipping the loaf out of the pan. Cut into 10 slices and enjoy.

6. Store in an airtight container in the fridge for up to 5 days.

Nutrition (per slice)
CALORIES: **63** FAT: **5.5g** PROTEIN: **13g** CARBS: **3.5g** FIBER: **2g** SUGAR ALCOHOLS: **2.5g**

GOAT CHEESE SOUFFLÉ

MAKES 4 soufflés   **PREP TIME:** 10 minutes   **COOK TIME:** 25 minutes

During the workweek, we are all about ease and speed in the kitchen; we like to whip up meals in under thirty minutes so we can get back to work. But weekends are a little different. If we're making brunch, we take our sweet time and let the morning last all day long. This soufflé is a little fancy and requires a few steps, but it's well worth it.

¼ cup blanched almond flour

½ teaspoon finely ground Himalayan pink salt

¼ teaspoon garlic powder

¼ teaspoon ground black pepper

¼ teaspoon xanthan gum

¼ cup plus 2 tablespoons heavy whipping cream

4 ounces fresh (soft) goat cheese, crumbled (about ½ cup)

2 tablespoons chopped fresh chives, plus more for garnish if desired

3 large eggs, room temperature, separated

1. Preheat the oven to 350°F. Grease four 4- to 6-ounce ramekins with coconut oil spray, then set them on a rimmed baking sheet.

2. In a large bowl, whisk together the almond flour, salt, garlic powder, pepper, and xanthan gum. Whisk in the cream until well combined. Whisk in the cheese, chives, and egg yolks until fully incorporated.

3. In a medium-sized mixing bowl, beat the egg whites with a hand mixer until stiff peaks form. Fold them into the almond flour mixture until combined.

4. Divide the mixture among the prepared ramekins and carefully place the baking sheet in the oven. Bake for about 25 minutes, until the soufflés have risen an inch or two above the rims and are golden brown.

5. Garnish with extra chives, if desired, and serve immediately.

6. We think these soufflés are best made fresh, but leftovers can be stored in an airtight container in the fridge for up to 3 days.

Nutrition (per soufflé)
CALORIES: 242   FAT: 21g   PROTEIN: 11.5g   CARBS: 2.4g   FIBER: 0.8g

BLUEBERRY CHIA SEED PUDDING

MAKES 4 servings   **PREP TIME:** 10 minutes, plus 30 minutes to chill

During the warmer months, it's nice to have recipes that don't require the oven or stove. This cool, creamy pudding will leave you feeling full and refreshed. Its consistency is similar to that of thick oatmeal or grits, which makes it a great option for breakfast or brunch.

PUDDING:

1½ cups unsweetened almond milk

½ cup chia seeds

¼ teaspoon liquid stevia

TOPPINGS:

½ cup heavy whipping cream

1½ ounces cream cheese (3 tablespoons), room temperature

Unsweetened coconut flakes

Fresh blueberries

1. Put the ingredients for the pudding in a bowl. Stir to combine using a spoon, then refrigerate for 30 minutes to allow the pudding to thicken.

2. Put the cream in a mixing bowl and whip using a hand mixer until stiff peaks form. Add the cream cheese and mix until fully combined.

3. Divide the pudding among four bowls or cups. Using a cookie scoop, scoop the whipped topping mixture onto the pudding and top with coconut flakes and blueberries. Serve immediately.

4. Store in an airtight container in the fridge for up to 10 days.

Nutrition (without coconut or blueberries)
CALORIES: 289   FAT: 25g   PROTEIN: 5g   CARBS: 13g   FIBER: 8g

Mains

MEXICAN SKILLET DINNER / 180

AVOCADO EGG SALAD / 182

CHICKEN PARMESAN / 183

EGGPLANT LASAGNA / 184

CAULIFLOWER CHILI / 186

SPICED KEEMA / 188

SALMON TOPPED WITH AVOCADO BRUSCHETTA / 190

ITALIAN HERBED MEATBALLS / 192

CREAMY PESTO SHRIMP / 194

DRY-RUBBED RIBS / 196

PORCINI AND BLUE CHEESE–ENCRUSTED STEAK / 198

FRENCH ONION CHICKEN BAKE / 200

LEMONY ROASTED DRUMSTICKS / 202

LAMB SHOULDER CHOPS / 204

CHILI WITH BACON / 206

CAULIFLOWER CRUST PEPPERONI PIZZA / 208

ONE-PAN CHICKEN WITH LEMON-GARLIC CREAM SAUCE / 210

OVEN-BRAISED SHORT RIBS / 212

INDIAN SPICED WINGS / 214

STEAK ROLL-UPS / 216

CAULIFLOWER NACHOS / 218

MEXICAN SKILLET DINNER

MAKES 8 servings   **PREP TIME:** 10 minutes   **COOK TIME:** 30 minutes

Parents love skillet dinners because they're one-pot cooking and easy cleanup, and kids love them because every bite is filled with different flavors. This is a great recipe for cooking ahead and then portioning out during the week for quick weeknight dinners. This recipe will also freeze well for up to a month!

1 pound ground beef (80/20)

½ medium white onion, diced

1 small red or green bell pepper, diced

1 teaspoon finely ground Himalayan pink salt

1 teaspoon chili powder

1 teaspoon garlic powder

1 teaspoon ground cumin

1 teaspoon onion powder

½ teaspoon dried oregano leaves

3 cups riced cauliflower (about 12 ounces)

1 cup shredded cheddar cheese (about 4 ounces), divided

¾ cup cherry tomatoes (about 3 ounces), quartered, divided

FOR GARNISH (OPTIONAL):

Chopped fresh cilantro

Full-fat sour cream

1. Preheat the oven to 350°F and heat a 12-inch cast-iron or other oven-safe skillet over medium-high heat. (If don't own an oven-safe skillet, see the note below.)

2. Brown the ground beef in the hot skillet, using a spoon to break it apart into crumbles as it cooks. When it's partially cooked, add the onion, bell pepper, salt, and spices and stir to combine.

3. Sauté until the beef is cooked through and the onion and bell pepper are tender. Add the riced cauliflower, half of the cheese, and half of the tomatoes. Stir to combine and cook for 3 to 5 minutes, until the cauliflower is tender.

4. Top with the remaining cheese and tomatoes and transfer the skillet to the oven. Bake for 10 to 12 minutes, until the cheese is fully melted. If desired, garnish with fresh cilantro and/or sour cream prior to serving.

5. Store in an airtight container in the fridge for up to 5 days.

note: If you don't own an oven-safe skillet, complete Steps 2 and 3 using any type of large skillet, then transfer the meat and vegetable mixture to a 13 by 9-inch casserole dish for the baking step. Top with the remaining cheese and tomatoes and bake as directed in Step 4.

Nutrition
CALORIES: 261   FAT: 22g   PROTEIN: 12g   CARBS: 5g   FIBER: 2g

AVOCADO EGG SALAD

MAKES 4 servings **PREP TIME:** 10 minutes, plus 1 hour to chill

A great way to increase the fat in egg salad is to add mashed avocado! It gives the salad the same creaminess that mayonnaise does, plus some fiber and nutrients that mayo is lacking.

8 large eggs, hard-boiled

2 medium-sized ripe avocados

¼ medium red onion, diced

Juice of ½ lemon

2 tablespoons mayonnaise

2 tablespoons minced fresh chives

1½ teaspoons finely ground Himalayan pink salt

1 teaspoon garlic powder

½ teaspoon ground black pepper

¼ teaspoon paprika

FOR GARNISH (OPTIONAL):

Sliced fresh chives

1. Peel the hard-boiled eggs and chop finely or roughly, according to your preference. (We like chunks of egg in our egg salad!) Put the chopped eggs in a large mixing bowl.

2. Peel the avocados and put the flesh in another bowl. Mash using a fork. Add the remaining ingredients to the mashed avocado and combine using a spoon.

3. Add the avocado mixture to the chopped eggs and combine using the spoon or a rubber spatula. Refrigerate for 1 to 2 hours prior to serving. Garnish with sliced fresh chives if desired.

4. Store in an airtight container in the fridge for up to 5 days.

Nutrition

CALORIES: **335**   FAT: **28g**   PROTEIN: **14g**   CARBS: **8.7g**   FIBER: **5.3g**

CHICKEN PARMESAN

MAKES 4 servings   **PREP TIME:** 10 minutes   **COOK TIME:** 25 minutes

Chicken Parmesan is a classic dish that you probably thought couldn't be duplicated in a low-carb version. However, pork rinds make for the perfect breading, whether you are frying or baking the chicken!

2 tablespoons extra-virgin olive oil, for the dish

1 tablespoon Italian seasoning

1 teaspoon red pepper flakes

½ cup grated Parmesan cheese (about 1½ ounces)

1 ounce pork rinds, ground

4 (6-ounce) boneless, skinless chicken breasts

½ cup marinara sauce

1 cup shredded mozzarella cheese (about 4 ounces)

1. Preheat the oven to 400°F. Coat the bottom and sides of a 1¾-quart baking dish with the oil.

2. In a medium-sized mixing bowl, mix together the Italian seasoning, red pepper flakes, Parmesan cheese, and ground pork rinds using a spoon.

3. Pat the chicken dry with a paper towel. Place the chicken in the prepared dish. Top with the marinara sauce, mozzarella cheese, and pork rind mixture.

4. Bake for 25 minutes, or until the chicken is fully cooked through. Serve immediately.

5. Store in an airtight container in the fridge for up to 5 days.

Nutrition

CALORIES: **386**   FAT: **22.5g**   PROTEIN: **39.5g**   CARBS: **4.5g**   FIBER: **0g**

EGGPLANT LASAGNA

MAKES 4 servings   **PREP TIME:** 20 minutes   **COOK TIME:** 40 minutes

Eggplant is very underrated in the low-carb community. It's comparable in heartiness and texture to a pasta noodle, so it works great in lasagna.

1½ pounds eggplant

Finely ground Himalayan pink salt

¾ pound ground beef (80/20)

½ cup tomato sauce

1 cup full-fat ricotta cheese

¼ cup grated Parmesan cheese

1 large egg

1 teaspoon minced garlic

½ teaspoon ground black pepper

¾ cup shredded mozzarella cheese (about 3 ounces)

tip:
If you're using a mandoline, first use a knife to cut the eggplant in half lengthwise, so that you have a flat surface to work with.

1. Preheat the oven to 350°F and grease a 3-quart casserole dish with coconut oil spray.

2. Using a mandoline or a sharp knife, slice the eggplant lengthwise into ⅛-inch-thick planks (or as thin as possible) to resemble lasagna noodles. Lay the eggplant slices on a cutting board in an even layer and sprinkle generously with salt to help draw out the moisture. After 10 minutes, pat the eggplant slices dry using a paper towel.

3. Heat a large skillet over medium-high heat. Brown the ground beef in the skillet, stirring often to crumble, until it is cooked through, then add the tomato sauce and stir to combine. Once the sauce is heated through, remove the pan from the heat and set aside.

4. In a medium-sized mixing bowl, whisk together the ricotta, Parmesan, egg, garlic, pepper, and ¾ teaspoon of salt; set aside.

5. Spread half of the meat mixture on the bottom of the casserole dish and layer half of the eggplant slices on top. Spread half of the ricotta mixture over the eggplant, then sprinkle with half of the mozzarella cheese. Repeat the layers once more.

6. Bake for 30 minutes, or until the cheese has browned. Serve immediately.

7. Store in an airtight container in the fridge for up to 5 days.

Nutrition
CALORIES: 480   FAT: 33.6g   PROTEIN: 30.6g   CARBS: 14.8g   FIBER: 4.8g

CAULIFLOWER CHILI

MAKES 4 servings   **PREP TIME:** 10 minutes   **COOK TIME:** 20 minutes

This is the perfect recipe for vegetarians who want to enjoy a hot bowl of chili on a cold winter day. It uses cauliflower as the base and may even convert some of you die-hard meat lovers!

1 medium head cauliflower (about 1 pound), cored and broken into large florets

¼ cup coconut oil, ghee, or tallow

1 small green bell pepper, diced

½ small white onion, diced

1 large tomato, diced

¾ cup vegetable broth, divided

2 teaspoons minced garlic

1½ teaspoons chili powder

1½ teaspoons ground cumin

1 teaspoon finely ground Himalayan pink salt

½ teaspoon ground black pepper

FOR SERVING:

¼ cup shredded cheddar cheese

3 tablespoons full-fat sour cream

1. Pulse the cauliflower florets in a food processor until you have small pieces about the size of peas. Don't process long enough to rice it.

2. Heat a large Dutch oven or other heavy pot over medium heat. Melt the oil in the pot, then add the bell pepper and onion and sauté for 3 to 5 minutes, until soft.

3. Add the tomato and ½ cup of the broth and cover partially with a lid (make sure the lid is tilted to let a little steam out). Turn the heat to high and cook for 5 minutes.

4. Add the cauliflower, garlic, spices, salt, pepper, and the remaining ¼ cup of broth and stir to combine. Cover and cook for 5 minutes, then remove the lid and cook for another 5 minutes to slightly reduce and thicken the chili. Serve immediately topped with cheddar cheese and sour cream.

5. Store in an airtight container in the fridge for up to 1 week.

note: *If you're not vegetarian, feel free to add 1 pound of ground beef or pork to up the fat and add some protein! You can also use low-sodium chicken broth in place of the vegetable broth.*

Nutrition (with toppings)

CALORIES: 387   FAT: 31g   PROTEIN: 11.5g   CARBS: 12.5g   FIBER: 4g

SPICED KEEMA

MAKES 4 servings   **PREP TIME:** 10 minutes   **COOK TIME:** 20 minutes

We love the smell of Indian food cooking in our home, and keema was one of Megha's favorites growing up in an Indian household. Traditionally, it uses peas and sometimes even potatoes, but this low-carb version will make you forget all about your peas and potatoes!

1 tablespoon coconut oil

1 small yellow onion (about 3½ ounces), diced

1 small serrano pepper, halved lengthwise and seeded

2 teaspoons minced garlic

1½ teaspoons finely ground Himalayan pink salt

1 tablespoon garam masala

2 teaspoons ground cumin

1 teaspoon ginger powder

1 teaspoon ground coriander

1 teaspoon turmeric powder

¼ teaspoon ground cinnamon

1 pound ground beef (80/20)

2 small Roma tomatoes, diced

3 tablespoons roughly chopped fresh cilantro leaves, plus more for garnish

1. Heat a large skillet over medium heat. Melt the oil in the skillet, then add the onion and sauté for 3 to 5 minutes, until softened.

2. Add the serrano pepper, garlic, salt, and spices and combine using a spoon. Cook for 1 to 2 minutes, until fragrant.

3. Turn the heat up to medium-high and add the ground beef. Brown the meat until completely cooked through, 6 to 8 minutes, using a wooden spoon to break it apart as it cooks.

4. Turn down the heat to medium and add the tomatoes. Cover with a lid and cook for 5 minutes, or until the tomatoes have broken down and reduced.

5. Remove from the heat and fold in the cilantro. Garnish with additional cilantro and serve immediately.

6. Store in an airtight container in the fridge for up to 1 week.

Nutrition
CALORIES: 321   FAT: 26.5g   PROTEIN: 20.4g   CARBS: 5.7g   FIBER: 1.3g

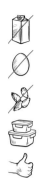

SALMON TOPPED WITH AVOCADO BRUSCHETTA

MAKES 4 servings   **PREP TIME:** 10 minutes   **COOK TIME:** 10 minutes

Traditional bruschetta is served with bread and guilt, but we all know that the best part is the fresh tomato topping! Who needs bread's empty calories when you can use salmon as your "bread" base while getting in some healthy fats, too?

SALMON:

1 tablespoon avocado oil or tallow

4 (6-ounce) skin-on salmon fillets

½ teaspoon finely ground Himalayan pink salt

½ teaspoon ground black pepper

AVOCADO BRUSCHETTA:

1 cup cherry tomatoes (about 5 ounces), quartered

1 large ripe avocado, diced

2 tablespoons chopped fresh basil

½ teaspoon finely ground Himalayan pink salt

¼ teaspoon ground black pepper

1 tablespoon extra-virgin olive oil

FOR SERVING (OPTIONAL):

Lime or lemon wedges

1. Cook the salmon: Heat the avocado oil in a large skillet over medium-high heat. Season the salmon with the salt and pepper. Once the oil is hot, place the fillets in the skillet skin side down. Cook for 3 minutes, or until the skin is crispy, then flip and cook for 3 minutes on the other side. Remove from the skillet and set on a plate.

2. Make the bruschetta: Put the tomatoes, avocado, basil, salt, and pepper in a medium-sized mixing bowl. Pour in the olive oil and stir together using a spoon.

3. Top the salmon fillets with the bruschetta and serve with lime wedges, if desired.

4. Store the salmon and bruschetta in separate airtight containers in the fridge; the salmon will keep for up to 5 days, the bruschetta for up to 3 days.

Nutrition

CALORIES: 460   FAT: 28.4g   PROTEIN: 44.5g   CARBS: 5.7g   FIBER: 3.8g

ITALIAN HERBED MEATBALLS

MAKES 16 meatballs (8 per serving)   **PREP TIME:** 10 minutes   **COOK TIME:** 15 minutes

Meatballs have been on the menu at our house at least twice a week lately. It's great to prep them in bulk and heat them up for a quick meal. Topping them with tomato sauce and Parmesan cheese is one of our favorite ways to serve them!

1 pound ground beef (90/10)

¼ cup grated Parmesan cheese

¼ cup ground pork rinds

2 teaspoons minced garlic

1½ tablespoons fresh basil leaves, or 1½ teaspoons dried basil

1½ teaspoons fresh oregano leaves, or ½ teaspoon dried oregano leaves

1½ teaspoons fresh rosemary leaves, or ½ teaspoon dried rosemary leaves

1½ teaspoons fresh thyme leaves, or ½ teaspoon dried thyme leaves

1 teaspoon finely ground Himalayan pink salt

1 teaspoon onion powder

½ teaspoon ground black pepper

½ teaspoon red pepper flakes

1 large egg

1. Preheat the oven to 375°F.

2. Put all the ingredients in a bowl and mix together using your hands. Using a 1½-tablespoon cookie scoop or your hands, make 16 evenly sized meatballs, about 1¼ inches in diameter, and place them on a rimmed baking sheet.

3. Bake for 15 to 17 minutes, until cooked through. Serve immediately.

4. Store in an airtight container in the fridge for up to 10 days.

note: We like to use 90/10 ground beef for meatballs so the excess fat doesn't drain off. The more fat that drains off, the less fat you end up consuming!

Nutrition
CALORIES: 532   FAT: 31g   PROTEIN: 56g   CARBS: 2.6g   FIBER: 0g

CREAMY PESTO SHRIMP

MAKES 4 servings **PREP TIME:** 10 minutes **COOK TIME:** 10 minutes

When you've had a long day but you don't want to feed your family takeout, this recipe will hit the spot! Shrimp cooks up really quickly, and adding a creamy pesto sauce balances the fat-to-protein ratio perfectly—and it's all ready in twenty minutes!

PESTO:

Leaves from 2 bunches fresh basil

2 cloves garlic

½ cup grated Parmesan cheese (about 1½ ounces), plus more for garnish if desired

⅓ cup raw walnuts

½ cup extra-virgin olive oil

½ teaspoon finely ground Himalayan pink salt

¼ teaspoon ground black pepper

¼ cup heavy whipping cream

SHRIMP:

1 tablespoon avocado oil

1 pound raw jumbo shrimp, peeled and deveined, tails on

½ teaspoon finely ground Himalayan pink salt

½ teaspoon ground black pepper

15 cherry tomatoes (about 4½ ounces), halved

FOR GARNISH (OPTIONAL):

Sprig of basil

1. Make the pesto: Put all the pesto ingredients except the cream in a blender or food processor and pulse until smooth. Add the cream and pulse briefly to combine.

2. Cook the shrimp: Heat the avocado oil in a large skillet over medium-high heat. Pat the shrimp dry, then season with the salt and pepper. Add the shrimp and tomatoes to the hot skillet and cook for 2 to 3 minutes per side, until the shrimp has turned pink and the tomatoes have softened.

3. Pour the pesto over the shrimp and tomatoes and cook for 2 to 3 minutes, until heated through, stirring to combine. Serve immediately, garnished with Parmesan cheese and a sprig of basil, if desired.

4. Store in an airtight container in the fridge for up to 5 days.

Nutrition
CALORIES: **485** FAT: **45g** PROTEIN: **17.5g** CARBS: **5.3g** FIBER: **1g**

DRY-RUBBED RIBS

MAKES 4 servings **PREP TIME:** 5 minutes, plus 15 minutes to rest
COOK TIME: 2 hours 40 minutes

Who doesn't love ribs? When you realize how easy they are to make at home, football Sundays will change forever. We love to get these going in the morning to have them ready by game time (or lunchtime)!

SEASONING RUB:

1 tablespoon finely ground Himalayan pink salt

1½ teaspoons chili powder

1½ teaspoons garlic powder

1½ teaspoons ground black pepper

1½ teaspoons ground cumin

1½ teaspoons onion powder

1½ teaspoons paprika

1 teaspoon cayenne or chipotle pepper

3 pounds pork ribs

1. Preheat the oven to 250°F.

2. Put the ingredients for the seasoning rub in a small bowl and stir to combine.

3. Pat the racks of ribs dry using paper towels and set them on a piece of foil large enough to wrap the ribs in.

4. Pour the seasoning rub on both sides of the ribs and rub it in using your hands, coating the entire racks.

5. Wrap the foil tightly around the ribs, then wrap it once more using another large piece of foil, ensuring there are no gaps or holes. The ribs will steam in the sealed foil.

6. Place the wrapped ribs on a rimmed baking sheet and bake for 2 hours. After 2 hours, remove the ribs from the oven, allow them to cool for 10 minutes, and then unwrap them.

7. Place a baking rack in the rimmed baking sheet and increase the oven temperature to 350°F. Place the unwrapped ribs on the baking rack and bake for another 40 minutes, until the ribs are tender and have reached an internal temperature of 195°F. Remove from the oven and allow to rest for 5 minutes before serving.

8. Store in an airtight container in the fridge for up to 1 week.

Nutrition

CALORIES: 460   FAT: 34.6g   PROTEIN: 33.4g   CARBS: 1.9g   FIBER: 0.3g

PORCINI AND BLUE CHEESE–ENCRUSTED STEAK

MAKES 2 servings   **PREP TIME:** 5 minutes   **COOK TIME:** 10 minutes

This recipe was inspired by a celebratory dinner we had the day we found out Megha was pregnant. The porcini mushrooms add a subtle earthy flavor to the steak, while the blue cheese adds a tangy creaminess that you wouldn't expect to pair perfectly with steak, but does!

½ ounce dried porcini mushrooms

2 (8-ounce) boneless rib-eye steaks, about 1 inch thick

1 teaspoon finely ground Himalayan pink salt

½ teaspoon ground black pepper

1 tablespoon high-heat cooking fat, such as tallow

2 ounces blue cheese, crumbled (about ½ cup)

1. Heat a large cast-iron or other heavy skillet over medium-high heat.

2. Pulse the dried mushrooms in a clean coffee or spice grinder until finely ground. Pour onto a plate.

3. Pat the steaks dry and season with the salt and pepper. Press both sides of the steaks into the ground dried mushrooms.

4. Melt the fat in the hot skillet. Add the steaks to the skillet and cook for 5 minutes per side for medium-rare steaks, or until the internal temperature reaches around 135°F. (Adjust the cooking time as needed for steaks that are thinner or thicker than 1 inch.)

5. Transfer the steaks to a cutting board, top each with 1 ounce of crumbled blue cheese, and tent with foil or cover with a large bowl. Allow to rest for 5 minutes before serving.

tips:

The cheese will melt somewhat as the steaks rest. If you prefer the cheese very melted, place the cheese-topped steaks under the oven broiler just until melted, then tent and rest as described.

To make this a balanced meal, serve the steaks with a side salad and the dressing of your choice.

Nutrition

CALORIES: 573   FAT: 39g   PROTEIN: 51g   CARBS: 5.5g   FIBER: 2.5g

FRENCH ONION CHICKEN BAKE

MAKES 4 servings   **PREP TIME:** 5 minutes   **COOK TIME:** 40 minutes

French onion soup at the local café is always a must, but ordering it without the bread doesn't really do it justice. Here, we've taken the basics of a French onion soup and turned it into the perfect family dinner. With chicken as the base, you won't miss the bread at all!

4 (6-ounce) boneless, skinless chicken breasts

1 teaspoon finely ground Himalayan pink salt

½ teaspoon ground black pepper

4 tablespoons (½ stick) unsalted butter, divided

½ medium yellow onion, thinly sliced

1 cup low-sodium beef broth

¼ teaspoon xanthan gum

4 slices mozzarella cheese

4 slices provolone cheese

FOR GARNISH (OPTIONAL):

Chopped fresh parsley

tip:
Swap out the chicken breasts for some boneless chicken thighs to up the fat and juiciness of this recipe!

1. Preheat the oven to 375°F and heat a 12-inch cast-iron or other oven-safe skillet over medium-high heat.

2. Pat the chicken breasts dry with paper towels and season with the salt and pepper. Melt 2 tablespoons of the butter in the hot pan. Add the chicken to the skillet and cook for 5 minutes on each side, until slightly browned. (It will not be fully cooked through at this point.) Remove from the skillet and set aside.

3. Turn the heat under the skillet down to medium. Melt the remaining 2 tablespoons of butter in the pan, then add the onion slices. Cook, stirring frequently, until all of the onion slices are very tender and browned, at least 20 minutes. Turn the heat down further if they begin to brown too quickly.

4. Add the broth to the hot skillet with the onions and scrape up the browned bits on the bottom of the pan with a wooden spoon. Add the xanthan gum and simmer, stirring continuously, until slightly thickened, about 1 minute.

5. Return the chicken to the skillet and ladle some of the onion mixture on top of each breast. Cover each breast with one slice of mozzarella and one slice of provolone.

6. Transfer the skillet to the oven and bake for 8 to 10 minutes, until the cheese is fully melted and the chicken is cooked through. Serve immediately, garnished with chopped parsley, if desired.

7. Store in an airtight container in the fridge for up to 5 days.

Nutrition
CALORIES: **536**   FAT: **28.3g**   PROTEIN: **63.5g**   CARBS: **2.3g**   FIBER: **0.2g**

LEMONY ROASTED DRUMSTICKS

MAKES 3 servings   **PREP TIME:** 5 minutes, plus 2 hours to marinate
COOK TIME: 25 minutes

Drumsticks are the underrated cut of chicken, and Matt loves to make them any chance he gets. You can't go wrong with a lemon-herb seasoning, and bone-in meat always comes out juicy and tender when roasted in the oven!

6 chicken drumsticks

MARINADE:

Grated zest of 1 lemon

Juice of 1 lemon

¼ cup plus 2 tablespoons extra-virgin olive oil

1 tablespoon fresh rosemary leaves, or 1 teaspoon dried rosemary leaves

2 teaspoons fresh oregano leaves, or ½ heaping teaspoon dried oregano leaves

1 tablespoon garlic powder

1½ teaspoons onion powder

½ teaspoon finely ground Himalayan pink salt

½ teaspoon ground black pepper

FOR GARNISH:

1 teaspoon fresh rosemary leaves, or ¼ heaping teaspoon dried rosemary leaves

¾ teaspoon fresh oregano leaves, or ¼ teaspoon dried oregano leaves

½ teaspoon finely ground Himalayan pink salt

1. Place the drumsticks in a gallon-sized zip-top bag and add the ingredients for the marinade. Seal and shake vigorously, ensuring all the chicken is coated, then place in the fridge to marinate for 2 hours.

2. Preheat the oven to 425°F and line a rimmed baking sheet with parchment paper.

3. Place the drumsticks on the lined baking sheet and sprinkle with the garnishes. Bake for 25 minutes, or until fully cooked through. (When done, the internal temperature of the drumsticks will have reached 165°F.) Serve immediately.

4. Store in an airtight container in the fridge for up to 5 days.

Nutrition
CALORIES: 492   FAT: 38.7g   PROTEIN: 32g   CARBS: 3.5g   FIBER: 0.3g

LAMB SHOULDER CHOPS

MAKES 4 servings   **PREP TIME:** 10 minutes   **COOK TIME:** 10 minutes

When lamb is on the menu, it's best to keep it simple. We use fresh rosemary and garlic to turn these quick-cooking lamb chops into a flavorful meal that will impress your friends and family.

2 pounds lamb shoulder chops, about ½ inch thick

1½ teaspoons finely ground Himalayan pink salt

1 teaspoon ground black pepper

Leaves from 2 sprigs fresh rosemary, chopped, plus more for garnish if desired

2 teaspoons minced garlic

2 tablespoons tallow or lard

FOR GARNISH (OPTIONAL):

Flake or coarsely ground sea salt

1. Heat a large skillet over medium heat.

2. Pat the lamb chops dry with paper towels and season with the salt and pepper. Coat the chops in the rosemary and garlic, pressing the seasonings firmly into the chops with your hands.

3. Melt the fat in the hot skillet, then add the seasoned chops to the pan and cook for 5 minutes on each side for medium-done chops.

4. Transfer the chops to a cutting board, tent with aluminum foil, and allow to rest for 5 minutes prior to serving. If desired, slice for easier serving and top with additional fresh rosemary and sea salt. Serve immediately.

5. Store in an airtight container in the fridge for up to 5 days.

tip:
These lamb chops pair great with our Garlic Green Beans (page 250)!

Nutrition
CALORIES: 686   FAT: 51.7g   PROTEIN: 51g   CARBS: 0.3g   FIBER: 0g

CHILI WITH BACON

MAKES 6 servings   **PREP TIME:** 10 minutes   **COOK TIME:** 1 hour 50 minutes

This chili recipe is one of the first recipes we posted on our food blog, KetoConnect, and it still holds true to chili perfection today. It's fatty and hearty, with a little kick of spice!

5 slices bacon, chopped

2 pounds ground beef (80/20)

1 small white onion, diced

1 small green bell pepper, diced

1 medium Roma tomato, diced

2 teaspoons minced garlic

1 teaspoon finely ground Himalayan pink salt

1 tablespoon chili powder

2 teaspoons ground cumin

1 teaspoon dried oregano leaves

½ teaspoon ground black pepper

2 medium jalapeño peppers, finely diced (see Tips)

1 teaspoon Worcestershire sauce

2½ cups low-sodium chicken or beef broth

FOR GARNISH (OPTIONAL):

Full-fat sour cream

Chopped fresh cilantro

1. Heat a Dutch oven or other heavy pot over medium-high heat. Put the chopped bacon in the pot and cook until the bacon is 90 percent cooked through. Add the ground beef, using a wooden spoon to break it apart as it cooks.

2. Once the ground beef is cooked through, add the onion, bell pepper, tomato, garlic, salt, and spices. Stir to incorporate all of the seasonings.

3. Add the jalapeños, Worcestershire sauce, and broth and stir once more. Cover with a lid and simmer for 90 minutes. After 90 minutes, remove the lid and simmer for 10 more minutes to allow the liquid to reduce. Serve immediately, topped with sour cream and cilantro, if desired.

4. Store in an airtight container in the fridge for up to 1 week.

tips:

If you miss beans in your chili, canned black soybeans are a good low-carb option to add to this recipe!

If you like less heat, seed one or both of the jalapeños.

Nutrition

CALORIES: 499   FAT: 39.5g   PROTEIN: 30g   CARBS: 4g   FIBER: 1g

CAULIFLOWER CRUST PEPPERONI PIZZA

MAKES 4 servings   **PREP TIME:** 10 minutes   **COOK TIME:** 30 minutes

After countless tries to make a great cauliflower crust, Matt was convinced it was impossible—until he realized that it's all about the thickness. Make sure you roll out the crust as thinly as you can to get it to crisp up in the oven! We've suggested some of our favorite toppings below, but feel free to substitute whatever you like.

CRUST:

1 large head cauliflower, cored and cut into chunks

2 large eggs

½ cup shredded mozzarella cheese (about 2 ounces)

¼ cup grated Parmesan cheese

½ teaspoon finely ground Himalayan pink salt

½ teaspoon dried oregano leaves

½ teaspoon garlic powder

½ teaspoon onion powder

¼ teaspoon red pepper flakes

TOPPINGS:

¾ cup tomato sauce

½ cup shredded mozzarella cheese (about 2 ounces)

2 ounces pepperoni

1. Preheat the oven to 425°F.

2. Put the chunks of cauliflower in a food processor and process until the pieces are the size of grains of rice.

3. Transfer the riced cauliflower to a large bowl and add the remaining crust ingredients. Combine using your hands or a spoon until everything is fully incorporated.

4. Transfer the dough to a baking sheet and spread it out until it's ¼ inch thick, either using your hands or by placing a sheet of parchment paper on top and rolling it out using a rolling pin.

5. Bake for 17 to 20 minutes, until the edges are starting to brown and the crust is cooked through.

6. Top with the tomato sauce, mozzarella, and pepperoni and bake for an additional 10 minutes. Slice and serve immediately.

7. Store in an airtight container or wrapped in plastic wrap in the fridge for up to 5 days or in the freezer for up to 3 weeks. Reheat in a preheated 300°F oven until heated through.

Nutrition
CALORIES: 296   FAT: 20g   PROTEIN: 17g   CARBS: 14g   FIBER: 4.3g

ONE-PAN CHICKEN WITH LEMON-GARLIC CREAM SAUCE

MAKES 4 servings   **PREP TIME:** 5 minutes   **COOK TIME:** 25 minutes

One-pan recipes mean easy preparation and easy cleanup! This recipe uses fresh lemon juice, garlic, and cream to transform boring, low-fat chicken into a delicious, high-fat meal.

CHICKEN:

4 boneless, skinless chicken thighs

1 teaspoon finely ground Himalayan pink salt

½ teaspoon ground black pepper

1 tablespoon coconut oil, for the pan

SAUCE:

¼ cup (½ stick) unsalted butter

2 teaspoons minced garlic

1 small shallot, diced

1 cup low-sodium chicken broth

½ cup heavy whipping cream

Juice of ½ lemon

¼ teaspoon finely ground Himalayan pink salt

¼ teaspoon ground black pepper

4 lemon slices, to top the chicken

FOR GARNISH (OPTIONAL):

Chopped fresh parsley

1. Preheat the oven to 350°F. Heat a large oven-safe skillet over medium-high heat.

2. Pat the chicken thighs dry with paper towels and season with the salt and pepper.

3. Melt the coconut oil in the hot pan, then add the thighs and sear on both sides, 3 to 4 minutes per side. (The chicken will not be cooked through at this point.) Transfer the seared chicken to a plate and set aside.

4. Make the sauce: Put the butter, garlic, and shallot in the same skillet and sauté over medium heat for 1 to 2 minutes, until fragrant.

5. Add the chicken broth, cream, lemon juice, salt, and pepper to the skillet and stir to combine using a wooden spoon. Simmer for 3 to 5 minutes to reduce, then return the chicken thighs to the skillet.

6. Top each thigh with a slice of lemon. Transfer the skillet to the oven and bake for 10 minutes, or until the chicken is cooked through. Serve immediately, garnished with chopped parsley if desired.

7. Store in an airtight container in the fridge for up to 5 days.

Nutrition

CALORIES: 448   FAT: 33g   PROTEIN: 33.8g   CARBS: 3.5g   FIBER: 0.3g

OVEN-BRAISED SHORT RIBS

MAKES 4 servings   **PREP TIME:** 5 minutes, plus 10 minutes to rest
COOK TIME: 2 hours 40 minutes

This slow braising recipe requires a large heavy pot with a tight-fitting lid. A Dutch oven is ideal. A tight-fitting lid ensures that the meat comes out tender and falling off the bone!

3½ pounds short ribs

2 tablespoons tallow or lard

1 large shallot, finely diced

2 teaspoons minced garlic

⅓ cup soy sauce or coconut aminos

½ teaspoon finely ground Himalayan pink salt

½ teaspoon ground black pepper

3 cups low-sodium chicken or beef broth

FOR GARNISH (OPTIONAL):

Fresh thyme leaves

1. Preheat the oven to 325°F and heat a Dutch oven or other large heavy pot over medium heat.

2. Pat the short ribs dry with paper towels and set aside.

3. Melt the tallow in the hot pot, then add the shallot and garlic. Sauté for 2 to 3 minutes, until fragrant.

4. Working in batches to avoid crowding the pot, sear the short ribs on all sides, about 1 minute per side.

5. Return all the seared short ribs to the pot and add the remaining ingredients. Cover with the lid and place in the oven. Cook for 2½ hours, or until the ribs are fall-off-the-bone tender. Allow to rest for 10 minutes with the lid on before serving. Garnish with fresh thyme, if desired.

6. Store in an airtight container in the fridge for up to 5 days.

Nutrition (including broth)
CALORIES: 728   FAT: 63g   PROTEIN: 34g   CARBS: 4.8g   FIBER: 0.2g

INDIAN SPICED WINGS

MAKES 4 servings   **PREP TIME:** 10 minutes   **COOK TIME:** 45 minutes

Matt has always believed that homemade wings trump all takeout wings. When you make them yourself, you have full control over the spice rub, and you can ensure that they aren't fried in peanut oil. We like to bake our wings and use baking powder to make them extra crispy!

2 pounds chicken wings

1 tablespoon baking powder

1 tablespoon finely ground Himalayan pink salt

1½ tablespoons paprika

1 tablespoon ground coriander

1 tablespoon ground cumin

1½ teaspoons garlic powder

1½ teaspoons ginger powder

½ teaspoon ground cinnamon

¼ teaspoon cayenne pepper

¼ teaspoon ground black pepper

FOR SERVING (OPTIONAL):

Lemon wedges

1. Preheat the oven to 225°F. Grease a baking rack with coconut oil spray and place it on a rimmed baking sheet.

2. Pat the chicken wings dry using paper towels and place them in a gallon-sized zip-top bag. Add the baking powder, seal the bag, and shake to coat the wings thoroughly.

3. In a small bowl, mix together the salt and spices, then add the seasoning mixture to the bag with the wings. Seal and shake vigorously to coat the wings as evenly as possible.

4. Place the wings in a single layer on the baking rack and bake for 30 minutes. Increase the oven temperature to 425°F and bake for an additional 15 minutes, until crispy and browned.

5. Transfer the wings to a serving platter and serve immediately, with lemon wedges on the side if desired.

6. Store in an airtight container in the fridge for up to 5 days. We prefer to reheat our wings in a preheated 200°F oven until heated through, 10 to 15 minutes.

tip:
If you love wings and are looking for a good takeout option, we recommend Buffalo Wild Wings. They fry their wings in beef tallow!

Nutrition
CALORIES: 593   FAT: 39g   PROTEIN: 54g   CARBS: 3.5g   FIBER: 1.5g

STEAK ROLL-UPS

MAKES 6 servings   **PREP TIME:** 10 minutes   **COOK TIME:** 25 minutes

Flank steak is very lean, but sometimes it's all you have on hand, or it's on sale at the grocery store. In that case, you can easily increase the fat by not only cooking the steak in fat but also stuffing it with cheese and olives. If your steaks are thick, feel free to pound them out or have your butcher slice them thin for you.

FILLING:

¾ cup full-fat ricotta cheese

½ cup grated Parmesan cheese (about 1½ ounces)

¼ cup fresh parsley leaves, chopped

3 ounces pitted Kalamata olives, roughly chopped

1 large egg

1 tablespoon minced garlic

STEAK:

1½ pounds flank steak, about ¼ inch thick (2 long pieces)

1 teaspoon finely ground Himalayan pink salt

½ teaspoon ground black pepper

2 tablespoons tallow or coconut oil, for the pan

FOR GARNISH (OPTIONAL):

Extra-virgin olive oil

Fresh cilantro leaves

Crumbled Cotija cheese

1. Preheat the oven to 400°F and heat a large cast-iron or other heavy oven-safe skillet over medium-high heat.

2. Make the filling: Place all the filling ingredients in a medium-sized bowl and mix with a spoon. Set aside.

3. Lay the flank steaks on a cutting board with the long sides facing you and spread the filling on each piece. Starting on a short end, roll the steaks up and season with the salt and pepper.

4. Melt the tallow in the hot skillet. Place the steak roll-ups in the skillet.

5. Bake for 20 minutes, or until the meat is cooked through, then broil for 3 minutes to brown the top. Remove from the oven, transfer both roll-ups to a cutting board, and allow to rest for 5 minutes before slicing and serving. If desired, drizzle with olive oil and sprinkle with some fresh cilantro and crumbled Cotija cheese.

6. Store in an airtight container in the fridge for up to 3 days.

Nutrition

CALORIES: 358   FAT: 19.5g   PROTEIN: 41g   CARBS: 4g   FIBER: 0g

CAULIFLOWER NACHOS

MAKES 4 servings   **PREP TIME:** 10 minutes   **COOK TIME:** 25 minutes

It can be hard to get everyone out of bed on Sunday morning, especially if you were out dancing all night or enjoyed some wine with friends. Simply start cooking these nachos and everyone in the house will follow the smell of bacon to the kitchen in no time.

Florets from 1 medium head cauliflower, cut into ¼-inch-thick slices

1½ tablespoons extra-virgin olive oil

1 teaspoon finely ground Himalayan pink salt

½ teaspoon chili powder

½ teaspoon garlic powder

½ teaspoon ground cumin

1 cup shredded cheddar cheese or Monterey Jack cheese (about 4 ounces)

¼ cup cooked and chopped bacon

TOPPINGS:

¼ cup pico de gallo or quartered cherry tomatoes

¼ cup guacamole

FOR GARNISH/SERVING (OPTIONAL):

Chopped fresh cilantro

Lime wedges

1. Preheat the oven to 425°F.

2. Place the cauliflower slices on a rimmed baking sheet and top with the olive oil, salt, chili powder, garlic powder, and cumin. Gently mix around using your hands, ensuring the cauliflower is well coated.

3. Bake for 15 minutes, or until the cauliflower is tender.

4. Turn the oven temperature down to 350°F and top the cauliflower with the shredded cheese and bacon. Bake for another 10 minutes, or until the cheese is fully melted.

5. Top with the pico de gallo and guacamole. If desired, garnish with cilantro and serve with lime wedges. Serve immediately.

6. Store in an airtight container in the fridge for up to 3 days. Reheat in a preheated 200°F oven until heated through and the cheese has melted again.

Nutrition (with toppings)
CALORIES: **313**   FAT: **24g**   PROTEIN: **15g**   CARBS: **11g**   FIBER: **5g**

Sides & Savory Snacks

CREAMY BRUSSELS SPROUTS WITH BACON / 222

ROSEMARY PARMESAN BISCUITS / 224

CHOPPED CAPRESE SALAD / 226

BACON GARLIC ASPARAGUS / 227

CREAM OF BROCCOLI SOUP / 228

PROSCIUTTO BRIE RASPBERRY CUPS / 230

PIZZA ROLLS / 232

KUNG PAO BRUSSELS SPROUTS / 234

BUTTERED MUSHROOMS / 236

ZUCCHINI BASIL MUFFINS / 238

CHEESY CREAMED SPINACH / 240

BATTERED ONION RINGS / 242

PIMENTO CHEESE / 244

PIZZA DIP / 246

BACON CAULIFLOWER GRATIN / 248

GARLIC GREEN BEANS / 250

AVOCADOS IN SPICY CILANTRO SAUCE / 252

BUFFALO CHICKEN–STUFFED MUSHROOMS / 254

WHOLE ROASTED CAULIFLOWER WITH PARMESAN CHEESE SAUCE / 256

SALMON JERKY / 258

CREAMY BRUSSELS SPROUTS WITH **BACON**

MAKES 6 servings   **PREP TIME:** 10 minutes   **COOK TIME:** 30 minutes

When you want to take a friendship to the next level, you give someone a nickname. We eat Brussels sprouts so often that it was only right to start calling them "Brussies." After trying this creamy rendition with bacon, you just might start calling Brussels sprouts "Brussies," too.

5 slices bacon, roughly chopped

1½ pounds Brussels sprouts

2 teaspoons minced garlic

2 tablespoons unsalted butter

¾ cup heavy whipping cream

¼ cup shredded mozzarella cheese

¾ teaspoon finely ground Himalayan pink salt

½ teaspoon ground black pepper

½ teaspoon red pepper flakes

¼ cup grated Parmesan cheese

1. Preheat the oven to 375°F.

2. Cook the bacon in a large oven-safe skillet over medium-high heat until the fat has rendered and the bacon is crispy. When done, transfer the bacon to a paper towel–lined plate and remove half of the bacon fat from the pan (reserve for another use or discard).

3. While the bacon is cooking, cut the Brussels sprouts in half. Add the halved Brussels to the bacon fat in the hot skillet and cook for 7 to 10 minutes, until tender and slightly browned. Turn the heat down to medium-low and add the garlic and butter.

4. Once the butter has melted and the garlic is fragrant, 30 to 60 seconds, return the bacon to the pan and add the cream, mozzarella, salt, black pepper, and red pepper flakes. Stir to combine using a wooden spoon.

5. Once the mozzarella has fully melted and everything is coated, remove the skillet from the heat and top with the grated Parmesan. Place in the oven and bake for 10 minutes, or until slightly browned and bubbly. Serve immediately.

6. Store in an airtight container in the fridge for up to 5 days.

Nutrition
CALORIES: 280   FAT: 23g   PROTEIN: 8.8g   CARBS: 11.5g   FIBER: 4.2g

ROSEMARY PARMESAN BISCUITS

MAKES 8 biscuits **PREP TIME:** 10 minutes, plus 10 minutes to cool
COOK TIME: 30 minutes

Winters get pretty cold in Michigan, where Matt grew up. Soups and stews were a nice way to warm up after a wicked day out in the wind. And if you were lucky, there were freshly baked biscuits for dipping!

4 large eggs

¼ cup heavy whipping cream

¼ cup (½ stick) unsalted butter, melted but not hot

¼ cup unsweetened almond milk

½ cup coconut flour

⅓ cup golden flax meal

1½ teaspoons baking powder

½ teaspoon finely ground Himalayan pink salt

½ cup grated Parmesan cheese (about 1½ ounces)

1½ tablespoons fresh rosemary leaves, chopped

1. Preheat the oven to 350°F and grease 8 wells of a standard-size 12-well muffin tin with coconut oil spray.

2. In a large mixing bowl, whisk together the eggs, cream, melted butter, and almond milk.

3. In a separate bowl, whisk together the coconut flour, flax meal, baking powder, and salt, then add the dry mixture to the egg mixture. Whisk the wet and dry ingredients together until you achieve a doughlike consistency.

4. Fold in the Parmesan cheese and rosemary and divide the dough evenly among the 8 greased muffin wells, filling each about three-quarters of the way full. If desired, top each muffin with a sprinkle of grated Parmesan before placing in the oven.

5. Bake for 30 minutes, or until a toothpick inserted in the center of a biscuit comes out clean. Allow to cool for 10 minutes prior to handling.

6. Store in an airtight container in the fridge for up to 1 week.

Nutrition (per biscuit)
CALORIES: 222   FAT: 17g   PROTEIN: 8.4g   CARBS: 8.3g   FIBER: 5.1g

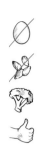

CHOPPED CAPRESE SALAD

MAKES 4 servings   **PREP TIME:** 10 minutes, plus 1 hour to chill

We traveled to Rome last summer, and instead of eating pizza, pasta, and gelato, we indulged in simple Italian delicacies. The cherry tomatoes, fresh mozzarella, and extra-virgin olive oil are what inspired this delicious salad.

5 ounces cherry tomatoes, halved

5 ounces fresh mozzarella cheese, chopped into bite-sized pieces

2 to 3 tablespoons chopped fresh basil leaves

3 tablespoons extra-virgin olive oil

½ teaspoon finely ground Himalayan pink salt

¼ teaspoon ground black pepper

1. Put all the ingredients in a medium-sized mixing bowl and toss to evenly coat the tomatoes and cheese in the olive oil. Refrigerate for 1 hour prior to serving.

2. Store in an airtight container in the fridge for up to 3 days.

Nutrition

CALORIES: **198**   FAT: **17.8g**   PROTEIN: **6.7g**   CARBS: **1.5g**   FIBER: **0.5g**

BACON GARLIC ASPARAGUS

MAKES 2 servings   **PREP TIME:** 5 minutes   **COOK TIME:** 15 minutes

The first time Matt invited me over for dinner, the first course he served was bacon-wrapped asparagus. How romantic! Bacon was his way to my heart. This recipe is a deconstructed version of that appetizer.

4 slices bacon, chopped

3 cloves garlic, minced

1 medium shallot, chopped

1 pound fresh asparagus, tough ends removed, chopped into thirds

tip:
We like to top this side dish with butter to up the fat and add some creaminess!

1. In a large skillet over medium-high heat, fry the bacon until it is 90 percent of the way cooked through and slightly crispy, then add the garlic and shallot and sauté for 1 to 2 minutes, until fragrant.

2. Add the chopped asparagus to the pan and cook for 5 to 7 minutes, until the asparagus is tender and bright green. Serve immediately.

Nutrition
CALORIES: **240**   FAT: **18.8g**   PROTEIN: **9.2g**   CARBS: **10g**   FIBER: **3.3g**

CREAM OF BROCCOLI SOUP

MAKES 4 servings   **PREP TIME:** 10 minutes   **COOK TIME:** 30 minutes

Megha loves to make large batches of soup and store them in the freezer for when Matt is away or she's looking for something delicious to heat up quickly. This cream of broccoli soup is one of her favorites, and it's quick and easy to whip up any night of the week!

2 tablespoons coconut oil

1 small white onion, diced

1 small shallot, diced

1½ cups broccoli florets, chopped (about 12 ounces)

4 cups low-sodium chicken broth

1½ teaspoons finely ground Himalayan pink salt

½ teaspoon ground black pepper

¼ cup heavy whipping cream

1. Heat a stockpot over medium heat. Melt the oil in the pot, then add the onion and shallot and cook for 5 to 7 minutes, until very tender but not browned. Add the chopped broccoli, broth, salt, and pepper and turn the heat up to medium-high.

2. Bring to a boil, then lower the heat to medium-low and cover the pot. Simmer for 20 minutes, or until the broccoli is very tender.

3. Remove from the heat and use an immersion blender to blend the soup until it has a smooth and creamy consistency. Place the pot back over medium heat, then add the cream and stir to combine. Once heated through, remove from the heat and serve.

4. Store in an airtight container in the fridge for up to 5 days.

Nutrition

CALORIES: **167**   FAT: **12.5g**   PROTEIN: **6.4g**   CARBS: **9.3g**   FIBER: **2.6g**

PROSCIUTTO BRIE RASPBERRY CUPS

MAKES 16 cups (4 per serving) **PREP TIME:** 10 minutes, plus 10 minutes to cool
COOK TIME: 12 minutes

Megha's perfect night requires the following items: charcuterie, some cheese, a little wine, and her pets. Oh, and Matt. This recipe was inspired by countless nights of good company and good eats.

8 thin slices prosciutto (about 4 ounces), halved

3 ounces Brie cheese, cut into 16 evenly sized pieces

8 raspberries, halved

1. Preheat the oven to 350°F. Grease 16 wells of a mini muffin tin with coconut oil spray.

2. Fold each prosciutto half in half to form a quarter-moon shape and place each, point end down, in a greased mini muffin cup, overlapping the cut ends to form a cone shape.

3. Place a piece of Brie in each of the prosciutto-lined cups and top with a raspberry half.

4. Bake for 10 to 12 minutes, until the cheese has fully melted. Allow to cool for 10 minutes prior to serving to allow the prosciutto to harden and the cheese to cool.

5. Store in an airtight container in the fridge for up to 2 days.

Nutrition

CALORIES: 124   FAT: 8.4g   PROTEIN: 10.8g   CARBS: 0.4g   FIBER: 0g

PIZZA ROLLS

MAKES 12 servings **PREP TIME:** 15 minutes, plus 10 minutes to cool
COOK TIME: 12 minutes

Pizza seems to be a Friday night affair for many families, but we believe every night has the potential to be pizza night. Add some tomato, pepperoni, and cheese to any dish to put a pizza twist on it!

DOUGH:

1½ cups shredded mozzarella cheese (about 6 ounces)

1 ounce cream cheese (2 tablespoons)

¾ cup blanched almond flour

1 large egg

1 teaspoon dried oregano leaves

½ teaspoon garlic powder

½ teaspoon onion powder

FILLING:

6 slices cheddar cheese

¼ cup tomato sauce

2 ounces sliced pepperoni

FOR GARNISH (OPTIONAL):

Chopped fresh basil or parsley

1. Preheat the oven to 400°F. Line a baking sheet with parchment paper, then grease the parchment paper with coconut oil spray.

2. Make the dough: Put the mozzarella and cream cheese in a medium-sized microwave-safe bowl. Microwave in 30-second increments until fully melted, about 60 seconds total.

3. Add the almond flour, egg, oregano, garlic powder, and onion powder to the melted cheeses and combine using a rubber spatula or your hands until you have a soft and sticky dough. If necessary, heat the dough in the microwave for another 15 to 20 seconds to incorporate all the ingredients.

4. Transfer the dough to the prepared baking sheet. Grease another sheet of parchment paper with coconut oil spray and place it greased side down on top of the dough. Roll out the dough as thinly as possible into a rectangle.

5. Remove the top sheet of parchment paper and layer on the cheese slices, covering as much of the dough as possible. Top with the tomato sauce and then the pepperoni.

6. Starting from the side closest to you, roll up the dough. As you roll it, make sure to tuck in the sides to prevent any spillage.

7. Cut the roll into 1-inch-thick slices. Lay the slices cut side down on the lined baking sheet. Bake for 10 to 12 minutes, until the dough is cooked through and the cheese has melted.

8. Allow to cool and harden for 5 to 10 minutes prior to serving. If desired, garnish with fresh basil or parsley.

9. Store in an airtight container in the fridge for up to 5 days.

Nutrition

CALORIES: 172   FAT: 14g   PROTEIN: 45.4g   CARBS: 3g   FIBER: 0.8g

KUNG PAO BRUSSELS SPROUTS

MAKES 4 servings   **PREP TIME:** 10 minutes   **COOK TIME:** 20 minutes

After going keto, we had to find ways to replicate our favorite dishes while keeping the carbs low. We've explored our favorite cultures and cuisines to learn what sorts of traditional ingredients give their dishes the flavors we crave. Toasted sesame oil, ginger, and rice wine vinegar are staples in Chinese cuisine.

BRUSSELS SPROUTS:

1 pound Brussels sprouts, halved

2 tablespoons extra-virgin olive oil

½ teaspoon finely ground Himalayan pink salt

½ teaspoon ground black pepper

SAUCE:

¼ cup low-sodium chicken broth

¼ cup soy sauce or coconut aminos

1 tablespoon Sriracha sauce

1 teaspoon unseasoned rice wine vinegar

½ teaspoon garlic powder

¼ teaspoon ginger powder

¼ teaspoon liquid stevia

½ teaspoon toasted sesame oil

⅛ teaspoon xanthan gum

FOR GARNISH (OPTIONAL):

Chopped peanuts

Sesame seeds

Sliced scallions

1. Preheat the oven to 425°F.

2. Roast the Brussels sprouts: On a rimmed baking sheet, toss the Brussels with the olive oil and season with the salt and pepper. Place in the oven and roast the Brussels until tender and slightly crispy, about 20 minutes.

3. While the Brussels sprouts are in the oven, make the sauce: In a saucepan over medium heat, combine the broth, soy sauce, Sriracha, rice wine vinegar, and spices. Simmer for 5 to 7 minutes to reduce slightly, then whisk in the stevia, sesame oil, and xanthan gum. Simmer for about 1 minute, whisking continuously, or until it has the consistency of a thick sauce. Slide the pan off the heat.

4. When the Brussels sprouts are done, transfer them to a serving bowl, pour the sauce over them, and toss to combine. Serve immediately, or return the sauced Brussels to the baking sheet and broil for 2 minutes to make them extra crispy, if desired.

5. If desired, garnish with peanuts, sesame seeds, and scallions prior to serving.

6. Store in an airtight container in the fridge for up to 5 days.

Nutrition (without garnishes)
CALORIES: 129   FAT: 7.8g   PROTEIN: 5.5g   CARBS: 12g   FIBER: 4.5g

BUTTERED MUSHROOMS

MAKES 4 servings   **PREP TIME:** 5 minutes   **COOK TIME:** 15 minutes

Steak night is a ritual in our house, and it starts with setting the mood. We turn on some music, fire up the stove, and get some garlic and mushrooms browning in butter. These buttery mushrooms are almost as crucial as a perfectly seared steak.

¼ cup (½ stick) unsalted butter

½ medium yellow onion, chopped

2 teaspoons minced garlic

1 pound small button mushrooms, stemmed

2 tablespoons dry white wine

2 tablespoons chopped fresh parsley leaves, divided

1 teaspoon chopped fresh thyme leaves

Finely ground Himalayan pink salt and ground black pepper

1. Melt the butter in a large skillet over medium-high heat. Add the onion and garlic and sauté until the onion is softened and the garlic is fragrant and slightly browned, about 3 minutes.

2. Add the mushrooms and cook until they have released their juices and are fully cooked and tender, and any mushroom juice has evaporated, 5 to 7 minutes.

3. Pour in the wine and cook for 2 minutes, or until most of it has evaporated. Stir in 1 tablespoon of the parsley and the thyme. Cook for 30 seconds, until fragrant.

4. Season to taste with salt and pepper. Sprinkle with the remaining 1 tablespoon of parsley and serve immediately.

5. Store in an airtight container in the fridge for up to 3 days.

Sides & Savory Snacks

Nutrition

CALORIES: 147   FAT: 12g   PROTEIN: 4.4g   CARBS: 4g   FIBER: 2g

ZUCCHINI BASIL MUFFINS

MAKES 6 muffins   **PREP TIME:** 10 minutes, plus 10 minutes to cool
COOK TIME: 22 minutes

Your mom might've made chocolate zucchini cake when you were little, but it wasn't just because she was trying to sneak some vegetables into your diet. She knew zucchini would make the cake super moist. This is exactly why we've "sneaked" some into this muffin recipe.

1 medium zucchini (about 7½ ounces), grated

3 large eggs

¼ cup coconut flour

½ teaspoon garlic powder

½ teaspoon onion powder

½ teaspoon finely ground Himalayan pink salt

1 teaspoon baking powder

½ cup grated Parmesan cheese (about 1½ ounces)

¼ cup finely chopped fresh basil leaves

1. Preheat the oven to 400°F. Line 6 wells of a standard-size 12-well muffin tin with paper liners or grease them with coconut oil spray.

2. Place the grated zucchini in a colander and squeeze out the excess liquid using your hands. Place the drained zucchini and the eggs in a large mixing bowl and whisk to combine.

3. In a separate bowl, whisk together the coconut flour, garlic powder, onion powder, salt, and baking powder, then add the dry ingredients to the bowl with the zucchini mixture and stir to combine.

4. Fold in the grated Parmesan and basil until fully incorporated. Divide the mixture evenly among the 6 prepared muffin wells, filling them about three-quarters of the way full.

5. Bake for 20 to 22 minutes, until slightly browned and a toothpick comes out clean when inserted in the middle of a muffin.

6. Allow to cool for 10 to 15 minutes prior to handling.

7. Store in an airtight container in the fridge for up to 5 days.

Nutrition (per muffin)
CALORIES: 100   FAT: 5.8g   PROTEIN: 6.7g   CARBS: 5g   FIBER: 2g

CHEESY CREAMED SPINACH

MAKES 4 servings   **PREP TIME:** 5 minutes   **COOK TIME:** 20 minutes

Back in the 1800s, it was rare for vegetables to be served without being covered in butter and salt, and for good reason. When you cover a vegetable like spinach in butter, cheese, and spices, you'll never want to eat it any other way again! Vegetables provide an easy way to add fat and variety to your keto meals.

2 tablespoons unsalted butter

1¼ pounds fresh spinach

½ teaspoon minced garlic

4 ounces cream cheese (½ cup)

¼ cup heavy whipping cream

¼ cup grated Parmesan cheese

¼ cup shredded mozzarella cheese

½ teaspoon finely ground Himalayan pink salt

½ teaspoon ground black pepper

1. Melt the butter in a large skillet over medium heat. Once melted, add the spinach in batches, adding more as it wilts.

2. Once all of the spinach has cooked down, add the garlic and cook for 1 to 2 minutes, until fragrant.

3. Add the cream cheese and heavy cream and stir using a wooden spoon until the cream cheese has completely melted into the spinach.

4. Add the remaining ingredients and stir as the cheese melts. Once the cheese is fully melted and heated through, remove from the heat and serve immediately.

5. Store in an airtight container in the fridge for up to 5 days.

Nutrition

CALORIES: 278   FAT: 24.5g   PROTEIN: 9.4g   CARBS: 8.5g   FIBER: 3.1g

BATTERED ONION RINGS

MAKES 3 servings   **PREP TIME:** 15 minutes   **COOK TIME:** 5 minutes

We used to live in San Francisco, where there's a hole-in-the-wall restaurant called Sam's Pizza and Burgers. They serve hot, greasy food late at night, and they encourage diners to dip their onion rings in ranch dressing instead of ketchup. Don't knock it until you've tried it!

Ghee, coconut oil, or tallow, for deep-frying

1 large yellow onion

DRY COATING:

¼ cup coconut flour

BATTER:

1 cup unflavored protein powder

3 large eggs

2 tablespoons hot water

1 teaspoon baking powder

¾ teaspoon finely ground Himalayan pink salt

½ teaspoon garlic powder

½ teaspoon paprika

¼ teaspoon ground black pepper

FOR GARNISH/SERVING (OPTIONAL):

Flake or coarsely ground sea salt

Sugar-free ketchup or ranch dressing

1. Attach a deep-fry thermometer to a medium-sized saucepan and fill the pan with enough ghee that it comes 2 inches up the side of the pan. Heat over medium-high heat until the temperature of the ghee reaches 330°F to 350°F. Set out a large plate lined with paper towels for the fried onion rings to rest on.

2. While the fat is heating, cut the onion into 3/8-inch-thick rings and prepare your batter station.

3. Set two medium-sized bowls side by side. Put the coconut flour in the one on the left. In the second bowl, whisk together the batter ingredients until smooth.

4. Dredge each onion ring in the coconut flour, then dunk it directly in the batter. Use a fork to remove the onion ring from the batter, letting any excess drip back into the bowl, and place it in the hot oil.

5. Fry the battered onion rings in small batches for 20 to 30 seconds on each side, until golden brown. Transfer to the paper towel–lined plate..

6. Serve immediately. If desired, garnish with sea salt and serve with your favorite dipping sauce on the side.

7. Store in an airtight container in the fridge for up to 3 days.

note: The macros for this recipe are approximate. It's difficult to pinpoint the exact amount of fat and protein in the finished onion rings because not all of the cooking fat and batter are used up in the process of coating and frying the onion rings.

Nutrition

CALORIES: **217**   FAT: **17g**   PROTEIN: **11g**   CARBS: **5.3g**   FIBER: **2g**

PIMENTO CHEESE

MAKES 8 servings   **PREP TIME:** 10 minutes, plus 1 hour to chill

Pimento cheese, also known as "the caviar of the South," is a special treat, and it's a great alternative to the usual cheese-slice-on-a-cracker routine. Looking for other uses for it? Pimento cheese can add some kick to your regular deviled eggs recipe: just mash some of this southern delicacy into the yolk mixture.

4 ounces cream cheese (½ cup), room temperature

4 ounces jarred diced pimentos, drained

½ cup mayonnaise

2 tablespoons minced fresh dill

1 tablespoon Dijon mustard

¼ teaspoon finely ground Himalayan pink salt

¼ teaspoon ground black pepper

1 cup shredded cheddar cheese (about 4 ounces)

1 cup shredded Monterey Jack cheese (about 4 ounces)

FOR GARNISH (OPTIONAL):

Sprig of fresh dill

FOR SERVING (OPTIONAL):

Low-carb crackers

Celery sticks or other veggie scoops

Pork rinds

1. Place the cream cheese, pimentos, mayo, dill, mustard, salt, and pepper in a large mixing bowl and combine using a rubber spatula.

2. Fold in the cheeses until fully incorporated.

3. Refrigerate for 1 to 2 hours before serving. Garnish with fresh dill, if desired, and serve with crackers, veggie scoops, and/or pork rinds, if desired.

4. Store in an airtight container in the fridge for up to 10 days.

Nutrition (cheese only)
CALORIES: 261   FAT: 25.6g   PROTEIN: 7.6g   CARBS: 2g   FIBER: 0.8g

PIZZA DIP

MAKES 6 servings   **PREP TIME:** 10 minutes   **COOK TIME:** 25 minutes

While you're making this dip, imagine you are making a real pizza. Don't be afraid to throw in your favorite pie toppings, like ham, onions, olives, or even a little pineapple. (If you go with pineapple, just be sure to count the carbs!)

1 (8-ounce) package cream cheese, room temperature

½ cup full-fat sour cream

1 teaspoon dried oregano leaves

½ teaspoon garlic powder

½ teaspoon onion powder

¼ teaspoon red pepper flakes

¼ teaspoon finely ground Himalayan pink salt

⅛ teaspoon ground black pepper

½ cup pizza sauce

2 ounces sliced pepperoni

½ cup shredded mozzarella cheese (about 2 ounces)

FOR GARNISH:

Chopped fresh basil or parsley

FOR SERVING:

Celery sticks

Pork rinds

Low-carb crackers

1. Preheat the oven to 350°F.

2. Put the cream cheese, sour cream, and seasonings in a bowl and stir to combine. Spread the cream cheese mixture in a 9-inch round or 8-inch square baking pan.

3. Spread the pizza sauce over the cream cheese mixture using a spoon. Layer the pepperoni on top of the sauce.

4. Bake for 15 minutes, or until the cream cheese mixture is melty.

5. Pull the pan out of the oven, sprinkle on the mozzarella, and bake for another 10 minutes, or until the mozzarella is fully melted.

6. Garnish with the chopped basil and serve immediately with celery sticks, pork rinds, and/or crackers.

7. Store in an airtight container in the fridge for up to 5 days.

Nutrition (dip only)
CALORIES: 262   FAT: 24.3g   PROTEIN: 7.2g   CARBS: 4.3g   FIBER: 0.3g

BACON CAULIFLOWER GRATIN

MAKES 10 servings   **PREP TIME:** 10 minutes   **COOK TIME:** 40 minutes

For this recipe, you will need two heads of cauliflower, or about 4 pounds total. Or you can swap out the cauliflower for broccoli or zucchini for simple yet tasty variations. If you use a less dense vegetable with a higher water content, like zucchini, there's no need to blanch it first.

GRATIN:

8 cups bite-sized cauliflower florets (about 2 heads)

3 tablespoons unsalted butter

2 teaspoons minced garlic

2 cups heavy whipping cream

3 cups shredded Monterey Jack cheese (about 12 ounces)

½ teaspoon finely ground Himalayan pink salt

½ teaspoon ground black pepper

10 slices bacon, cooked and chopped, divided

TOPPING:

¼ cup grated Parmesan cheese

¼ cup ground pork rinds

FOR GARNISH (OPTIONAL):

Chopped fresh parsley

1. Preheat the oven to 350°F.

2. Bring a large pot of water to a boil. Once it's boiling, add the cauliflower and cook for 3 minutes, until slightly tender. Drain and set aside.

3. Set the same pot over medium-high heat. Melt the butter in the pot, then add the garlic and cook until fragrant, 1 to 2 minutes. Add the cream and stir continuously until heated through, 2 to 3 minutes.

4. Turn the heat down to medium. Add the Monterey Jack, salt, and pepper and stir until the cheese has melted completely. Add the cauliflower and three-quarters of the chopped bacon and toss to coat.

5. Transfer the mixture to an 8-inch oven-safe skillet or similar-sized casserole dish and top with the remaining bacon.

6. Combine the Parmesan and pork rinds in a bowl and sprinkle the topping over the cauliflower mixture.

7. Bake for 25 minutes, or until the cheese is bubbly and the topping has browned. If desired, garnish with fresh parsley. Serve immediately.

8. Store in an airtight container in the fridge for up to 3 days.

Nutrition
CALORIES: 390   FAT: 34g   PROTEIN: 15.7g   CARBS: 6g   FIBER: 1.7g

GARLIC GREEN BEANS

MAKES 4 servings   **PREP TIME:** 5 minutes   **COOK TIME:** 7 minutes

This may be the fastest side dish in this entire cookbook. You can prepare it in minutes and have it ready to serve alongside any keto meal before running out the door to the next practice, class, or meeting.

¼ cup water

1 pound fresh green beans, trimmed

¼ cup (½ stick) unsalted butter

2 teaspoons minced garlic

¼ teaspoon finely ground Himalayan pink salt

⅛ teaspoon ground black pepper

FOR GARNISH (OPTIONAL):

Sliced almonds

1. In a large skillet, bring the water and green beans to a boil over high heat; continue to cook for 3 minutes, until the beans are bright green.

2. Pour the green beans into a colander to drain, then wipe the skillet dry with a paper towel.

3. Melt the butter in the skillet over medium heat. Add the garlic and cook, stirring continuously, until fragrant, about 1 minute.

4. Return the green beans to the pan and season with the salt and pepper. Toss the beans to coat them in the butter, then remove from the heat. Garnish with sliced almonds prior to serving, if desired.

5. Store in an airtight container in the fridge for up to 5 days.

Nutrition

CALORIES: **140**   FAT: **11.8g**   PROTEIN: **2.2g**   CARBS: **8g**   FIBER: **3g**

AVOCADOS IN SPICY CILANTRO SAUCE

MAKES 4 servings **PREP TIME:** 10 minutes

We first tried this dish while on vacation in Hawaii. Eating avocados in such a new and refreshing way was a pleasant surprise. Try it alongside some grilled chicken!

SAUCE:

2 medium jalapeño peppers, seeded and roughly chopped

1 bunch fresh cilantro

Juice of 1 lime

¼ cup extra-virgin olive oil

1 small shallot, roughly chopped

Finely ground Himalayan pink salt and ground black pepper

2 large ripe avocados

FOR GARNISH:

Walnut halves

Jalapeño slices

1. Put all the sauce ingredients in a blender and pulse until well combined but still slightly chunky. Season to taste with salt and pepper (make sure to season it well because the sauce will be the seasoning for the avocados).

2. Slice the avocados in half, remove the pits, and peel. Lay them cut side down on a serving plate.

3. Pour the sauce over the avocados, coating them entirely. Garnish with walnuts and jalapeño slices.

note: This dish will keep well in the fridge for up to 12 hours if covered with plastic wrap.

Nutrition

CALORIES: 276 FAT: 27.3g PROTEIN: 2.5g CARBS: 9g FIBER: 5.5g

BUFFALO CHICKEN–STUFFED MUSHROOMS

MAKES 6 servings   **PREP TIME:** 10 minutes, plus 10 minutes to cool
COOK TIME: 15 minutes

One of our favorite things to do on a Sunday afternoon is to make up a few appetizers and spend the day together watching movies or football. This dish is a spicy twist on classic stuffed mushrooms.

1 pound baby bella mushrooms

FILLING:

1 cup finely chopped cooked chicken

2 ounces cream cheese (¼ cup), room temperature

¼ cup finely shredded cheddar cheese, plus more for the top if desired

¼ cup mayonnaise

2 tablespoons Frank's RedHot sauce

FOR SERVING (OPTIONAL):

Hot sauce

1. Preheat the oven to 400°F.

2. Clean the mushrooms and remove the stems. Scoop a little extra mushroom out of the center to make more room for the filling, then place the mushrooms cavity side down on a rimmed baking sheet. Bake for 5 minutes, or until they're slightly tender. Remove the mushrooms from the oven and allow to cool for 10 minutes prior to filling.

3. While the mushrooms are baking, make the filling: In a medium-sized mixing bowl, combine all the filling ingredients using a fork.

4. Fill each mushroom with some of the filling (you may have some filling left over). If desired, top with more cheddar cheese.

5. Bake for 10 minutes, or until the cheese on top has slightly browned. Serve immediately with hot sauce, if desired.

6. Store in an airtight container in the fridge for up to 3 days.

Nutrition
CALORIES: **181**   FAT: **13.3g**   PROTEIN: **13.5g**   CARBS: **3g**   FIBER: **0.8g**

WHOLE ROASTED CAULIFLOWER
WITH PARMESAN CHEESE SAUCE

MAKES 6 servings　　**PREP TIME:** 10 minutes　　**COOK TIME:** 45 minutes

If you want to impress someone with a "fancy" meal, this is the dish to bring to the table. Serve up an elegant and delicious side without all the fuss.

ROASTED CAULIFLOWER:

1 medium head cauliflower

2 tablespoons extra-virgin olive oil

½ teaspoon finely ground Himalayan pink salt

¼ teaspoon ground black pepper

GARLIC PARMESAN SAUCE:

¼ cup (½ stick) unsalted butter

2 teaspoons minced garlic

1 cup grated Parmesan cheese (about 3 ounces)

½ cup heavy whipping cream

Finely ground Himalayan pink salt and ground black pepper

¼ teaspoon xanthan gum

FOR GARNISH (OPTIONAL):

Finely chopped fresh parsley or dried parsley

Ground pork rinds

1. Preheat the oven to 375°F.

2. Trim the leaves and cut off some of the stalk from the head of cauliflower—just enough to allow it to sit upright on its base. Set it in a baking dish or oven-safe skillet. Brush the olive oil over the cauliflower and season it with the salt and pepper.

3. Loosely cover with foil and bake for 30 minutes. Remove the foil and bake for an additional 15 minutes, until the cauliflower is slightly browned on top and tender enough to pierce with a fork.

4. When the cauliflower is almost done, make the sauce: Heat a medium-sized heavy-bottomed saucepan over medium heat. Melt the butter in the hot pan, then add the garlic and sauté for 30 to 60 seconds, until fragrant. Add the Parmesan cheese and cream and whisk until everything has melted and come together. Season to taste with salt and pepper. Whisk in the xanthan gum and cook for 2 to 3 minutes, until the sauce has thickened, whisking continuously. Turn the heat to low to keep the sauce warm while the cauliflower finishes cooking, whisking every so often.

5. When the cauliflower is done, transfer it to a cutting board and top with the sauce. If desired, garnish with parsley and ground pork rinds. Serve immediately.

6. Store in an airtight container in the fridge for up to 3 days.

note: We like to serve this dish on a large cutting board styled with a chef's knife and some forks for a fun, family-style presentation!

Nutrition

CALORIES: **271**　　FAT: **24g**　　PROTEIN: **7g**　　CARBS: **7.8g**　　FIBER: **2g**

SALMON JERKY

MAKES 16 servings   **PREP TIME:** 5 minutes, plus 2 to 4 hours to marinate
COOK TIME: 6 to 8 hours

Fish jerky was a common meal back when people were hunter-gatherers. Fish was plentiful in the lakes, oceans, and streams, and the best way to preserve it so that it would last throughout the winter or stay fresh in the summer was to smoke it or hang it to dry.

3 pounds skin-on salmon fillets

½ cup soy sauce or coconut aminos

2 tablespoons apple cider vinegar or lemon juice

1 tablespoon liquid smoke

2 teaspoons garlic powder

2 teaspoons onion powder

2 teaspoons red pepper flakes

1 teaspoon ginger powder

1 teaspoon ground black pepper

½ teaspoon finely ground Himalayan pink salt

1. Slice the salmon into ½-inch-thick pieces and place in a gallon-sized zip-top bag.

2. Add the remaining ingredients, seal the bag, and shake to coat the salmon thoroughly. Place in the refrigerator to marinate for 2 to 4 hours.

3. Preheat the oven to 170°F and place a baking rack on a rimmed baking sheet.

4. Remove the salmon from the bag and pat it dry using paper towels. Place the salmon pieces on the baking rack, making sure to leave some space between them to allow air to circulate around them. Dehydrate the salmon in the oven for 6 to 8 hours, until dry to the touch.

5. Store in a zip-top bag in the fridge for up to 2 weeks.

Nutrition
CALORIES: 180   FAT: 11g   PROTEIN: 18g   CARBS: 1g   FIBER: 0g

Desserts & Sweet Snacks

ALMOND COCONUT CRUMB CAKE

MAKES one 9 by 5-inch loaf cake (8 servings)
PREP TIME: 10 minutes, plus 20 minutes to cool   **COOK TIME:** 30 minutes

This is the dessert you've been waiting for. The cake is moist and wonderfully dense, and the topping is crumbly and crunchy. Be careful, though: you may find yourself wanting to eat the entire cake in one sitting!

CAKE:

½ cup (1 stick) unsalted butter

1 cup blanched almond flour

½ cup unsweetened coconut flakes

2 large eggs

2 teaspoons baking powder

1 teaspoon vanilla extract

¼ teaspoon liquid stevia

¼ teaspoon finely ground Himalayan pink salt

TOPPING:

¼ cup heavy whipping cream

1 teaspoon unflavored beef gelatin powder

½ cup raw almonds, chopped

2 tablespoons granular erythritol

2 tablespoons unsweetened coconut flakes

10 drops liquid stevia

1. Preheat the oven to 350°F and grease a 9 by 5-inch loaf pan with coconut oil spray.

2. Make the cake: Place the butter in a large microwave-safe bowl and microwave on high until melted. Add the remaining ingredients for the cake and combine using a hand mixer. Pour the mixture into the greased loaf pan and smooth the top using a rubber spatula.

3. Make the topping: In a small bowl, stir the cream and gelatin together. Allow to sit for 5 minutes, then add the remaining ingredients. Mix using a spoon.

4. Spoon the topping mixture evenly over the top of the cake batter.

5. Bake for 30 minutes, or until the topping has hardened and is slightly browned. Allow to cool for 20 minutes prior to removing it from the pan. Cut into 8 slices and enjoy!

6. Store in an airtight container in the fridge for up to 1 week.

Nutrition
CALORIES: 333 FAT: 32g PROTEIN: 7g CARBS: 8.5g FIBER: 3.8g SUGAR ALCOHOLS: 3g

PUMPKIN COLLAGEN FUDGE

MAKES 8 pieces **PREP TIME:** 10 minutes, plus 2 hours to chill

Matt grew up going to "Fudge Island"—Mackinac Island in Michigan—with his family, and fudge has been one of his favorite treats ever since. This recipe uses pumpkin puree to replicate the dense, rich consistency of fudge without all the high-sugar condensed milk!

½ cup natural creamy almond butter

½ cup unflavored collagen peptides

¼ cup coconut flour

¼ cup 100% pure pumpkin puree

2 teaspoons ground cinnamon

½ teaspoon ground nutmeg

½ teaspoon liquid stevia

¼ teaspoon finely ground Himalayan pink salt

1. Line a mini (6 by 3-inch) loaf pan with parchment paper, leaving some overhanging for easy removal of the fudge.

2. Put all the ingredients in a medium-sized mixing bowl. Mix using a fork or rubber spatula until fully incorporated.

3. Transfer the fudge mixture to the lined loaf pan. Spread evenly using a rubber spatula.

4. Refrigerate for 2 hours or until set. Remove from the pan, cut into 8 pieces, and enjoy.

5. Store in an airtight container or a zip-top bag in the fridge or freezer for up to 1 month. It can be eaten straight from the freezer without thawing.

Nutrition (per piece)

CALORIES: 159   FAT: 9g   PROTEIN: 6g   CARBS: 5.5g   FIBER: 3.3g

PEANUT BUTTER PECAN FAT BOMBS

MAKES 1 dozen fat bombs   **PREP TIME:** 10 minutes, plus 2 hours to freeze

We share a love of peanut butter, but only one of us can control herself around it. Matt totally avoids the nutty spread because he'll end up finishing the entire jar, but Megha likes to portion it out and savor every bite.

¼ cup (½ stick) unsalted butter

¼ cup natural peanut butter

¼ teaspoon finely ground Himalayan pink salt

¼ teaspoon liquid stevia

½ cup raw pecans, chopped

Special equipment: 24-well silicone mini muffin tin or similar-sized fat bomb mold

1. Place the butter in a small microwave-safe bowl and microwave on high until melted.

2. Add the peanut butter, salt, and stevia to the melted butter and combine using a spoon until fully incorporated.

3. Distribute the fat bomb mixture evenly among 12 wells of a silicone mini muffin tin (or fat bomb mold), filling the wells to the top. Sprinkle on the chopped pecans, dividing them as evenly as possible among the fat bombs. Freeze for 2 hours or until solid.

4. Store in an airtight container or a zip-top bag in the freezer for up to 1 month. These are best eaten straight from the freezer!

Nutrition (per fat bomb)
CALORIES: **101**   FAT: **10g**   PROTEIN: **1.5g**   CARBS: **2g**   FIBER: **0.8g**

FUDGY AVOCADO BROWNIES

MAKES 9 brownies   **PREP TIME:** 10 minutes, plus 15 minutes to cool   **COOK TIME:** 30 minutes

Brownies wear the dessert crown, so replicating that royal balance of moist, chewy, and chocolaty with low carbs is the ultimate challenge. Avocado to the rescue! This fatty fruit helps keep these decadent treats moist.

2 medium-sized ripe avocados (about 7½ ounces), peeled, halved, and pitted

4 large eggs

1 teaspoon liquid stevia

1 cup blanched almond flour

½ cup cocoa powder

¼ cup granular erythritol

1 teaspoon baking powder

½ teaspoon finely ground Himalayan pink salt

1 tablespoon coconut oil

2 ounces unsweetened baking chocolate (100% cacao)

1. Preheat the oven to 350°F and line an 8-inch square baking pan with parchment paper.

2. In a large bowl, mash the avocados. Add the eggs and stevia and combine using a whisk or fork until fully incorporated.

3. In a medium-sized mixing bowl, whisk together the almond flour, cocoa powder, erythritol, baking powder, and salt, then add the dry ingredients to the avocado mixture. Whisk to fully combine the wet and dry ingredients.

4. Put the coconut oil and unsweetened chocolate in a small microwave-safe bowl. Microwave in 30-second increments until completely melted, about 60 seconds total. Stir until the chocolate is fully combined with the oil.

5. Slowly whisk the melted chocolate into the batter until fully combined.

6. Pour the batter into the lined baking pan and spread evenly using a rubber spatula.

7. Bake for 30 minutes, or until a toothpick comes out clean when inserted into the center. Allow to cool for 15 minutes prior to handling. Cut into 9 brownies and enjoy.

8. Store in an airtight container or a zip-top bag in the fridge for up to 1 week.

Nutrition (per brownie)
CALORIES: 232 FAT: 20.5g PROTEIN: 7.3g CARBS: 9.4g FIBER: 6g SUGAR ALCOHOLS: 5g

PUMPKIN SPICE CREAM CHEESE COOKIES

MAKES 15 cookies   **PREP TIME:** 10 minutes, plus 15 minutes to cool   **COOK TIME:** 18 minutes

We're here to make sure you don't feel deprived of pumpkin this fall. Everyone deserves a little pumpkin spice when school starts up again and the weather cools.

¾ cup coconut flour

⅓ cup granular erythritol

2 tablespoons pumpkin pie spice

1 teaspoon baking powder

¼ teaspoon finely ground Himalayan pink salt

4 ounces cream cheese (½ cup), room temperature

¼ cup (½ stick) unsalted butter, room temperature

2 large eggs, room temperature

1 teaspoon vanilla extract

½ teaspoon liquid stevia

1. Preheat the oven to 350°F and line a baking sheet with parchment paper.

2. In a medium-sized mixing bowl, whisk together the coconut flour, erythritol, pumpkin pie spice, baking powder, and salt until combined.

3. In a large bowl, combine the cream cheese, butter, eggs, vanilla extract, and stevia using a hand mixer until fully incorporated. Start the mixer on the medium setting, then move it to high to create a consistent texture.

4. Add the dry ingredients to the wet ingredients in two batches and combine using the hand mixer.

5. Using a 1½-tablespoon cookie scoop, scoop 15 cookies onto the lined baking sheet, spacing them about 1 inch apart. Flatten using your hands or a rubber spatula. The cookies will not spread in the oven.

6. Bake for 15 to 18 minutes, until the cookies have browned slightly on the edges. Allow to cool on the baking sheet for 5 minutes, then gently transfer to a cooling rack using a spatula to cool for an additional 10 minutes.

7. Store in an airtight container or a zip-top bag in the fridge for up to 1 week.

Nutrition (per cookie)
CALORIES: 86 FAT: 7.3g PROTEIN: 2g CARBS: 3.5g FIBER: 2g SUGAR ALCOHOLS: 4g

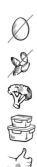

LEMON BLUEBERRY CHEESECAKE FAT BOMBS

MAKES 10 fat bombs   **PREP TIME:** 10 minutes, plus 2 hours to freeze

These fat bombs are a nice change from the classic peanut butter–and–chocolate recipes constantly floating through the Instagram feed. Cream cheese and lemon zest are a match made in keto heaven!

3 tablespoons coconut oil

3 tablespoons unsalted butter

5 ounces cream cheese, room temperature

Grated zest of 1 lemon

Juice of 1 lemon

½ ounce fresh blueberries, coarsely mashed

¼ teaspoon finely ground Himalayan pink salt

15 drops liquid stevia

TOPPING (OPTIONAL):

10 fresh blueberries

Special equipment: 24-well silicone mini muffin tin or similar-sized fat bomb mold

1. Put the coconut oil and butter in a medium-sized microwave-safe bowl and microwave on high until melted.

2. Add the cream cheese to the melted oil and butter and combine using a hand mixer on medium speed. Add the lemon zest, lemon juice, mashed berries, salt, and stevia. Mix to combine once more.

3. Distribute the fat bomb mixture evenly among 10 wells of a silicone mini muffin tin (or fat bomb mold), filling the wells to the top. If desired, top each fat bomb with an additional blueberry. Freeze for 2 hours or until solid.

4. Store in an airtight container or a zip-top bag in the freezer for up to 1 month. These are best eaten straight out of the freezer.

Nutrition (per fat bomb)

CALORIES: 104   FAT: 11.4g   PROTEIN: 0.1g   CARBS: 1g   FIBER: 0.2g

CHOCOLATE PEANUT BUTTER PIE

MAKES one 9½-inch pie (10 servings)   **PREP TIME:** 15 minutes, plus 4 hours to chill
COOK TIME: 13 minutes

Who says you have to have cake on your birthday? Nothing says "party" like peanut butter pie. Blow out those candles and indulge in a rich slice of silken chocolaty goodness with a flaky peanut butter crust.

PEANUT BUTTER CRUST:

1 cup natural creamy peanut butter

½ cup powdered erythritol

½ teaspoon liquid stevia

1 large egg

CHOCOLATE FILLING:

2 (8-ounce) packages cream cheese, room temperature

¼ cup full-fat sour cream

¼ cup (½ stick) unsalted butter

2 ounces unsweetened baking chocolate (100% cacao), chopped

½ cup powdered erythritol

3 tablespoons cocoa powder

2 teaspoons vanilla extract

½ teaspoon finely ground Himalayan pink salt

¾ cup heavy whipping cream

¼ teaspoon liquid stevia

FOR GARNISH (OPTIONAL):

Shaved unsweetened chocolate

Whipped cream

1. Preheat the oven to 350°F and grease a 9½-inch deep-dish pie pan with coconut oil spray.

2. Make the crust: Put the crust ingredients in a large bowl and mix using a hand mixer on high speed until fully incorporated. Transfer to the greased pie pan and spread evenly on the bottom and up the sides of the pan using a rubber spatula.

3. Poke holes in the crust using a fork and bake for 12 minutes, until browned and hard around the edges. Allow to cool completely before adding the filling.

4. Make the filling: In a large mixing bowl, combine the cream cheese and sour cream using a hand mixer on high speed.

5. Place the butter and chocolate in a small microwave-safe bowl and microwave on high in 30-second increments until the butter has melted, about 60 seconds total. Mix using a spoon until the chocolate has fully melted into the butter.

6. Add the erythritol, cocoa powder, vanilla extract, and salt to the cream cheese mixture and combine using the hand mixer on high speed. Slowly pour the melted chocolate mixture into the cream cheese mixture as you continue to mix using the hand mixer. Once fully incorporated, set aside.

7. In a medium-sized mixing bowl, whip the cream with the hand mixer until stiff peaks form. Add the stevia and mix once more to combine. Fold the whipped cream into the chocolate filling mixture until fully incorporated.

8. Pour the filling into the cooled pie crust and spread evenly using a rubber spatula. Refrigerate for 4 hours before serving. To serve, cut into 10 slices and garnish with shaved chocolate and dollops of whipped cream, if desired.

9. Store in an airtight container in the fridge for up to 5 days.

Nutrition
CALORIES: 456 **FAT:** 44.3g **PROTEIN:** 10g **CARBS:** 11.7g **FIBER:** 6.2g **SUGAR ALCOHOLS:** 19g

COCONUT BALLS

MAKES 10 balls   **PREP TIME:** 10 minutes, plus 20 minutes to freeze   **COOK TIME:** 21 minutes

We love keeping these in our freezer for when we need just a small treat after dinner. They're made with simple ingredients and aren't extremely decadent, which means it's easy to stop after just one.

COCONUT BALLS:

1 cup unsweetened shredded coconut

2 tablespoons coconut flour

¼ teaspoon liquid stevia

3 large egg whites

CHOCOLATE TOPPING:

2 tablespoons coconut oil

1½ ounces unsweetened baking chocolate (100% cacao), chopped

⅛ teaspoon liquid stevia

1. Preheat the oven to 350°F and line a baking sheet with parchment paper.

2. Make the coconut balls: In a medium-sized mixing bowl, whisk the shredded coconut, coconut flour, stevia, and egg whites until fully incorporated.

3. Using your hands, roll the mixture into 10 evenly sized balls, about 1¼ inches in diameter, and place them on the lined baking sheet.

4. Bake for 20 minutes, or until slightly browned. Let cool on the pan.

5. When the balls have cooled, make the chocolate topping: Place the coconut oil and chocolate in a small microwave-safe bowl and microwave on high in 30-second increments until heated through, about 60 seconds total. Combine using a spoon until the chocolate has completely melted into the oil. Add the stevia and stir once more.

6. Drizzle the cooled coconut balls with the chocolate topping. Place in the freezer to harden, 15 to 20 minutes.

7. Serve immediately or store in an airtight container in the fridge for up to 5 days. These are best eaten straight from the fridge.

Nutrition (per ball)
CALORIES: 112   FAT: 11g   PROTEIN: 2.4g   CARBS: 4.2g   FIBER: 2.5g

BUTTER COOKIES

MAKES 10 cookies   **PREP TIME:** 10 minutes, plus 15 minutes to cool   **COOK TIME:** 10 minutes

If you're an active keto baker, you probably have every single one of these ingredients in your kitchen right now. Don't wait another minute! Make these cookies now and they'll be out of the oven and into your mouth in less than forty minutes.

¼ cup (½ stick) unsalted butter

1 cup blanched almond flour

¼ cup granular erythritol

15 drops liquid stevia

½ teaspoon vanilla extract

1. Preheat the oven to 350°F and line a baking sheet with parchment paper.

2. Place the butter in a large microwave-safe bowl and microwave on high until melted. Add the almond flour, erythritol, stevia, and vanilla extract and combine using a rubber spatula or your hands until a stiff dough forms.

3. Using your hands, roll the dough into 10 evenly sized balls, about 1½ inches in diameter, and place them on the lined baking sheet, spacing them about 1½ inches apart. Using a fork, press down on the cookies to flatten them and create a crisscross pattern on top.

4. Bake for 10 minutes, or until slightly browned on the edges. Allow to cool on the pan for 15 minutes prior to handling.

5. Store in an airtight container in the fridge for up to 1 week.

Nutrition (per cookie)
CALORIES: **113** FAT: **11g** PROTEIN: **2.5g** CARBS: **2g** FIBER: **1g** SUGAR ALCOHOLS: **4.8g**

CARROT CAKE

MAKES one 3-layer, 8-inch cake (12 servings)
PREP TIME: 15 minutes, plus 1 hour 15 minutes to cool and chill   **COOK TIME:** 40 minutes

Yes, carrots can be keto. Being in ketosis is all about limiting carbohydrates and fueling with ketones, so if you can fit carrots into your daily macros, you have nothing to worry about. One of the best ways to eat them is in cake form.

CAKE:

2 cups blanched almond flour

½ cup coconut flour

½ cup granular erythritol

2 teaspoons baking powder

2 teaspoons ground cinnamon

½ teaspoon finely ground Himalayan pink salt

2 large carrots (about 8 ounces), grated (about 1½ cups)

6 large eggs

½ cup (1 stick) unsalted butter, melted but not hot

½ cup heavy whipping cream

1½ teaspoons vanilla extract

½ teaspoon liquid stevia

¾ cup raw pecans, chopped

ICING:

1 (8-ounce) package cream cheese, room temperature

½ cup (1 stick) unsalted butter, room temperature

½ cup powdered erythritol

½ teaspoon liquid stevia

FOR GARNISH (OPTIONAL):

½ cup chopped raw pecans

1. Preheat the oven to 325°F and grease three 8-inch cake pans with coconut oil spray. If you don't have three pans, you can bake one cake layer at a time.

2. Make the cakes: In a medium-sized bowl, whisk together the flours, erythritol, baking powder, cinnamon, and salt. Add the grated carrots and stir to combine.

3. In a large mixing bowl, whisk together the eggs, melted butter, cream, vanilla extract, and stevia.

4. Add the flour mixture to the wet ingredients in two batches and whisk until fully incorporated. Fold in the chopped pecans using a rubber spatula.

5. Divide the cake batter evenly among the greased cake pans, filling each a little less than halfway full. Spread evenly using a rubber spatula and bake for 40 minutes, or until a toothpick comes out clean when inserted into the center.

6. While the cakes are baking, make the icing: Place the icing ingredients in a medium-sized bowl and combine using a hand mixer on medium speed until fluffy and incorporated.

7. When the cakes are done, set the pans on a cooling rack and allow the cakes to cool completely.

8. Run a knife around the edge of one of the cooled cakes to loosen it, then remove it from the pan and place it on a cake plate. Top the first cake with one-third of the icing. Repeat with the remaining two cakes and icing until all three cakes are stacked and there is icing between the layers and on the top. Sprinkle chopped pecans on top of the cake, if desired.

9. Refrigerate for 1 hour before serving. Cut into 12 slices and enjoy.

10. Store in an airtight container in the fridge for up to 5 days.

Nutrition
CALORIES: 464 FAT: 44g PROTEIN: 9.5g CARBS: 9g FIBER: 4.8g SUGAR ALCOHOLS: 16g

CRUNCHY CHOCOLATE COOKIES

MAKES 15 cookies   **PREP TIME:** 10 minutes, plus 15 minutes to cool   **COOK TIME:** 11 minutes

The kids are home from school and they're hungry. Get them in the kitchen measuring the butter, cracking the egg, and mixing the dough for these chocolate cookies. Delicious homemade cookies will be cooling on the counter soon enough. The salt topping gives these cookies an adult angle; if you don't think the little ones will like it, simply omit it.

6 tablespoons (¾ stick) unsalted butter, melted but not hot

1 large egg

¼ cup plus 2 tablespoons granular erythritol

1 cup blanched almond flour

¼ cup cocoa powder

¼ teaspoon baking soda

¼ teaspoon finely ground Himalayan pink salt

TOPPING (OPTIONAL):

Sea salt flakes

1. Preheat the oven to 350°F and line two baking sheets with parchment paper.

2. In a large bowl, whisk together the melted butter, egg, and erythritol.

3. Add the almond flour, cocoa powder, baking soda, and salt and whisk until fully incorporated.

4. Using a 1½-tablespoon cookie scoop, scoop out 15 evenly sized balls, about 1¼ inches in diameter, and place on the lined baking sheets, spacing them 2 inches apart. Use the palm of your hand or your fingers to flatten the cookies to a ¼-inch thickness.

5. Bake for 8 to 11 minutes, until slightly browned on the edges. Allow to cool for 15 minutes prior to handling.

6. Store in an airtight container in the fridge for up to 1 week.

Nutrition (per cookie)
CALORIES: 95   FAT: 9g   PROTEIN: 2g   CARBS: 1.7g   FIBER: 1g   SUGAR ALCOHOLS: 5g

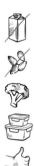

CHOCOLATE AVOCADO COOKIES

MAKES 1 dozen cookies   **PREP TIME:** 10 minutes, plus 10 minutes to cool   **COOK TIME:** 9 minutes

These are the softest, fudgiest, gooiest cookies you'll ever eat on the keto diet. That was a pretty bold statement, but we are serious.

2 medium-sized ripe avocados (about 7½ ounces), halved, peeled, and pitted

2 large eggs

½ teaspoon liquid stevia

1 cup cocoa powder

½ cup unsweetened shredded coconut

⅓ cup granular erythritol

1 teaspoon baking powder

½ teaspoon finely ground Himalayan pink salt

TOPPING (OPTIONAL):

Sugar-free chocolate chips

tip:
Megha likes to top these cookies with chopped pecans as well as chocolate chips before baking!

1. Preheat the oven to 350°F and line two baking sheets with parchment paper.

2. Mash the avocados in a large mixing bowl. Add the eggs and stevia and whisk to combine.

3. In a separate large bowl, whisk together the remaining ingredients, then add the dry ingredients to the avocado mixture and whisk to fully incorporate.

4. Using a 1½-tablespoon cookie scoop, scoop out 12 evenly sized balls, about 1¼ inches in diameter, and place on the lined baking sheets, spacing them 1½ inches apart.

5. Using your hands, flatten the cookies (they will not spread in the oven). If desired, top with chocolate chips.

6. Bake for 8 to 9 minutes, until firm and a toothpick comes out clean when inserted into a cookie. Allow to cool for 10 minutes before handling.

7. Store in an airtight container in the fridge for up to 1 week.

Nutrition (per cookie)
CALORIES: 97 FAT: 8.5g PROTEIN: 2.5g CARBS: 5.7g FIBER: 4g SUGAR ALCOHOLS: 5g

CHOCOLATE PECAN POUND CAKE

MAKES one 8 by 4-inch loaf cake (8 servings)
PREP TIME: 10 minutes, plus 20 minutes to cool   **COOK TIME:** 35 minutes

Pound cake is good, but chocolate pecan pound cake is great. If you want to take this coffee time treat to dinner party level, feel free to top it with a simple keto glaze or chocolate icing, or spread some butter on a warm piece and enjoy!

4 ounces cream cheese (½ cup), room temperature

¼ cup (½ stick) unsalted butter, room temperature

¼ cup granular erythritol

⅛ teaspoon liquid stevia

2 large eggs

1 cup blanched almond flour

2 tablespoons cocoa powder

2 tablespoons coconut flour

1½ teaspoons baking powder

¼ teaspoon finely ground Himalayan pink salt

¼ teaspoon xanthan gum

⅓ cup raw pecans, chopped, divided

1. Preheat the oven to 350°F and grease an 8 by 4-inch loaf pan with coconut oil spray.

2. In a large bowl, combine the cream cheese and butter using a hand mixer on high speed until completely incorporated. Add the erythritol, stevia, and eggs and combine once more.

3. In a medium-sized bowl, whisk together the remaining ingredients except the pecans. Add the dry ingredients to the wet ingredients in two batches, combining with the hand mixer on medium speed after each addition.

4. Once the wet and dry ingredients are fully incorporated, use a rubber spatula to fold in one-quarter of the chopped pecans.

5. Transfer the batter to the greased loaf pan and spread evenly using the rubber spatula. Top with the remaining pecans and bake for 30 to 35 minutes, until a toothpick comes out clean when inserted in the middle of the cake.

6. Allow the cake to cool in the pan for 15 minutes before flipping it out of the pan. Allow to cool for 5 more minutes, then cut into 8 slices and serve.

7. Store in an airtight container in the fridge for up to 1 week.

Nutrition
CALORIES: 249 FAT: 23.5g PROTEIN: 6g CARBS: 5g FIBER: 2.8g SUGAR ALCOHOLS: 6g

PEANUT BUTTER COOKIES

MAKES 1 dozen cookies **PREP TIME:** 10 minutes, plus 15 minutes to cool **COOK TIME:** 15 minutes

The gelatin is what makes these cookies irresistibly chewy, but if you don't have any on hand, don't worry about it. The flavor will still be perfect; you'll just end up with crispier cookies.

⅓ cup natural peanut butter

1 large egg

1 teaspoon vanilla extract

¼ teaspoon liquid stevia

¼ teaspoon finely ground Himalayan pink salt

1 cup blanched almond flour

¼ cup coconut flour

¼ cup granular erythritol

2 teaspoons unflavored beef gelatin powder (optional)

1. Preheat the oven to 350°F and line a baking sheet with parchment paper.

2. In a large mixing bowl, combine the peanut butter, egg, vanilla extract, stevia, and salt using a spoon or fork.

3. Add the remaining ingredients and stir until fully incorporated; the mixture should have a doughlike consistency.

4. Form the mixture into 12 evenly sized balls, about 1¼ inches in diameter, and place them on the lined baking sheet, spacing them 1½ inches apart. Flatten the cookies using your hand.

5. Bake for 13 to 15 minutes, until browned on the edges and firm to the touch. Allow to cool for 15 minutes before handling.

6. Store in an airtight container in the fridge for up to 1 week.

Nutrition (per cookie)
CALORIES: **121** FAT: **12g** PROTEIN: **4.5g** CARBS: **4.8g** FIBER: **2.3g** SUGAR ALCOHOLS: **4g**

PECAN PIE COOKIES

MAKES 10 cookies   **PREP TIME:** 10 minutes, plus 20 minutes to cool   **COOK TIME:** 17 minutes

We've turned pecan pie into a cookie so it's easier to enjoy this family favorite. No keto crust to fuss with, just cookies covered with gooey pecan filling.

COOKIES:

¼ cup plus 1 tablespoon unsalted butter, melted but not hot

2 tablespoons heavy whipping cream

1 tablespoon cream cheese, room temperature

1 large egg

¼ cup granular erythritol

¼ teaspoon liquid stevia

⅓ cup coconut flour

1 tablespoon unflavored beef gelatin powder

1 teaspoon baking powder

FILLING:

¼ cup plus 1 tablespoon raw pecans, finely chopped

2 tablespoons powdered erythritol

1 tablespoon heavy whipping cream

1 teaspoon unflavored beef gelatin powder

tip:
Store the leftover filling in a zip-top bag in the fridge for up to 1 week for your second batch of these cookies. Trust us, you'll be making more once the first batch is gone!

1. Preheat the oven to 350°F and line a baking sheet with parchment paper.

2. Make the cookies: In a large mixing bowl, whisk together the melted butter, heavy cream, cream cheese, egg, erythritol, and stevia. In a small bowl, whisk together the remaining ingredients for the cookies, then add the dry ingredients to the wet mixture and whisk until it has a doughlike consistency. Set aside.

3. Make the filling: Put the filling ingredients in a small bowl and combine using a spoon. Allow the filling mixture to thicken while you shape the cookies.

4. Using a 1½-tablespoon cookie scoop or your hands, divide the dough into 10 evenly sized portions. Using your hands, form each portion into a cookie shape, about 1½ inches in diameter, and place on the lined baking sheet. The cookies will not spread in the oven.

5. Make a small divot in the center of each cookie, then fill it with some of the pecan mixture. (You will have some filling left over.)

6. Bake for 15 to 17 minutes, until the edges have browned. Allow to cool for 15 to 20 minutes prior to handling.

7. Store in an airtight container in the fridge for up to 5 days.

Nutrition (per cookie)
CALORIES: 136 FAT: 12g PROTEIN: 2g CARBS: 3g FIBER: 1.5g SUGAR ALCOHOLS: 7g

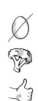

DOUBLE CHOCOLATE CHIP COOKIE DOUGH

MAKES 12 servings   **PREP TIME:** 10 minutes

A cookie dough that is safe to eat raw! If you like a little crunch in your cookie dough, as Matt does, toss in some chopped pecans, walnuts, or peanuts.

1 (8-ounce) package cream cheese, room temperature

½ cup (1 stick) unsalted butter, room temperature

¼ cup powdered erythritol

¼ cup plus 2 tablespoons blanched almond flour

¼ cup cocoa powder

¼ teaspoon finely ground Himalayan pink salt

¼ teaspoon liquid stevia

¼ teaspoon vanilla extract

¼ cup sugar-free chocolate chips

1. Place the cream cheese and butter in a medium-sized mixing bowl and combine using a hand mixer on high speed. Add the remaining ingredients except the chocolate chips and combine once more until fully incorporated.

2. Using a rubber spatula, fold in the chocolate chips.

3. Using a 1½-tablespoon cookie scoop, divide the dough into 12 equal portions.

4. Serve immediately or store in the fridge in an airtight container for later consumption.

5. Store in an airtight container in the fridge for up to 3 days or in the freezer for up to 1 month.

Nutrition
CALORIES: 172 FAT: 17.5g PROTEIN: 3.6g CARBS: 4.8g FIBER: 2g SUGAR ALCOHOLS: 5g

BLUEBERRY MUG CAKE

MAKES 1 serving   **PREP TIME:** 5 minutes   **COOK TIME:** 90 seconds

You're going to want to bookmark this page because this recipe never gets old. We make it all the time, and at any time of day: for an after-dinner dessert, an afternoon snack, and even for breakfast. A fresh blueberry cake is just minutes away. Or swap out the blueberries for raspberries for a different take on this easy treat!

1 ounce cream cheese (2 tablespoons), room temperature

1 tablespoon unsalted butter, melted but not hot

1 large egg

2 tablespoons coconut flour

¼ teaspoon finely ground Himalayan pink salt

¼ teaspoon liquid stevia

½ teaspoon baking powder

1 ounce fresh blueberries, plus more for serving if desired

FOR GARNISH (OPTIONAL):

Powdered erythritol

1. Combine the cream cheese and melted butter in an 8-ounce mug using a fork. Add the remaining ingredients except the blueberries and combine with the fork until fully incorporated.

2. Gently stir in the blueberries. Microwave on high for 60 to 90 seconds, until cooked through. When done, a toothpick will come out clean when inserted into the center of the cake.

3. Flip the mug over on a plate to release the cake. You may have to shake the mug a little to get the cake to fall out. Dust with powdered erythritol and serve with additional blueberries, if desired. Serve immediately.

Desserts & Sweet Snacks

Nutrition

CALORIES: 344   FAT: 29g   PROTEIN: 10g   CARBS: 12.5g   FIBER: 5.5g

PECAN SNOWBALL COOKIES

MAKES 15 cookies   **PREP TIME:** 10 minutes, plus 15 minutes to cool   **COOK TIME:** 30 minutes

If these cookies don't take you back in time to childhood holidays, that's okay. They will still satisfy your sweet tooth and fill the house with the delicious aroma of toasted pecans.

½ cup (1 stick) unsalted butter, melted but not hot

1 large egg

½ teaspoon liquid stevia

½ teaspoon vanilla extract

1 cup raw pecans

½ cup coconut flour

½ cup powdered erythritol, divided

¼ cup unsweetened shredded coconut

1. Preheat the oven to 300°F and line a baking sheet with parchment paper.

2. In a large mixing bowl, whisk the melted butter, egg, stevia, and vanilla extract until combined.

3. Put the pecans in a food processor and process until finely ground. Add the ground pecans, coconut flour, ¼ cup of the erythritol, and the shredded coconut to the butter mixture and mix until it has a doughlike consistency.

4. Using your hands, roll the dough into 15 evenly sized balls, about 1¼ inches in diameter, and place on the lined baking sheet. They will not spread in the oven.

5. Bake for 27 to 30 minutes, until browned. Allow to cool for 5 minutes, then roll each cookie in the remaining ¼ cup of powdered erythritol. Let cool for 10 more minutes prior to serving.

6. Store in an airtight container or a zip-top bag in the fridge for up to 1 week or in the freezer for up to 2 weeks.

Nutrition (per cookie)
CALORIES: **128** FAT: **13g** PROTEIN: **1.7g** CARBS: **3g** FIBER: **2g** SUGAR ALCOHOLS: **6.5g**

RASPBERRY CREAM CHEESE COOKIES

MAKES 1 dozen cookies   **PREP TIME:** 10 minutes, plus 15 minutes to cool   **COOK TIME:** 10 minutes

Don't worry, raspberry lovers, we didn't forget about you. We believe these tart, sweet, and juicy berries are Mother Nature's candy, and they belong in cookies. But you can also swap out the raspberries for some pecans or walnuts for a nutty twist on this recipe!

6 ounces cream cheese (¾ cup), room temperature

¼ cup (½ stick) butter, room temperature

1 large egg

2 tablespoons lemon juice

1 teaspoon vanilla extract

¼ teaspoon liquid stevia

½ cup coconut flour

¼ cup powdered erythritol

12 fresh raspberries

1. Preheat the oven to 350°F and line a baking sheet with parchment paper.

2. In a large mixing bowl, cream the cream cheese and butter using a hand mixer on medium speed until light and fluffy. Add the remaining ingredients except the raspberries and mix until fully combined.

3. Using a 1½-tablespoon cookie scoop, scoop out 12 evenly sized balls, about 1¼ inches in diameter, and place on the lined baking sheet, spacing them about 1½ inches apart.

4. Using a fork, press each cookie to flatten it and create a crisscross pattern on top. Place a raspberry in the center of each cookie.

5. Bake for 8 to 10 minutes, until the edges start to brown slightly. Allow to cool for 15 minutes prior to serving.

6. Store in an airtight container in the fridge for up to 5 days.

Nutrition (per cookie)
CALORIES: **113** FAT: **10g** PROTEIN: **2.2g** CARBS: **4g** FIBER: **1.8g** SUGAR ALCOHOLS: **4g**

LOW-CARB GRAHAM CRACKERS

MAKES 6 servings **PREP TIME:** 10 minutes, plus 30 minutes to cool **COOK TIME:** 12 minutes

These graham crackers would make the perfect base for a cheesecake: you can crush them, flatten them into a cake pan, and bake until golden brown before pouring the cheesecake batter into the crust.

1½ cups blanched almond flour

1 teaspoon ground cinnamon

½ teaspoon baking soda

1 large egg

¼ cup (½ stick) unsalted butter, melted

¼ teaspoon liquid stevia

¼ teaspoon xanthan gum

1. Preheat the oven to 350°F and line a baking sheet with parchment paper.

2. In a large bowl, combine all the ingredients using a whisk until the mixture has the consistency of a thick dough.

3. Transfer the dough to the lined baking sheet and form it into a ball using your hands. Place another piece of parchment paper on top and roll the dough into a square or rectangle, ¼ to ½ inch thick.

4. Using a sharp knife, gently score the rolled-out dough to create graham cracker squares (no need to cut all the way through). If desired, use a fork to poke two sets of holes in the crackers prior to baking.

5. Bake for 10 to 12 minutes, until the edges have browned. Depending on how thick the crackers are, they may need more or less time, so keep an eye on them starting at about 8 minutes. Allow to cool for 20 to 30 minutes before breaking into squares and serving.

6. Store in an airtight container or a zip-top bag in the fridge for up to 2 weeks or on the counter for up to 1 week.

Nutrition
CALORIES: 261   FAT: 23.5g   PROTEIN: 7g   CARBS: 5g   FIBER: 3g

Allergen Index

RECIPES	PAGE	🥛	∅	🥜	🥦	🍱	👍
SWEET ASIAN BBQ SPATCHCOCKED CHICKEN	98	✓	✓	✓			
CHICKEN POT PIE SOUP	100		✓	✓			
CHICKEN AND RICOTTA STUFFED PEPPERS	102		✓	✓			✓
LOADED CHICKEN SALAD	104			✓			✓
BARBACOA	106	✓	✓	✓			
BARBACOA LETTUCE WRAPS	108		✓	✓			✓
ASIAN CABBAGE BOWL	110	✓	✓	✓			✓
BARBACOA BREAKFAST SKILLET	112			✓			
MUSTARD-RUBBED PORK TENDERLOIN	114	✓	✓	✓			
PORK TENDERLOIN IN MUSHROOM CREAM SAUCE	116		✓	✓			
PORK FRIED RICE	118		✓	✓			
OMELET FOR TWO	120						
SOY-GLAZED SALMON	122	✓	✓	✓			✓
SALMON SALAD	124	✓		✓			✓
MIXED GREENS SALAD with SALMON AND SESAME DRESSING	126	✓	✓	✓			✓
SPICE-RUBBED BRISKET	128	✓	✓	✓			
BRISKET SANDWICH	130			✓			✓
BRISKET BREAKFAST SKILLET	132	✓		✓			✓
SUPREME PIZZA BREAKFAST CASSEROLE	136			✓		✓	✓
OVERNIGHT PROTEIN "OATS"	138		✓			✓	✓
HERBED RICOTTA BREAKFAST CASSEROLE	140			✓		✓	
CHILE RELLENOS CASSEROLE	142			✓	✓	✓	
CINNAMON MORNING MUFFINS	144				✓	✓	✓
MOCHA EGG COFFEE	146	✓		✓	✓		✓
DUTCH BABY FOR TWO	147			✓			✓
CHEDDAR AND SAUSAGE SCONES	148				✓		
MINI BREAKFAST CAKES with LEMON WHIPPED CREAM	150				✓		
JALAPEÑO POPPER EGG BITES	152			✓		✓	✓
SOUR CREAM BISCUITS	154				✓		
RASPBERRY CRUMBLE CHEESECAKE	156			✓	✓		
MEGHA'S FAMOUS SMOOTHIE BOWL	158		✓		✓		✓
GOAT CHEESE SHAKSHUKA	160			✓	✓		✓
5-MINUTE BREAKFAST SANDWICH	162			✓			
POPCORN CHICKEN	164			✓		✓	✓
COCONUT FLOUR PANCAKES	166			✓	✓		✓
SOUTHERN GRITS	168			✓			✓
LEMON POPPY SEED WAFFLES	170				✓		✓
ALMOND BUTTER PROTEIN LOAF	172					✓	✓
GOAT CHEESE SOUFFLÉ	174				✓		
BLUEBERRY CHIA SEED PUDDING	176		✓		✓		✓
MEXICAN SKILLET DINNER	180		✓	✓		✓	✓
AVOCADO EGG SALAD	182	✓		✓	✓	✓	✓
CHICKEN PARMESAN	183		✓	✓			
EGGPLANT LASAGNA	184			✓		✓	
CAULIFLOWER CHILI	186		✓	✓	✓	✓	
SPICED KEEMA	188	✓	✓	✓			
SALMON TOPPED WITH AVOCADO BRUSCHETTA	190	✓	✓	✓		✓	✓
ITALIAN HERBED MEATBALLS	192			✓		✓	✓
CREAMY PESTO SHRIMP	194						
DRY-RUBBED RIBS	196	✓	✓	✓		✓	

MEGHA BAROT and MATT GAEDKE

RECIPES	PAGE	🥛	⊘	🌿	🥦	🥡	👍
PORCINI AND BLUE CHEESE–ENCRUSTED STEAK	198		✓	✓			
FRENCH ONION CHICKEN BAKE	200		✓	✓		✓	
LEMONY ROASTED DRUMSTICKS	202	✓	✓	✓		✓	✓
LAMB SHOULDER CHOPS	204	✓	✓	✓			
CHILI WITH BACON	206	✓	✓	✓		✓	✓
CAULIFLOWER CRUST PEPPERONI PIZZA	208		✓			✓	✓
ONE-PAN CHICKEN with LEMON-GARLIC CREAM SAUCE	210		✓	✓			✓
OVEN-BRAISED SHORT RIBS	212	✓	✓	✓		✓	
INDIAN SPICED WINGS	214	✓	✓	✓			
STEAK ROLL-UPS	216		✓				
CAULIFLOWER NACHOS	218		✓				
CREAMY BRUSSELS SPROUTS with BACON	222		✓	✓			✓
ROSEMARY PARMESAN BISCUITS	224				✓	✓	
CHOPPED CAPRESE SALAD	226		✓	✓	✓		✓
BACON GARLIC ASPARAGUS	227	✓	✓	✓			✓
CREAM OF BROCCOLI SOUP	228		✓	✓		✓	
PROSCIUTTO BRIE RASPBERRY CUPS	230		✓	✓			✓
PIZZA ROLLS	232						
KUNG PAO BRUSSELS SPROUTS	234	✓	✓	✓			
BUTTERED MUSHROOMS	236		✓	✓	✓		✓
ZUCCHINI BASIL MUFFINS	238			✓	✓	✓	
CHEESY CREAMED SPINACH	240		✓	✓	✓		✓
BATTERED ONION RINGS	242	✓		✓	✓		
PIMENTO CHEESE	244			✓	✓	✓	✓
PIZZA DIP	246		✓	✓			✓
BACON CAULIFLOWER GRATIN	248		✓	✓			
GARLIC GREEN BEANS	250		✓	✓	✓	✓	✓
AVOCADOS IN SPICY CILANTRO SAUCE	252	✓	✓		✓		
BUFFALO CHICKEN–STUFFED MUSHROOMS	254			✓			
WHOLE ROASTED CAULIFLOWER with PARMESAN CHEESE SAUCE	256		✓	✓	✓		
SALMON JERKY	258	✓	✓	✓		✓	
ALMOND COCONUT CRUMB CAKE	262						
PUMPKIN COLLAGEN FUDGE	264	✓	✓			✓	✓
PEANUT BUTTER PECAN FAT BOMBS	266		✓		✓	✓	✓
FUDGY AVOCADO BROWNIES	268	✓			✓	✓	
PUMPKIN SPICE CREAM CHEESE COOKIES	270			✓	✓		
LEMON BLUEBERRY CHEESECAKE FAT BOMBS	272		✓	✓	✓	✓	✓
CHOCOLATE PEANUT BUTTER PIE	274				✓		
COCONUT BALLS	276	✓		✓	✓		
BUTTER COOKIES	278		✓		✓	✓	✓
CARROT CAKE	280				✓		
CRUNCHY CHOCOLATE COOKIES	282				✓	✓	
CHOCOLATE AVOCADO COOKIES	284	✓		✓	✓	✓	✓
CHOCOLATE PECAN POUND CAKE	286				✓	✓	
PEANUT BUTTER COOKIES	288	✓			✓	✓	✓
PECAN PIE COOKIES	290						
DOUBLE CHOCOLATE CHIP COOKIE DOUGH	292		✓		✓		✓
BLUEBERRY MUG CAKE	294			✓	✓		
PECAN SNOWBALL COOKIES	296				✓	✓	
RASPBERRY CREAM CHEESE COOKIES	298			✓	✓		
LOW-CARB GRAHAM CRACKERS	300				✓	✓	

Recipe Index

MEAL PREP

98

Sweet Asian BBQ Spatchcocked Chicken

100

Chicken Pot Pie Soup

102

Chicken and Ricotta Stuffed Peppers

104

Loaded Chicken Salad

106

Barbacoa

108

Barbacoa Lettuce Wraps

110

Asian Cabbage Bowl

112

Barbacoa Breakfast Skillet

114

Mustard-Rubbed Pork Tenderloin

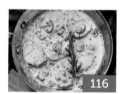
116

Pork Tenderloin in Mushroom Cream Sauce

118

Pork Fried Rice

120

Omelet for Two

122

Soy-Glazed Salmon

124

Salmon Salad

126

Mixed Greens Salad with Salmon and Sesame Dressing

128

Spice-Rubbed Brisket

130

Brisket Sandwich

132

Brisket Breakfast Skillet

MEGHA BAROT AND MATT GAEDKE

BREAKFAST & BRUNCH

 136

Supreme Pizza Breakfast Casserole

 138

Overnight Protein "Oats"

 140

Herbed Ricotta Breakfast Casserole

 142

Chile Rellenos Casserole

 144

Cinnamon Morning Muffins

 146

Mocha Egg Coffee

 147

Dutch Baby for Two

 148

Cheddar and Sausage Scones

 150

Mini Breakfast Cakes with Lemon Whipped Cream

 152

Jalapeño Popper Egg Bites

 154

Sour Cream Biscuits

 156

Raspberry Crumble Cheesecake

 158

Megha's Famous Smoothie Bowl

 160

Goat Cheese Shakshuka

162

5-Minute Breakfast Sandwich

 164

Popcorn Chicken

 166

Coconut Flour Pancakes

 168

Southern Grits

 170

Lemon Poppy Seed Waffles

 172

Almond Butter Protein Loaf

 174

Goat Cheese Soufflé

 176

Blueberry Chia Seed Pudding

MAINS

 180
Mexican Skillet Dinner

 182
Avocado Egg Salad

 183
Chicken Parmesan

 184
Eggplant Lasagna

 186
Cauliflower Chili

 188
Spiced Keema

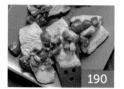 190
Salmon Topped with Avocado Bruschetta

 192
Italian Herbed Meatballs

 194
Creamy Pesto Shrimp

 196
Dry-Rubbed Ribs

 198
Porcini and Blue Cheese–Encrusted Steak

 200
French Onion Chicken Bake

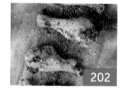 202
Lemony Roasted Drumsticks

 204
Lamb Shoulder Chops

 206
Chili with Bacon

 208
Cauliflower Crust Pepperoni Pizza

 210
One-Pan Chicken with Lemon-Garlic Cream Sauce

 212
Oven-Braised Short Ribs

 214
Indian Spiced Wings

 216
Steak Roll-Ups

 218
Cauliflower Nachos

SIDES & SAVORY SNACKS

222

Creamy Brussels Sprouts with Bacon

224

Rosemary Parmesan Biscuits

226

Chopped Caprese Salad

227

Bacon Garlic Asparagus

228

Cream of Broccoli Soup

230

Prosciutto Brie Raspberry Cups

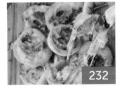

232

Pizza Rolls

234

Kung Pao Brussels Sprouts

236

Buttered Mushrooms

238

Zucchini Basil Muffins

240

Cheesy Creamed Spinach

242

Battered Onion Rings

244

Pimento Cheese

246

Pizza Dip

248

Bacon Cauliflower Gratin

250

Garlic Green Beans

252

Avocados in Spicy Cilantro Sauce

254

Buffalo Chicken–Stuffed Mushrooms

256

Whole Roasted Cauliflower with Parmesan Cheese Sauce

258

Salmon Jerky

DESSERTS & SWEET SNACKS

Almond Coconut Crumb Cake — 262

Pumpkin Collagen Fudge — 264

Peanut Butter Pecan Fat Bombs — 266

Fudgy Avocado Brownies — 268

Pumpkin Spice Cream Cheese Cookies — 270

Lemon Blueberry Cheesecake Fat Bombs — 272

Chocolate Peanut Butter Pie — 274

Coconut Balls — 276

Butter Cookies — 278

Carrot Cake — 280

Crunchy Chocolate Cookies — 282

Chocolate Avocado Cookies — 284

Chocolate Pecan Pound Cake — 286

Peanut Butter Cookies — 288

Pecan Pie Cookies — 290

Double Chocolate Chip Cookie Dough — 292

Blueberry Mug Cake — 294

Pecan Snowball Cookies — 296

Raspberry Cream Cheese Cookies — 298

Low-Carb Graham Crackers — 300

General Index